THE HUNGRY FAN'S
GAME DAY
COOKBOOK

THE HUNGRY FAN'S
GAME DAY
COOKBOOK

165 RECIPES FOR EATING, DRINKING & WATCHING SPORTS

★ DAINA FALK ★

Oxmoor House®

Text ©2016 Daina Falk
Design/images ©2016 Time Inc. Books

Published by Oxmoor House, an imprint
of Time Inc. Books
225 Liberty Street, New York, NY 10281

Editorial Director: Anja Schmidt
Project Editor: Melissa Brown
Editorial Assistant: Nicole Fisher
Creative Director: Felicity Keane
Art Director: Christopher Rhoads
Designer: Steve Attardo
Junior Designer: AnnaMaria Jacob
Director of Photography: Iain Bagwell
Photographer: Greg Dupree
Prop Stylists: Kellie Gerber Kelly,
    Mindi Shapiro Levine
Food Stylists: Nathan Carrabba,
    Margaret Monroe Dickey, Ana Kelly,
    Catherine Crowell Steele
Workflow Manager: Alyson Moreland Haynes
Recipe Testers: Julia Levy, Callie Nash, Karen Rankin
Senior Production Manager: Greg A. Amason
Associate Project Manager: Hillary Leary
Copy Editors: Jacqueline Giovanelli, Sarah Scheffel
Proofreaders: Rebecca Brennan, Julie Gillis
Indexer: Carol Roberts
Fellow: Natalie Schumann

ISBN-13: 978-0-8487-4583-7
ISBN-10: 0-8487-4583-3
Library of Congress Control Number: 2016943633

First Edition 2016
Printed in the United States of America
10 9 8 7 6 5 4 3 2 1

Time Inc. Books products may be purchased for
business or promotional use. For information on bulk
purchases, please contact Christi Crowley in the Special
Sales Department at (845) 895-9858.

We welcome your comments and suggestions about
Time Inc. Books.
Please write to us at:
Time Inc. Books
Attention: Book Editors
P.O. Box 62310
Tampa, Florida 33662-2310

Photography Credits: Getty Images: Tyler Olsen: **4;**
Ezra Shaw: **5;** David Madison: **8;** Yobro10: **58;** kevinrank:
98; Russell Sadur: **142;** Grant Halverson: **190;** Juan
Silva: **194;** gaspr13: **212;** Jostaphot: **230;** MistikaS: **242;**
Courtesy of author: 40; 46; 65; 70; Fangater bag, **72; 74;**
91; 119; 128; 172; 176; 179; 181; 198; 225

TABLE OF CONTENTS

INTRODUCTION

When I say I've been a Hungry Fan® from the womb, I mean it in the most literal sense possible. I learned not too long ago from my mom that my first time traveling with NBA basketball players was on a trip through Italy. . . in my mom's stomach. I think it's safe to say this early taste of sports and *molto delizioso* food from inside the womb set the scene for the rest of my life.

My father, David Falk, began his sports agent career in the 1970s, starting as an unpaid intern and ultimately becoming one of the most renowned agents in the industry, representing major sports stars and coaches like Michael Jordan; Boomer Esiason; Arthur Ashe; Patrick Ewing; Dikembe Mutombo; Coach K; Coach John Thompson, Jr.; and the list goes on. I share this not to brag about my dad (although I am so fiercely proud of him), but to give you some insight into what I was exposed to growing up. His heyday was in the 1990s, a very formative part of my childhood. On any given day we would have professional athletes staying in our guest room, calling our house (pre-cell phone), or passing lo mein across the table at dinner (so many of them liked eating Chinese takeout).

I grew up loving sports. But I've also always been a good eater. If it's in front of me, I'll eat it—from a lamb's head during Greek Easter dinner in Astoria, Queens (my first spring in NYC), to whatever delicious Japanese food I espied every 90 minutes or so during my first trip to Tokyo (except for when I was asleep, of course—though then I was probably dreaming of food). During college, I studied abroad and

furthered my passion for food—not just eating it, but also preparing it—in cooking classes in France and Italy. I learned classical techniques and enjoyed eating and cooking with the freshest of ingredients. After graduation, I was all set to move to Los Angeles for a job at a Beverly Hills talent agency when I was involved in a serious car accident. I relocated anyway, and the silver lining of what felt like a not-so-awesome situation was that my extensive post-accident physical therapy regime inspired me to adopt a healthier lifestyle (including eating fresh, organic ingredients, which is quite easy in LA)—and in the process I shed 60 pounds.

I'm proud to say that I'm in better, healthier shape than ever before. But on game day, all bets are off. My nutrition professor in college once said (and this has stuck with me) that stress is far more dangerous to one's health than being slightly overweight. (Note the emphasis on the word "slightly.") Thus, I say eat healthy six days a week—but on game day, enjoy yourself! I like to think of game day as a calorie-free zone where you can eat and drink exactly what you want. There's nothing better than cheering on your team at deafeningly loud decibels while chowing down on "sportsfood" yummies. (Fun fact: I originated the hashtag #sportsfood on Twitter and Facebook). Besides, I've got enough on my plate (pun intended) worrying about my team—I can't also be counting calories and fearing for my waistline.

There was a brief time, toward the end of college, when I contemplated being a sports agent like my dad. That didn't last. Nonetheless,

FANGATING™

A few years ago, I came up with the word Fangating™. It is such a mouthful to say "tailgating or homegating," so I just crafted the word "fangating™" to mean both. Whether you're at home or in the parking lot outside the stadium—or even on the moon—if you're eating, drinking, hanging with friends and family, and watching sports, you're officially fangating™. (Use it and pass it on!)

I knew I wanted to work in sports—I just wanted to pave my own path. I spent a lot of time thinking about how to do that—asking myself what I am passionate about, what I know, what I'm good at, etcetera—and I came to recognize this exciting intersection where sports and food meet. It's a giant, meaningful part of the sports fan experience. And since I've been a sports fan longer than I can remember, I realized I had found my calling.

I have this habit of keeping sticky notes and a pen by my bed. I find that I have some of my best ideas in the middle of the night. In the early morning hours of January 1, 2011, I finally went to bed after helping out at a huge multi-day/night concert in Miami. When I awoke later that day, I found I had left myself an interesting note. It simply said "Hungry Fan." I instantly knew it was the perfect name for me—and for you, the Hungry Fans of America; the people I consider the most passionate people I've ever had the pleasure of meeting. Hungry Fan gelled slowly. I stewed on the concept for nearly a year before soft-launching my website, HungryFan.com, in late 2011.

As "The Hungry Fan" (my moniker) and the face of the Hungry Fan brand, I like to say my job is to curate the fan experience. I actually trademarked the word "fangating™," and it's the word I use when describing the act of watching sports with friends and family while enjoying delicious food and drink. The term is meant to be location-neutral. You could be in a parking lot, at home, or on the moon—if you're eating, drinking, and watching sports, then you're fangating™. (Use it and pass it on!) My website's main purpose is to feature my fangating™ recipes, which I now pass along to you, conveniently bundled into one book for your reading and cooking pleasure. (It's way, way easier to cook from a recipe when it's in a book, if you ask me. I hate getting sauce splatter, oil smears, and chopped bits of whatever on my iPad or phone. It's terribly messy. Who wants a phone caked with BBQ sauce for days?)

Typically, the recipes I feature on my site are specifically crafted for matchups happening in the days following my post. For example, when my Dukies finally made their first bowl game in decades, they faced off against Cincinnati. So I published a blog featuring recipes for North Carolina–style BBQ (of which I ate plenty during my days in Durham) and Cincinnati sky-high chili. I like highlighting authentic, regional flavors and celebrating the variety of cultures throughout this nation.

This cookbook is an ode to every sports fan out there, regardless of gender, race, ethnicity, age, or team preference (even you, Carolina Tarheels). Whether it's basketball, football, baseball, hockey, tennis, soccer, NASCAR, or any other competitive sport that makes your heart beat a little faster or causes you to scream like a maniac and nibble without abandon, this cookbook is for you. Happy cooking—and even happier eating!

FRIENDLY FANGATING TIP: I've created something to make your tailgating meals easier: The Hungry Fan™ 3-in-1 Fangating™ Bag, or Fangater for short. Many of the recipes in this book can be started at home and then placed inside your Fangater to get you to your game. By the time you're there and set up with your tailgate, the dish will be ready to eat! Tailgating has never been so delicious.

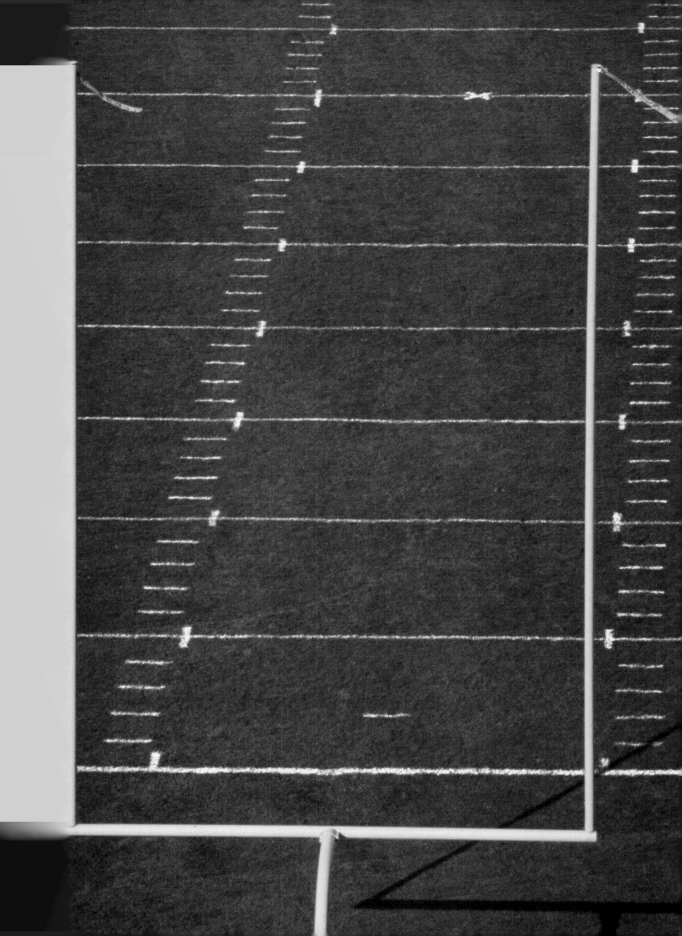

STARTERS

Sportsfood is meant to be shareable, accessible, tasty, and fun to eat. It's the less-fancy cousin of gourmet cuisine that tastes best made with quality ingredients and it can be dressed up to a degree. But at its core, sportsfood is rooted in time-honored (often regional) traditions and ought to be enjoyed by everyone.

To me, a starter is essentially a smaller plate of food intended to whet your appetite for the main event. In this book, starter refers to the snacks you might serve before the rack of baby back ribs comes off the grill or before you bust out the make-your-own burger bar. It's what you eat during the first half of the game before the bigger, more filling dishes are ready to eat during the second half.

Starters are the perfect food to set out during an intense game; they're what I like to nervously munch on as the minutes wind down and I hope my team ends up on top. There is such satisfaction in salty, crunchy chips. And they're perfect to pop quickly, one after the next, especially when your team is down. I can easily get away with watching an entire game just munching on many of the starters featured in this chapter. They're not the most filling of dishes—and aren't intended to be—unless you eat them in quantity (which I am known to do).

This chapter focuses on finger foods, chips, and dips. All of these recipes can be made for individual portions (party for one!) or to feed everyone you invited to your Super Bowl party, for instance. Simply double or triple the recipes as needed to serve large groups. Going for a more fancy-schmancy look? Many of these recipes can also make great hors d'oeuvres in a more upscale party setting. Passed or plated, these dishes are sure to please.

BLIND DATES

MAKES **12**

Here in New York, we couldn't have been more excited for Super Bowl XLVIII—the first to be held in the Big Apple since the Super Bowl era began. For the big game, I teamed up with Celebrations.com and put together a killer Super Bowl food guide with party ideas and recipes. They asked me to think outside the box, and after tinkering around in the kitchen a bit, I came up with these easy, elegant, and downright decadent hors d'oeuvres. They're like devils on horseback—on steroids. They are insanely, ridiculously addictive, and when you pop 'em in your mouth, it's a rush of flavors—salty, sweet, creamy, crunchy, cheesy, and spicy—all at once. There's something in this recipe for everyone—and chances are, you'll be whipping up another batch before halftime. Good luck only having one or two of these. I ate my whole first batch and I'm not ashamed to admit it!

Parchment paper

6 strips of bacon (preferably nitrate-free), cut in half crosswise

1 ounce creamy Gorgonzola cheese

2 ounces mascarpone cheese

Toothpicks, soaked for 30 minutes

12 Medjool dates, pitted

$1/_2$ cup heavy cream

4 ounces bittersweet chocolate

Cayenne pepper, to taste

1. Line a baking sheet with aluminum foil and another baking sheet with parchment paper.

2. Place the bacon on the foil baking sheet, and bake it in the oven while preheating to 400°F, about 15 minutes.

3. Meanwhile, stuff some cheese into each date, alternating between the two cheeses and placing the dates on the paper-lined baking sheet. (When filling with the mascarpone, spoon it into a zip-top bag, snip a small hole in the corner, and squeeze the cheese into the date.)

4. When the bacon is ready, quickly wrap each date with a piece of bacon, securing it with a toothpick.

5. Simmer the heavy cream in a small saucepan over low. Remove from the heat, add the chocolate, and stir until smooth. Add the cayenne to taste for a nice zing of spice.

6. Dip the dates into the chocolate, being sure to coat each one entirely, and return them to the paper-lined baking sheet.

7. Let set at room temperature, or place in the fridge to set quickly.

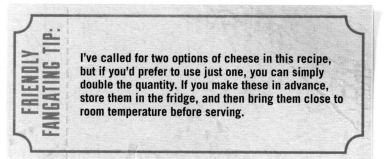

FRIENDLY FANGATING TIP: I've called for two options of cheese in this recipe, but if you'd prefer to use just one, you can simply double the quantity. If you make these in advance, store them in the fridge, and then bring them close to room temperature before serving.

ANDOUILLE-STUFFED DATES

CONTRIBUTOR: **WILL WITHERSPOON** | MAKES **30**

Will Witherspoon is one of the most unique football players you'll ever meet. He made a name for himself playing linebacker in the NFL for 11 years for the Carolina Panthers, the St. Louis Rams, the Philadelphia Eagles, the Tennessee Titans, and ultimately finished his career back with the Rams. But what you might not know is that Will is also a farmer, environmentalist, and frequent expert presenter on Capitol Hill. "Spoon," as his friends call him, is the proud owner of Shire Gate Farm in Owensville, Missouri. What's so special about Shire Gate is that it's certified Animal Welfare Approved (AWA), which means the grass-fed White Park Cattle and other animals found there are raised sustainably without antibiotics. Whenever I call and check in with Spoon, he'll tell me of a new gelding he acquired or a new henhouse he's building. I am so impressed with Will and his efforts to clean up the food supply, and I'm also grateful to be his friend—he has sent me lots of delicious grass-fed beef and some of the andouille sausage featured in this recipe. You have my word—it's the bee's knees.

30 dates

1 pound bacon

1 pound andouille sausage, preferably Shire Gate Farm brand, casing removed

2 cups Pomì tomato sauce, warmed

1. Preheat the oven to 375°F.

2. Split open the dates on one side, and remove the seeds. Cut the strips of bacon in half crosswise.

3. Stuff approximately 1 tablespoon andouille sausage into each date. (The amount of sausage will vary according to size of date.) Then wrap each stuffed date in bacon.

4. Place the wrapped dates in a baking dish. Bake until the bacon is crispy, about 40 minutes, flipping over halfway through.

5. Once the bacon is crisp, transfer the dates to a serving platter, and serve with the warmed tomato sauce for dipping.

TASTY TIDBITS

In 2012, much to my delight, Rodale, the publisher of *Men's Health* and *Women's Health* magazines, named Spoon number 7 on their list of the world's "Top 50 Sexiest Environmentalists." He placed behind Gretchen Bleiler, Jessica Alba, Matt Damon, Alicia Silverstone, Ryan Gosling, and Kate Middleton. Needless to say, the teasing went on for…years.

SHEPHERD'S PIE QUESADILLA BITES

MAKES **48**

A few years ago, Selection Sunday and March Madness were both scheduled on either side of March 17th, better known as St. Patrick's Day. In the spirit of the Irish, I gave my March Madness recipes an Irish spin (or lilt, as I like to say). Quesadilla bites are a great dish to serve at an NCAA hoops watch party—and no forks are necessary! These Irish-themed quesadillas are filled with a traditional Irish recipe—shepherd's pie. When I first served them, they were a hit. (I think I ate about a dozen myself.) Since then, Selection Sunday has continued to fall on or near St. Paddy's Day, and now my March Madness always begins with these little bites of the Irish classic.

4 large (or 6 to 8 small-medium) potatoes, peeled

8 tablespoons (1 stick) Irish (salted) butter, plus 1 tablespoon for frying

$1/4$ cup heavy cream

1 teaspoon sea salt

$1^1/2$ teaspoons freshly ground black pepper

Several sprigs of chives, minced

12 (8-inch) flour tortillas

1 cup shredded Dubliner cheese

1 cup shredded mild white Cheddar cheese

MEAT FILLING

1 tablespoon extra virgin olive oil

$3/4$ cup Guinness Stout

$3/4$ cup diced yellow onions

$3/4$ cup diced carrots

Several stalks of chives, minced

1 teaspoon ground nutmeg

1 teaspoon ground cinnamon

2 tablespoons Worcestershire sauce

1 pound ground beef, preferably grass-fed

$1/2$ cup fresh or frozen English peas, or more to taste

1 teaspoon sea salt

1 teaspoon freshly ground black pepper

1. First, make the meat filling: Combine the olive oil and Guinness in a large skillet over medium. Add the onions and carrots, and sauté until the onions are translucent and the veggies have sucked up most of the liquid, about 10 minutes. Add the chives, nutmeg, cinnamon, Worcestershire sauce, and beef, stirring constantly, until the meat is cooked, about 7 minutes. Be sure to mash the meat while stirring to avoid large chunks. Stir in the peas, salt, and pepper, and transfer the filling to a bowl.

2. Meanwhile, boil the potatoes until soft enough to mash. Drain and mash the potatoes, then add the butter, cream, salt, pepper, and half of the chives. Mix well, and set aside.

3. Assemble the quesadillas: Lay 1 flour tortilla out on a plate. Spread with $1/2$ cup of the mashed potatoes and about $3/4$ cup of the meat filling. Top with a generous sprinkle of each cheese. Place another tortilla on top. Repeat with the remaining 10 tortillas and fillings.

4. In the same large skillet used to make the meat filling, melt 1 tablespoon of the butter over medium-low, slide the quesadilla into the skillet, and increase the heat to medium-high. Brown for 2 minutes, then carefully flip over and brown the other side (adding more butter if necessary) for another 2 minutes. Repeat with the remaining quesadillas and butter.

5. Cut each quesadilla into 8 triangular pieces, and top with a sprinkle of chives. Serve!

WISCONSIN-STYLE FRIED CHEESE CURDS

MAKES ABOUT **20**

These are my ode to America's "cheeseheads." Truth be told, I haven't spent a lot of time in Wisconsin. But when I think about die-hard sports fans—my favorite kind—I immediately conjure a picture in my head of this guy I saw on TV during a Green Bay game late in the season with his shirt off. He was wearing a beanie hat and had a long, bushy beard. . . with icicles on it. That's die-hard. That's devotion and insanity mixed together into one loyal NFL fan package that the Packers are lucky to call their own.

Growing up, I was a fan of mozzarella sticks—like no one's business. My mom kept a steady stash of them in our freezer, and before I learned how to cook I used to zap 'em in our microwave as a snack. When I was a little older, I tried my first cheese curds and I was hooked. This is my Wisconsin-style, cheese-curd-lovin' spin on mozzarella sticks. You can find cheese curds at your local cheesemonger or at some gourmet markets. Maybe one day I'll figure out how to freeze them and sell them like the mozzarella sticks I ate as a kid. Until then, I'd argue that these really are best when fresh.

2 quarts avocado oil, for frying

³/₄ cup all-purpose flour

¹/₄ cup whole milk

³/₄ cup beer, preferably dark such as Guinness

¹/₂ teaspoon Lawry's seasoned salt

¹/₄ teaspoon cayenne pepper

2 large eggs, beaten

1 pound cheese curds

1. Heat the oil over high in a large saucepan or electric fryer until it reaches 375°F on a deep-fry thermometer.

2. Meanwhile, combine the flour, milk, beer, salt, cayenne, and egg in a large mixing bowl, and whisk until well blended; your batter should be light and liquidy. Dunk the curds into the batter, coat well, and then remove, using a slotted spoon to drain excess batter.

3. Drop the curds one by one in the hot oil (to avoid clumping), and deep-fry until they're golden brown, about 2¹/₂ minutes. Transfer to a paper towel–lined tray to drain off excess oil. Serve!

HEALTHY JALAPEÑO POPPERS

SERVES **8**

As football season carries on into the late fall and winter (much like the beginnings of the NBA and NHL seasons), the temperatures in most parts of the United States and Canada, where the games take place, start to creep down lower and lower. In recent years, it's gotten so stinkin' cold that our weather experts have actually invented new terms such as "polar vortex" to describe patterns of intense freezing.

My response to that pesky polar vortex? Eat spicy food! It'll warm you up from the inside out. I happen to love jalapeño poppers—they're fried and creamy and oh so delicious. But because I was poppin' 'em so often, and because extraordinary motivation is needed to get to the gym in those colder months, I decided I needed to figure out how to make my poppers healthier. Instead of frying the poppers, I baked them. The end result is a fun and zesty finger food that's noticeably lighter—but just as satisfying.

8 jalapeño peppers

4 ounces Neufchâtel cheese, softened

1 cup shredded pepper Jack cheese, plus more for sprinkling, optional

2 medium Fresno chiles, membranes and seeds removed, finely chopped

1/2 teaspoon sea salt

3 tablespoons minced fresh cilantro

1 1/2 teaspoons ground cumin

1/2 cup whole-wheat panko or gluten-free breadcrumbs

1. Preheat the oven to 375°F.

2. Slice the jalapeños in half vertically, and remove the seeds and membranes.

3. Mix both cheeses, the chiles, salt, 2 tablespoons of the cilantro, and the cumin in a bowl. Combine the remaining tablespoon cilantro with the panko in a separate bowl.

4. Fill the jalapeños with the cheese mixture, and then coat them with the panko mixture. Transfer to a baking sheet, and sprinkle with additional pepper Jack, if desired.

5. Bake for 30 minutes. If using cheese on top, broil for only a few additional minutes to brown the cheese.

6. Serve warm and enjoy.

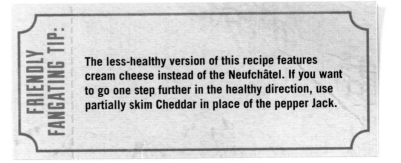

FRIENDLY FANGATING TIP: The less-healthy version of this recipe features cream cheese instead of the Neufchâtel. If you want to go one step further in the healthy direction, use partially skim Cheddar in place of the pepper Jack.

CHICKEN WINGS WITH BALSAMIC BBQ SAUCE

CONTRIBUTORS: ROY AND PADDY HIBBERT | MAKES **24**

I know NBA All-Star Roy Hibbert can eat. I've seen it with my own eyes, and it's impressive. It's really no surprise. Roy is seven-foot-two, so there's a lot to feed. I've known Roy since he was drafted out of Georgetown in 2008. I remember coming home to visit my parents, and there he was, sitting in my family's kitchen. Since then, Roy's really gotten into food—particularly the nutritional science behind it.

When I asked Roy to share a recipe with me for this book, he generously sent two. (You'll find the other recipe on page 182.) Roy's mom, Paddy, helped create both recipes. Mrs. Hibbert is from Trinidad, and you'll find the Caribbean influence in both dishes. This is a great recipe for the summertime, when the weather's ideal for grilling.

2 pounds chicken wings, cut apart at the joints, tips discarded, and washed

1 teaspoon sea salt

1 teaspoon freshly ground black pepper

1 tablespoon Mrs. Dash seasoning

3 tablespoons garlic powder

1 tablespoon ground ginger

Olive oil spray

BALSAMIC BBQ SAUCE

$^1\!/_2$ cup balsamic vinegar

$^1\!/_2$ cup olive oil

2 tablespoons Dijon mustard

1 tablespoon honey

1 tablespoon Mrs. Dash seasoning

1. Whisk together all the barbecue sauce ingredients in a small bowl.

2. Place the chicken wings in a large zip-top bag, and season with the salt, pepper, Mrs. Dash, garlic, and ginger. Then pour the barbecue sauce on top. Seal and let marinate overnight in the refrigerator.

3. When you're ready to grill, cover a grill rack with aluminum foil, making holes in it so heat can penetrate it, and then spray the foil with the olive oil spray.

4. Heat your gas grill to high (400°F); if using a charcoal grill, get it really hot. Using tongs, transfer the marinated chicken wings to the prepared rack, reserving the extra marinade, and then reduce the flame to medium (about 300°F). Turn every 5 minutes until the wings develop somewhat of a crust. Continue cooking, basting the wings with the marinade, until the chicken is well done and toasty brown, about 25 minutes.

TASTY TIDBITS

I remember the press storm a few years back after Roy did a total diet makeover. He began working with a nutritionist to improve his diet, and his game took off: Roy put up more points, blocked more shots, and dished more assists than in any previous year with the Pacers—and he became an All-Star for the first time.

BUFFALO WINGS

MAKES **36**

Buffalo wings are hands-down my favorite sportsfood. They're tangy, they've got kick, and while they may be messy, I think they're fun to eat. (And yes, I will nibble on the bones as well. Maybe I'm weird but I learned it from my mom—and she learned it from her grandmother.) This recipe makes 36. I'm pretty confident in saying I could eat them all myself. If I'm with my sister, you best shut your doors and latch your windows: The two of us together are a Buffalo wing–eating tornado. Together, we have single-handedly scavenged the United States for delicious and even so-so wings. Here's a heads-up: If your wings are dry, we won't be happy.

Most Buffalo wing recipes call for frying the chicken, but my healthier take involves baking them. And, for those of you who are gluten-free, I've got you covered with the oat flour so you can eat these. And my sneaking suspicion—not to toot my own horn or anything—is that you will love them.

3 tablespoons vegetable or olive oil

36 chicken wing pieces, cut into two pieces (the "flat" and the "drum"), skin removed, if desired, or just drumettes

$1^1/_4$ teaspoons sea salt

1 cup oat or all-purpose flour

$1^1/_2$ tablespoons white vinegar

$^1/_4$ teaspoon cayenne pepper

$^1/_8$ teaspoon garlic powder

$^1/_2$ teaspoon Worcestershire sauce

2 teaspoons Tabasco sauce

6 tablespoons Louisiana hot sauce

1. Preheat the oven to 425°F. Line one or two baking sheets with foil, and grease with 2 tablespoons of the oil.

2. Toss the wings with the remaining oil and 1 teaspoon of the salt in a bowl. Put into a large zip-top bag, add the flour, and seal. Shake well to coat the chicken evenly.

3. Remove the wings from the bag, shaking off any excess flour, and spread them evenly on the prepared baking sheet(s) in one layer. (Don't stack the wings!) Bake for about 20 minutes, turn the wings over, and bake for another 20 minutes, or until the wings are browned on the outside and cooked through.

4. Meanwhile, mix the vinegar, cayenne, garlic powder, Worcestershire, Tabasco, hot sauce, and the remaining $^1/_4$ teaspoon of the salt in a small saucepan. Bring to a simmer over low heat, stirring occasionally, about 3 minutes.

5. After the wings are cooked, transfer them into a large mixing bowl. Pour the sauce over the hot wings, and toss to coat completely. Serve immediately.

COCONUT-CRUSTED SHRIMP WITH SWEET AND SOUR SAUCE

SERVES **4**

I came up with this recipe for one of my Super Bowl–themed TV cooking demos a few years ago and was inspired by my days at Duke. My friends and I used to watch sports at one particular restaurant where coconut shrimp was the house specialty, and I remember eating more shrimp than I care to admit. (You may be noticing an ongoing theme in this book: I've long been a bottomless pit when it comes to sportsfood.) This recipe is sort of Caribbean meets Asian and has always been a people-pleaser when I serve it. No forks needed! Use your fingers to eat and dunk these fried yummies.

Vegetable and sesame oil (2 parts veggie, 1 part sesame), for frying

1 cup panko breadcrumbs

1 teaspoon red pepper flakes, or more for added heat

1 cup sweetened shredded coconut

1 teaspoon baking powder

1 large egg

1 teaspoon sea salt

$\frac{1}{3}$ cup water

$\frac{1}{2}$ cup all-purpose flour

1 pound medium to large shrimp, peeled, deveined, tails removed, and patted dry

DIPPING SAUCE

2 tablespoons rice wine vinegar

2 teaspoons cornstarch

$\frac{1}{2}$ cup pineapple juice

2 tablespoons sweet chili sauce

$\frac{1}{2}$ teaspoon red pepper flakes, or to taste

1. Fill a large pot 2 to 3 inches deep with the vegetable and sesame oil combination. Heat over high until it reaches 325°F on a deep-fry thermometer.

2. While the oil heats, prep the shrimp. Combine the panko breadcrumbs, red pepper flakes, and coconut in a wide bowl or shallow dish. Whisk together the baking powder, egg, salt, and water in another shallow dish. Place the flour in a third shallow dish.

3. Dip the shrimp one at a time in the flour, then in the baking powder mixture, and finally dredge in the panko mixture.

4. Working in batches, fry the shrimp in the hot oil for 1 to 2 minutes or until golden brown. Keep warm in a low oven while making the sauce.

5. Make the dipping sauce: Combine the vinegar and cornstarch in a small saucepan, and whisk, cooking over medium-low, until they emulsify. Add the pineapple juice, sweet chili sauce, and red pepper flakes to the saucepan, and whisk together briefly. Bring to a quick boil—you will see the mixture start to shrink down. Decrease the temperature to low, and let sit for a few minutes, stirring occasionally.

6. Serve the shrimp on a plate aside a bowl of the dipping sauce and enjoy.

FRIENDLY FANGATING TIP:

If you don't have a deep-fry thermometer, don't fret. You can heat the oil over medium heat and just keep an eye on it. If it starts to smoke, it's too hot. You want to heat the oil to just before that smoke point. If the oil starts to smoke, lower the heat just a tad.

HONEY-SRIRACHA-TERIYAKI DRUMSTICKS

MAKES **6**

I've already expounded on my deep love and adoration for Buffalo wings. I won't carry on with that further. You get it. At least I hope you get it. A big part of my love for Buffalo wings is certainly the flavor—but I am also just a huge fan of wings. I like the eating process. In an effort to come up with other flavors, simply so I had more wings to eat, I tinkered in the kitchen and came up with these Sriracha teriyaki drumsticks.

Let's face it. Sriracha is probably the best hot sauce on the market. And I find it hard to get enough Asian food in my diet, so I went for the teriyaki, too. I made my first batch of these with wingettes and drumettes. Tasty. But I wanted more. So I went back to the grocery store and bought large drumsticks. I drowned them in my marinade, and air-fried them up. They made me so happy. It's a lot of chicken, and these will fill you up, especially when done as drumsticks. They're great as a starter or even as an entrée at your tailgate or watch party.

¼ cup green onions, cut into thin rounds, plus more for garnish

¼ cup teriyaki sauce

1 tablespoon Sriracha chili sauce

½ teaspoon black pepper

1½ teaspoons honey

2 teaspoons sesame oil

½ teaspoon red pepper flakes

All purpose-flour (or brown rice flour if you're keeping it gluten-free), for dredging

Shredded carrots, for serving

6 large chicken drumsticks (you can always use 12 drumettes instead)

1. Whisk together the green onions, teriyaki sauce, Sriracha chili sauce, black pepper, honey, sesame oil, and red pepper flakes in a mixing bowl. Place the flour in a shallow bowl.

2. Dredge the drumsticks (skin on or off, your call) in the flour, coating the entire piece of chicken in an even, thin layer of flour. Then dunk the drumsticks in the sauce, coating well.

3. Place all the drumsticks in an air fryer at 390°F for 10 minutes. Alternatively, bake in a preheated 425°F oven on a lightly greased, foil-lined baking sheet for 20 minutes, and then flip. Bake for another 25 minutes, checking to ensure the chicken is cooked through.

4. Place the drumsticks atop a bed of shredded carrots. Top with additional green onion slices and serve.

CAJUN SHRIMP SKEWERS

CONTRIBUTOR: **KEETH SMART** | MAKES **16**

This recipe is fitting for a guy like Keeth Smart—he is an American silver-medal-winning sabre fencer. (Get it? Skewers—sabres?) Hailing from Brooklyn, New York, Keeth competed for the United States in the 1999 Pan American Games, where his team won a bronze. In 2002 and 2004, Keeth won the US National Sabre Championship and in 2003, he became the first American to be the top-ranked fencer worldwide. Keeth competed in three Summer Olympic Games, earning his silver in Beijing in 2008.

It's your choice how to cook the shrimp in Keeth's recipe. You can grill them on a gas or charcoal barbecue, or you can broil them in your oven.

16 (6-inch) wooden skewers

3 bell peppers (yellow, red, and/or orange)

3 cloves garlic, minced

1 teaspoon kosher salt

2 tablespoons fresh lemon juice

2 tablespoons olive oil

2 teaspoons Cajun seasoning

2 pounds large shrimp, cleaned, deveined, and shells discarded

1. Soak the wooden skewers in water for about 30 minutes. (This helps prevent them from catching fire when you cook the shrimp.)

2. While the skewers are soaking, deseed and cut the bell peppers into 1-inch squares.

3. Combine the garlic and salt in a medium bowl. Stir well, and then add the lemon juice, olive oil, Cajun seasoning, and shrimp. Toss well to fully coat the shrimp.

4. Preheat your grill to medium-high or your broiler to high. Line a baking sheet with aluminum foil.

5. Alternating between the shrimp and bell pepper squares, stack the skewers until they're loaded up, roughly 3 to 4 shrimp and 5 to 6 peppers per skewer.

6. Place the skewers on the prepared baking sheet, pouring the remaining sauce on top of them.

7. Grill or broil the skewers for 3 minutes per side. Serve immediately (with a huge smile).

Cajun Shrimp Skewers,
vegetable skewers, and
Bacon-Wrapped Chicken
Skewers (page 24)

BACON-WRAPPED CHICKEN SKEWERS (PICTURED ON PAGE 23)

SERVES 6

I have a theory, and I'm pretty sure it's not wholly original, but here goes: If you add bacon to anything, everyone will eat it (save maybe for those who keep kosher and vegetarians). Americans love bacon. I love bacon. It's pretty much the tastiest thing ever invented. Have a kid who hates Brussels sprouts? Wrap the sprouts in bacon and I'd wager that your kid will eat 'em.

This is a simple chicken kebab recipe jazzed up with America's favorite pork product. The kebabs could qualify as an entrée, but I like to serve them as a tasty treat that everyone can eat with their fingers at any point during a fangate. Pick up a skewer and go to town because this recipe won't let you or your friends down!

1¼ pounds boneless, skinless chicken breasts

¾ cup fresh pineapple chunks

1 bell pepper, cut into 1-inch squares

10 white mushrooms, cut in half vertically

¼ cup low-sodium soy sauce

1 tablespoon extra-virgin olive oil

¼ cup red wine vinegar

1½ teaspoons onion powder

½ teaspoon garlic salt

1 teaspoon freshly ground black pepper (or kick it up a notch with ½ teaspoon red pepper flakes)

12 (9-inch) wooden skewers

2 whole jalapeño peppers, cut into thin rounds, seeds removed (see Tip)

6 slices bacon, each cut into 3 pieces

1. Cut the chicken into chunks, and place in a zip-top bag with the pineapple, bell peppers, and mushrooms. Add the soy sauce, oil, vinegar, onion powder, garlic salt, and pepper. Seal the bag, and mix, making sure everything is well coated. Place in the fridge to marinate for 45 minutes.

2. Meanwhile, soak the wooden skewers in water for 30 minutes.

3. Preheat your grill or a grill pan over medium-high.

4. To assemble the chicken skewers, place a jalapeño slice on each side of a chicken chunk. Wrap them in a slice of bacon and secure with 2 chunks of chicken per skewer. Repeat with the remaining jalapeño, chicken, and bacon on 5 other skewers. Then load the remaining 6 skewers, alternating the pineapple, peppers, and mushrooms.

5. Drizzle the chicken skewers with the remaining marinade, and grill for 25 to 30 minutes, until the bacon is crisp and the chicken is fully cooked, turning once. Grill the vegetable skewers until grill marks appear and the mushrooms are tender, about 15 minutes, turning once. Serve warm.

FRIENDLY FANGATING TIP: Use a knife or other kitchen instrument to remove the jalapeño's seeds. Do not use your fingernails! They will burn for hours, along with any body part you touch!

FRIED OYSTERS

MAKES **2 DOZEN**

I like to create with regionally relevant recipes for specific sporting events. A few years ago, the Wisconsin Badgers took on the Stanford Cardinals in the Rose Bowl. The Bay Area is known for its incredible seafood, including, notably, its oysters. So I came up with this recipe as my homage to Stanford's team. I have a special place in my heart for fried oysters, especially on top of a Caesar salad. But for the purposes of designing tasty, easy-to-serve finger food, I thought, why not just serve these puppies alone? I love that they're bite-sized, so you can pop them in your mouth, one after the next, with no effort whatsoever. You may want to double or triple this recipe if you know you've got guests who, like me, can down a dozen of these in five minutes or less.

24 small oysters, shucked

$^1/_2$ cup all-purpose flour

$^1/_2$ teaspoon paprika

Sea salt and freshly ground black pepper

2 large eggs, beaten

1 cup panko breadcrumbs

Vegetable oil, for frying

Hot sauce

Lemon wedges

Tartar sauce

1. Drain the shucked oysters so they're dry.

2. Prepare three shallow bowls—one with the flour, paprika, and salt and pepper to taste; one with the beaten eggs; and one with the panko breadcrumbs.

3. Pour about 2 inches vegetable oil into a medium pot. Heat over high until the oil shimmers or reaches 350°F on a deep-fry thermometer. It should not be smoking. If it is, it's too hot; turn the temperature down.

4. First coat the oysters in the flour and paprika mixture. Follow that with a dunk into the egg so they're fully coated. Finish with a coating of the panko crumbs.

5. Working in batches, fry the oysters in the hot oil until they're browned around the edges, flip them, and fry them until they're golden brown, $1^1/_2$ to 2 minutes total.

6. Using a slotted spoon, remove the fried oysters from the oil and drain on a paper towel–lined rack or plate. Season with more salt and pepper.

7. Serve with hot sauce, lemon wedges, and tartar sauce on the side.

FRIENDLY FANGATING TIP: I like to serve these with a chilled glass of Anchor Steam to keep the Bay Area theme going. Anchor Steam, which was first brewed in San Francisco in 1896, is one of my favorites. Other great Bay Area beers include Russian River, Gordon Biersch, and any of the Moonlight Brewing Company ales.

"GO FOR GOLD" CHICKEN AND CASHEW LETTUCE WRAPS

MAKES **16**

Shaun White, America's most famous snowboarder, has competed in three consecutive Winter Olympic Games. And he's got two gold medals to show for it. Pretty remarkable if you ask me. Shaun has publicly shared that his favorite cuisine is Chinese, so I created this recipe in homage to the King of Snowboarding. This is a delicious and athlete-approved spin on the classic chicken with cashew stir-fry. I cut down on the fat by using chicken breasts instead of thighs and opted to couch this protein-packed entrée in lettuce, rather than serving it traditionally atop white rice. This way you've got an easy and tasty finger food recipe for your fangate.

3 tablespoons vegetable oil

1¼ pounds boneless, skinless chicken breasts, chopped into ¼-inch pieces

2 tablespoons cornstarch

½ teaspoon crushed red pepper flakes

½ teaspoon sea salt

¼ cup finely chopped green onion bulbs, plus 2 tablespoons thinly sliced green onion tops

1 tablespoon minced garlic

1 tablespoon minced fresh ginger

8 ounces snow peas, ends and threads removed, thinly sliced on the diagonal (about 2 cups)

1 large red bell pepper, julienned (about 1 cup)

½ red onion, thinly sliced (about 1 cup)

2 stalks celery, peeled and diced

¼ cup chicken stock

¼ cup hoisin sauce

2 tablespoons low-sodium soy sauce

2 tablespoons rice vinegar

½ cup roasted cashews

Freshly ground black pepper

16 Boston bibb or butter lettuce leaves

1. Heat the oil in a wok or a large skillet over high.

2. Place the chicken, cornstarch, red pepper flakes, and salt in a large zip-top plastic bag, and shake to coat.

3. When the oil is hot, add the chicken, and cook for 5 to 6 minutes, until the chicken turns opaque and is lightly browned. Transfer to a paper towel–lined plate to drain.

4. Reduce the heat to medium-high. Add the green onion bulbs, garlic, ginger, snow peas, red bell peppers, onions, and celery to the wok, and cook for 3 to 4 minutes, stirring often, until tender-crisp. Transfer the vegetables to a plate.

5. Stir together the chicken stock, hoisin sauce, soy sauce, and vinegar in a small bowl. Add to the wok, and stir with a wooden spoon to remove any browned bits from the bottom of the pan. Reduce the heat, and simmer the sauce for 1 to 2 minutes, or until slightly thickened. Return the chicken and veggies to the wok, and toss to coat everything well. Add the green onion tops and roasted cashews, season with pepper, and toss again.

6. Transfer the stir-fry to a serving bowl with a spoon. Serve with the lettuce leaves for wrapping.

HEALTHY CHIPOTLE CHICKEN POTATO SKINS

SERVES 6

Potato skins are a sportsfood staple. But I've got to say—and forgive me for sounding whiny—I've been served terrible ones so many times. Why are they so hard to make well? I think part of the problem is that, more often than not, people overcook the potatoes. And then once the potatoes get cold—yuck. Of course, I like this recipe for 'tater skins—it's my own. But I've also opted to use sweet potatoes because I think they're a bit juicier, they've got more flavor, and I find them less starchy. They're also so much more nutritious than regular potatoes. Add my chipotle chicken mixture on top and you'll hit your protein quota and enjoy every bite—you'll need a fork and knife for these!

3 medium-sized organic sweet potatoes

¹/₄ cup plus 3 tablespoons extra virgin olive oil

³/₄ pound boneless, skinless chicken breasts (about 2 small breasts)

¹/₂ teaspoon sea salt and ¹/₂ teaspoon freshly ground black pepper, plus more for seasoning

2 tablespoons fresh lime juice

2 cloves garlic, minced

1 tablespoon minced chipotles in adobo

1 teaspoon dried oregano

1 teaspoon ground cumin

2 teaspoons chili powder

2 cups spinach, wilted (see Tip)

5 ounces sharp white Cheddar cheese, grated

Plain Greek yogurt (see Tip)

Chipotle hot sauce, optional

Cilantro sprigs, roughly chopped

1. Preheat the oven to 350°F.

2. Wash the sweet potatoes, and prick them all over with a fork. Brush the skins with 2 tablespoons of the olive oil. Place in a Pyrex dish or on a baking sheet, and bake them for 50 to 60 minutes or until fork-tender.

3. Place the chicken in a baking dish, rub with 1 tablespoon of the olive oil, and season with a small dash of salt and pepper. Place the chicken in the oven alongside the potatoes, and cook for 25 to 30 minutes, until cooked through. Set aside to cool.

4. Meanwhile, combine the remaining ¹/₄ cup olive oil, lime juice, garlic, chipotle pepper, oregano, cumin, chili powder, and ¹/₂ teaspoon each of the salt and pepper in a medium bowl. Set aside.

5. Once the chicken is cool enough to handle, shred it with a fork or your fingers. Then combine it with the spinach, and keep warm.

6. Cut the sweet potatoes in half lengthwise, and let cool for 5 to 10 minutes more.

7. Increase the oven temperature to 400°F.

8. Using a spoon, scrape out the insides of the potatoes, leaving only the skin and a ¹/₄-inch layer of potato flesh. (Be careful not to tear the skins.) Return the skins to the baking dish, and brush the insides with the chipotle and herb mixture. Bake for 5 to 10 minutes or until crisp.

9. Meanwhile, add the remaining chipotle and herb mix to the spinach and chicken, tossing to combine.

10. Once the skins are done, stuff them with the chicken mixture, top with grated cheese, and bake for another 5 to 10 minutes, until the cheese has melted and the skins are hot and crisp. Serve topped with Greek yogurt, the hot sauce, if desired, and chopped cilantro.

FRIENDLY FANGATING TIP:

Feel free to wilt your spinach in the microwave by putting it in a bowl with 1 teaspoon water and zapping it for 20-second intervals. I like to substitute Greek yogurt for sour cream. They taste almost exactly the same, but Greek yogurt is much healthier and lower in fat and calories.

EMPANADAS

CONTRIBUTOR: **BRYAN VOLPENHEIN** | MAKES ABOUT **12**

I'm so excited to include recipes from US Olympic Champion Bryan Volpenhein in this book. His Olympic career is impressive to say the least, and you can read his long list of achievements on the opposite page. But something else that's really remarkable about Bryan, aside from the fact that he is the nicest person you'll ever meet, is that he is also a classically trained chef. How he found the time, I do not know, because he got his culinary arts degree in between Olympic Games. Throughout this chapter, you'll find a couple of his recipes, and take it from me—like Bryan, they are serious winners.

2¼ cups all-purpose flour, plus more for flouring work surface

1½ teaspoons sea salt

8 tablespoons (2 sticks) cold, unsalted butter

2 large eggs

⅓ cup ice water

1 tablespoon white vinegar

1 tablespoon water

Empanada Filling of choice (page 31 or 33)

Sour cream, for serving

Homemade Salsa (page 57)

1. To make the empanada dough, sift the flour and salt into a large bowl. Cut the butter into ½-inch cubes, and add to the flour. Blend with your hand or a pastry cutter until the mixture looks crumbly and the butter is in flaky chunks (like piecrust dough).

2. Beat together 1 egg with the ice water and vinegar. Add to the flour mixture, and mix with a fork until just combined. (It will still look a little shaggy.) Turn the dough out onto a lightly floured surface, and gently knead until it comes together. You will only need a few turns.

3. Tightly wrap in plastic wrap, and chill for 1 hour. (If you chill it longer, you will need to let the dough warm up slightly before rolling it out.)

4. Preheat the oven to 350°F.

5. Prepare an egg wash: Beat the remaining egg with 1 tablespoon water.

6. On a floured surface, roll out the dough into a ¼-inch-thick rectangle. Cut with a 3½-inch ring mold into approximately 10 rounds. Collect the scraps, and roll them out to make a couple more.

7. Fill each round with 1 tablespoon of your favorite filling (recipes follow). Lightly brush the edges with the egg wash, and gently fold the dough over the filling, sealing the edges with a fork to make half-moon shapes. (The dough will stretch a little, but be careful of tearing the dough.)

8. Brush the tops of the empanadas with egg wash, and bake on a foil-lined baking sheet for about 35 minutes, or until golden brown.

9. Serve with sour cream and salsa.

SALSA VERDE (MAKES ABOUT 3 CUPS)

1 pound tomatillos

2 medium jalapeños

$\frac{1}{2}$ large sweet onion

4 cloves garlic

Juice of 2 limes

2 tablespoons cilantro sprigs

1. Peel the husks off the tomatillos, and cut them into quarters.

2. Seed and chop the jalapeños, peel the onion and garlic cloves, and roughly chop them.

3. Place the vegetables in a food processor or blender. Add the lime juice and cilantro. Pulse until smooth, about 4 to 6 pulses.

CHORIZO AND POTATO FILLING (MAKES ABOUT 2$\frac{1}{2}$ CUPS)

3 to 4 medium Yukon Gold potatoes

8 ounces fresh chorizo

2 tablespoons olive oil

1 tablespoon chopped fresh oregano

$\frac{1}{2}$ cup crumbled queso fresco

Sea salt and freshly ground black pepper

1. Cut the potatoes into $\frac{1}{4}$-inch cubes, and put them in a large pot. Cover with cold water and a large pinch of salt. Bring to a boil, and cook until fork-tender, about 3 minutes. Drain and let cool.

2. With a sharp paring knife, slice the chorizo lengthwise, and remove the casings.

3. Heat a medium sauté pan over medium-high. Sauté the chorizo until cooked through. Add the olive oil, potatoes, oregano, and cheese; toss to combine. Season with salt and pepper.

CHICKEN AND BEAN FILLING (MAKES ABOUT 2$\frac{1}{2}$ CUPS)

2 chicken thighs, with or without skin, cooked (preferably grilled)

$\frac{1}{2}$ cup canned pinto beans, drained

4 ounces shredded pepper Jack cheese

$\frac{1}{4}$ cup Salsa Verde (recipe above)

Sea salt and freshly ground black pepper

1. Remove the chicken meat from the bones, and finely chop. (I like the skin's flavor and crispiness so I leave it on, but you can remove it.)

2. Combine the chicken in a bowl with the beans, cheese, and salsa, and toss to combine. Season with salt and pepper.

TASTY TIDBITS

Three-time Olympian Bryan Volpenhein has won too many medals to count. Bryan is the only two-time winner (2002 and 2004) of the US Rowing Male Athlete of the Year Award. In 2012, he was named the men's coach for the US National/Olympic Team and coached our guys to the podium in both the 2013 and 2014 World Championships.

RELLENO EMPANADAS

CONTRIBUTORS: **ALESSIA AND ROCKY MCINTOSH** | MAKES **20**

If you're an NFL fan, you probably know Rocky from his eight-year career as a linebacker, during which he played for the Washington Redskins, the St. Louis Rams, and the Detroit Lions. Alessia and Rocky are college sweethearts from the University of Miami, and they are two of the kindest people you will ever meet. The two are friends and former classmates of mine from grad school, and I adore their beautiful family and their entrepreneurial and philanthropically minded spirits. During the first module of grad school, Alessia and Rocky hosted an event for their A GRAN Foundation at the Palm in Washington, D.C., to which our entire grad school cohort was invited. The food, as always, was great, but the highlight of the evening was that the normal waitstaff had been replaced by Rocky and several of his Redskins teammates (both retired and current).

20 (5¹⁄₂-inch) discs of empanada dough, thawed (check the Hispanic freezer section)

1 to 2 large eggs, beaten (to make an egg wash)

¹⁄₂ cup Mexican crema

1 tablespoon aji Amarillo (yellow pepper) paste

¹⁄₂ teaspoon ground cumin

RELLENO FILLING

1 tablespoon olive oil

1 pound lean ground beef or chicken

Sea salt and freshly ground black pepper

¹⁄₄ cup chopped green onions

1 tablespoon aji Amarillo (yellow pepper) paste

1 small red bell pepper, chopped

2 tablespoons raisins

3 boiled eggs, chopped

¹⁄₂ cup chopped Spanish olives, optional

¹⁄₂ cup chopped fresh parsley

1 tablespoon soy sauce

1. Preheat the oven to 400°F.

2. Make the relleno filling: Heat the olive oil in a saucepan over medium. Add the meat and salt and pepper to taste. Cook, stirring often and breaking up the meat until browned, 6 to 8 minutes. Add the green onions, aji paste, and red peppers, and cook another 4 minutes. Add the raisins, chopped eggs, olives, if desired, parsley, and soy sauce to the pan, and mix together well.

3. Remove the filling from the heat, and cool to room temperature. Once cooled, fill each of the discs of dough with 2 generous tablespoons of the filling, brush the edges of each disc with the egg wash, and fold them over to create half-moon shapes. Seal the edges with a fork (or you can also fold the edges down by hand). Lightly brush the entire surface of the empanadas with egg wash.

4. Place the empanadas on a baking sheet, and bake for 18 to 20 minutes, until they take on a golden brown color.

5. Meanwhile, stir together the crema, aji paste, and cumin in a small serving bowl, and serve alongside the empanadas.

FRIENDLY FANGATING TIP: Alessia says that the specialty ingredients for this recipe can be most easily found in the Hispanic section of your grocery store.

SWEET POTATO CHIPS

SERVES **10**

Growing up, I had a sweet tooth. And then at some point—I'm not entirely sure when—my love for sugar transitioned to salt. (I had become my mother.) Now I crave the salty crunchiness of chips. Store-bought chips have gotten better and better in the last few years. The ingredients are increasingly simple and cleaner. I'm all for buying those instead of making them yourself. But, if you do want to make your own chips (simply so you can control the ingredients and the healthiness of them, or so you can season them yourself so they taste exactly as you want them to), here's an easy recipe for homemade. I have opted to use sweet potatoes rather than regular potatoes. That's a personal preference—I prefer the taste of sweet potatoes (and the fact that they're lower in carbs, sugar, and calories, and have significantly more calcium, Vitamin A, and Vitamin C than regular potatoes). But feel free to use regular potatoes for this recipe. Either spud type will yield the taste and crunch you know and love.

Avocado oil, for frying

2 medium to large sweet potatoes, peeled and cut widthwise into ⅛-inch-thick slices

Freshly ground black pepper

SEASONED SALT*

1 tablespoon garlic powder

1 tablespoon onion powder

½ teaspoon ground turmeric

1 teaspoon brown sugar

½ teaspoon paprika

1 teaspoon sweet smoked paprika

1 teaspoon sea salt

*A nice store-bought alternative to the seasoned salt is Lawry's.

1. Make the seasoned salt: stir together all the ingredients in a small bowl. Set aside.

2. Heat the avocado oil in a large Dutch oven or deep fryer over high until it reaches 360°F on a deep-fry thermometer. Working in batches, add 1 cup of the potato slices to the hot oil, and fry them, stirring to distribute them evenly, for 2 to 3 minutes, or until golden. Transfer to a paper towel–lined tray. Repeat with the remaining potatoes, making sure the oil comes back up to 360°F before adding the next batch.

3. Sprinkle the taters (lightly!) with black pepper and the seasoned salt. Serve immediately.

FRIENDLY FANGATING TIP: The thinner you slice the spuds, the easier it is to cook them so they're nice and crunchy. Although I tend to lean toward a healthier approach, these chips only absorb about ¼ cup of the frying oil and come out perfectly crispy and golden brown. The easiest way to get a thin slice is to use a mandoline or hand slicer. Just be very careful.

A HEALTHY SPIN ON FRENCH ONION DIP

MAKES ABOUT **2 CUPS**

If you're like me, you hear dip and you cringe just a bit—the word brings to mind the processed gunk at the grocery store that has so many chemicals in it I'm fairly certain it could withstand nuclear winter. Not exactly what I want to put into my body. It's really not all that hard to make dip, nor is it difficult to make French onion dip healthier. The usual recipe calls for ingredients like butter, sour cream, and mayonnaise—a trifecta of saturated fat. I use extra virgin olive oil in place of butter (because it is rich in monounsaturated fat, which lowers your "bad" cholesterol) and low-fat Greek yogurt instead of the sour cream and mayo. Suddenly the calories come way down and you're indulging in good, healthy fats. As an added bonus, Greek yogurt will save you from having to take your daily probiotic since the yogurt has billions of healthy live cultures in it already! I make to you this promise: This dip does not taste like health food, and your friends and fellow tailgaters won't know the difference.

2 tablespoons extra virgin olive oil

1 large yellow onion, finely chopped

2 cloves garlic, minced

1 teaspoon kosher salt

2 teaspoons Worcestershire sauce

1¹/₂ cups low-fat plain Greek yogurt

¹/₈ teaspoon cayenne pepper, or to taste

¹/₄ teaspoon freshly ground black pepper

Sweet Potato Chips (page 34)

1. Sauté the onions in the olive oil in a skillet over medium-high until caramelized, 10 to 12 minutes. Add the garlic, sprinkle with the salt, and sauté for 2 minutes more. Remove from the heat, and let cool for a few seconds.

2. Add in the Worcestershire sauce, and use a wooden spoon to scrape the olive oil and salt bits off the bottom of the pan. Stir everything together, and set aside to cool.

3. Stir together the yogurt, cayenne, and black pepper in a mixing bowl. Stir in the room-temperature onion-and-garlic mixture.

4. Refrigerate before serving the dip with my Sweet Potato Chips, and you've got a killer (healthier) tailgating snack!

BLUE CHEESE DIP

MAKES ABOUT 2 CUPS

I came up with this recipe to accompany my Buffalo wings. Some people prefer Ranch dressing for dipping them, but I've never been much of a Ranch girl—it's blue cheese or bust. Since so many of the commercial blue cheese dressings available are packed with chemicals, I figured it's just healthier and yummier to make it myself. And since this dip takes about three minutes to make, it's almost as easy as buying a bottle of packaged dressing. I prefer Blue Castello cheese because it's very creamy and mixes easily into the yogurt.

$1\frac{1}{2}$ cups low-fat plain Greek yogurt or sour cream

$\frac{1}{3}$ cup blue cheese, crumbled (preferably Blue Castello)

$\frac{1}{2}$ teaspoon sea salt

1 heaping tablespoon minced fresh chives

$\frac{1}{8}$ teaspoon freshly ground black pepper, plus more for serving

2 tablespoons water

Simply combine all the ingredients in a mixing bowl. Stir well, transfer into your serving vessel, sprinkle with some freshly ground black pepper, and serve.

NOT JUST SHAKERS ON THE TABLE

When I was a little girl, my dad used to take me on Amtrak up to New York from time to time to watch the Knicks play. I have such wonderful memories of the old Madison Square Garden—the purple seats and the ring around the second tier where crazy fans used to run around with big poster cutouts of the letter D and a picket fence. It was almost magical.

I was such a huge Knicks fan. Patrick Ewing was my favorite player in the NBA, but I also knew everything about his rotating teammates, John Starks (who for some reason I called "Sparky" when I think I might have meant Starky), Charles Oakley (Oak), Allan Houston, Marcus Camby, Charlie Ward, Hubert Davis, Greg Anthony, Herb Williams, Anthony Mason (may he rest in peace), Derek Harper, and the list goes on. I'm pretty sure I was the only little girl in my elementary school begging my mom to let me stay up late on school nights to watch my team play. And when it came time for the playoffs, going to bed early wasn't even remotely a question.

When my dad took me to games, I got to wear a special pass around my neck that allowed me to stay after the game, walk on the court, and go into the tunnels outside the locker room. (When I was really, really little I actually got to go into the locker room with my dad, provided I covered my eyes.)

Sometimes, my dad would leave me with other grown-ups while he went to talk to the coaches or the players. On one such occasion, my dad left me with Patrick's wife at the time, Rita, and these two nice women who were with her. I sat on the laps of these two women I didn't know and was mesmerized by their cool leather tops and the really long, intricately painted nails of one of them. Frankly, I had a blast being one of the girls, but I was too young to really know who the two women were.

Fast forward to about a year later when I was in fifth grade. I was watching MTV after school one day and the music video for the song "Shoop" came on. There, standing on the Coney Island boardwalk in front of a Mercedes-Benz convertible, stood the two women from the Knicks game. Yup, you guessed it. Salt-N-Pepa, two of the greatest female rappers of our time. I wish I had known who they were at the game!

HAM-AND-CHEESE DIP

SERVES **6 TO 8**

Ham and cheese go together like chocolate and peanut butter, chips and salsa, or meat and potatoes. Who doesn't love a ham-and-cheese sandwich? I've been eating them since I can remember. But the first time I had a honey-glazed ham—a Christmas ham, if you will—was in college, and it blew my mind. It's so much better than the thin deli-style ham slices you can buy at the grocery store. In this recipe, I chop a hunk of honey-glazed ham into small cubes and add them to a trio of ooey-gooey melty yummy cheeses. And then for good measure, I throw in some beer. This recipe has a lot of complex flavors even though it's pretty simple. It's one of my favorite recipes in the whole book. You can serve this dip hot, warm, at room temperature, or even cold. I happen to think it's good at any temperature. And my guinea pigs—ahem, friends—agree.

2 tablespoons extra virgin olive oil

1/2 large onion, diced

2 Fresno chiles, seeded and minced

1/4 teaspoon sea salt

3/8 teaspoon freshly ground black pepper

8 ounces cream cheese

1 cup pale ale

1 pound honey-glazed ham, minced

1 cup grated Gruyère cheese

1 cup grated Emmentaler cheese

1 cup grated sharp Cheddar cheese

1/4 cup minced fresh chives, plus more for garnish

1 baguette, sliced into 1/2-inch-thick rounds and lightly toasted

1. Heat the olive oil in a large ovenproof skillet over medium-high. Add the onions, chiles, salt, and 1/8 teaspoon of the pepper, and sauté until the onions are soft and translucent, about 5 minutes.

2. Reduce the heat to medium, and add the cream cheese and beer, stirring well until the cheese melts and there are no more lumps. Let simmer in the pan for 5 minutes to cook off the beer.

3. Reduce the heat to low. Add in the ham, trio of cheeses, chives, and remaining 1/4 teaspoon pepper. (It's best to add in each cup of cheese one at a time, stirring well, before adding in the next cup.)

4. Transfer the dip to a lidded pot, and place in your Hungry Fan™ 3-in-1 Fangating™ Bag to cook for 30 minutes for the flavors to gel. Alternatively, place your ovenproof skillet in a 200°F oven for 30 minutes.

5. Serve with another sprinkle of chives and the toasted baguette rounds for dipping.

CHICKEN NACHOS

SERVES **10 TO 12**

This is the most popular recipe on my website to date—it's simple and super tasty. I love these nachos for so many reasons. Hot, gooey cheese? Yes, please. Juicy chicken? Yup. Easy to share at a tailgate or house party? You bet. That is, if you feel like sharing. I am a kindergarten graduate, and therefore I have learned, if not mastered, the art of sharing. But when it comes to these chicken nachos, I am known to be a nachos hog. You'll have to wrestle that plate of chicken nachos out of my kung fu grip. You can easily substitute the plain chicken breast with barbecue chicken (or even pork). See my barbecue recipes in Chapter 4.

Parchment paper

2 cups shredded cooked chicken breast

3 to 4 teaspoons fresh lemon juice

1 teaspoon sea salt

1 teaspoon freshly ground black pepper

3 tablespoons canola oil

2 cloves garlic, peeled and crushed

6 green onions, chopped

1 cup Homemade Salsa (page 57)

Half a 12-ounce bag corn tortilla chips

2 cups shredded sharp Cheddar cheese

$\frac{1}{2}$ large tomato, diced

2 tablespoons pimiento-stuffed olives, sliced, optional

1 cup Italian-Style Spinach Artichoke Dip (page 51), optional

$\frac{1}{4}$ cup roughly chopped fresh cilantro, optional

1. Preheat the oven to 350°F.

2. Toss the shredded chicken with the lemon juice, salt, and pepper. Set aside.

3. Heat the oil in a large skillet over medium. Add the garlic and green onions, and cook for 1 minute, until softened. Toss in the chicken, stir in the salsa, and cook until most of the moisture evaporates and the chicken is warmed through, 2 to 3 minutes.

4. Cover a baking sheet with parchment paper, and evenly spread out the tortilla chips on the sheet. (The parchment paper will save you some cleanup.) Scoop some chicken mixture on each individual chip (you'll get bonus points for presentation), or pile it on top of a bed of chips, bar style. Sprinkle with the shredded Cheddar cheese.

5. Bake for 10 minutes. Remove from the oven, and let sit for a few minutes. Top the nachos with the tomatoes and olives, along with dollops of the spinach artichoke dip and cilantro, if desired, for tasty goodness.

FRIENDLY FANGATING TIP: You know how when you dress a salad way ahead of time it gets soggy? Nachos are the same way. Here's a simple tip to keep your nachos fresh and crunchy: Assemble them immediately before serving! If you're tailgating outside the stadium, fear not: You can use a cast-iron skillet on your grill. Melt the cheese in the skillet, drizzle it onto your tortilla chips, and boom! Hot, crunchy nachos alfresco!

BBQ PULLED PORK NACHOS

SERVES **10 TO 12**

Here's another take on nachos. Really, you can make nachos however you'd like. All you need are tortilla chips, some cheese, and whatever else you want to layer on top. I slow-cook pork pretty often; it's so easy and immensely tasty. But all too often I make way too much, so this recipe arose from the leftovers. This is an easy dish to throw together last minute, as prep time and cook time combined are maybe 10 minutes. I assure you, though, that the ease of the recipe doesn't detract from its taste. This one will make your friends keep coming back for more.

Parchment paper

1 (8-ounce) bag corn tortilla chips

1½ cups (about 11½ ounces) BBQ Pulled Pork (page 127 or 148)

1 (15-ounce) can black beans, rinsed and drained

8 ounces finely shredded mozzarella cheese or queso blanco

2 green onions, finely chopped

1 to 2 fresh jalapeños, thinly sliced, to taste

¾ cup sweet yellow corn kernels (canned is fine; just drain it well)

½ avocado, peeled and cut into small chunks

1 cup Homemade Salsa (page 57)

½ cup sour cream (or low-fat plain Greek yogurt if you want to keep it healthier)

1 teaspoon chopped fresh chives, optional

1. Preheat the oven to broil. Line a rimmed baking sheet with parchment paper.

2. Spread out the tortilla chips on the prepared baking sheet. Evenly top with the pork, beans, cheese, and green onions.

3. Place under the broiler for 2 minutes, just until the cheese melts.

4. Top with the jalapeños, corn, and avocados. Serve with the salsa and sour cream on the side or dolloped on top. Sprinkle with the chives, if desired.

MEDITERRANEAN NACHOS

MAKES **1 LARGE PLATE**

I have to admit it—I'm a total nacho fiend. Whether I'm watching the game from the stands or on the couch at home, there are few things I find more satisfying than a plate of crunchy, cheesy nachos. I love playing around with different flavors, which is how I came up with my Mediterranean nachos—a healthier and more interesting riff on the classic dish. Preparing fresh hummus and tzatziki makes all the difference in this awesomely easy snack.

1 (8-ounce) bag baked pita chips

²/₃ cup thinly sliced romaine lettuce

¹/₂ cup Kalamata olives, chopped

²/₃ cup diced tomatoes

¹/₂ cup crumbled feta cheese

HUMMUS

1 (15.5-ounce) can chickpeas

3 tablespoons tahini

4 to 5 ice cubes

Juice of 1 lemon

2 cloves garlic, peeled and crushed

2 tablespoons extra virgin olive oil

TZATZIKI

1 cup reduced-fat (2%) plain Greek yogurt

2 cloves garlic, peeled and crushed

Juice of 1 lemon

2 tablespoons extra virgin olive oil

1 sprig dill, finely chopped

1 small cucumber, half minced, half diced

Sea salt and freshly ground black pepper

1. Make the hummus: Drain the chickpeas, and skin them by placing them in a single layer on a paper towel and rubbing gently; the skins will come right off with your fingers. Place in a food processor with the tahini, blend, and then drop in the ice cubes one by one to create a very smooth texture. Transfer to a bowl, and add the juice of 1 lemon, 2 crushed garlic cloves, and 2 tablespoons olive oil. Mix well. If you want a thinner consistency (similar to nacho cheese or refried beans), stir in 1 tablespoon water.

2. Make the tzatziki: Combine the Greek yogurt, 2 crushed garlic cloves, the juice of 1 lemon, and 2 tablespoons olive oil, the dill, minced cucumbers, and salt and pepper to taste in a bowl. Stir thoroughly so all ingredients are evenly incorporated.

3. Lay out the pita chips on a tray or serving plate. Top with ³/₄ cup of the hummus and ³/₄ cup of the tzatziki, and sprinkle with the diced cucumbers, lettuce, olives, tomatoes, and feta. Serve immediately with any leftover hummus and tzatziki on the side.

The adorable McIntosh kids, usually picky eaters, chow down on this nacho dish that their mom, my good friend Alessia, wife of star NFL linebacker Rocky McIntosh, made after seeing my demo on the Today show.

TACHOS

You've heard of nachos. You've heard of tater tots. Combining them creates sheer taste bud amazingness in the form of what I call "Tachos." The key to this recipe is that the tater tots must be served really crispy and hot. This dish is goopy, so you really want your tots to hold up to the cheesy yumminess like tortilla chips would.

6 ounces dried chorizo, diced

$^1/_2$ cup Negra Modelo, or another dark beer

16 ounces extra-sharp Cheddar cheese

1 serrano pepper, seeds and veins removed, minced

1 (4-ounce) can diced green chiles, drained

2 tablespoons thinly sliced green onions

3 cups tater tots

2 tablespoons plain Greek yogurt or sour cream

$^1/_4$ cup Homemade Salsa (page 57)

1 tablespoon minced fresh cilantro

Freshly ground black pepper, optional

1. Cook the chorizo over medium in a large saucepan for 8 to 10 minutes, until crisp and the fat has rendered. Transfer to a paper towel–lined plate to drain, and discard the rendered fat.

2. Heat the beer in the same saucepan over high for about 5 minutes to reduce it a bit. Reduce the heat to low, and add the cheese, stirring often as it melts into the beer. Once fully melted, add the fresh and canned chiles, 1 tablespoon of the green onions, and half the chorizo. Bring to a simmer for 7 to 10 minutes.

3. Transfer your lidded pan into your Hungry Fan 3-in-1 Fangating™ Bag, and let it cook and marinate in its own goodness for 1 hour. Alternatively, continue to simmer on your stovetop for 1 hour.

4. Meanwhile, bake the tater tots in a preheated oven according to package directions, making sure to cook them to their crispiest.

5. Remove the cheese sauce from the Fangating™ Bag, and stir very well, in case it has gotten a bit clumpy.

6. Place the tater tots on a large tray, and drizzle the cheese sauce on top. Dollop with the yogurt and salsa. Top with the remaining chorizo and green onions and the cilantro. Feel free to sprinkle with some freshly ground black pepper, too, and then serve immediately.

CINCINNATI SKYLINE CHILI DIP

CONTRIBUTOR: BRYAN VOLPENHEIN | SERVES **10 TO 12**

US Olympic Champion Bryan Volpenhein, or "Volp" as his friends call him, hails from Cincinnati and attended Ohio State University ("Go Buckeyes!"), where he rowed for the university's crew club. It therefore comes as no surprise that Volp makes a mean Skyline Chili. Cincinnati chili usually combines sweet and fairly hot spices and is typically served atop a bed of spaghetti. Volp has taken this chili one step further and has made it into a mean dip. Put away the forks, people. This is meant to be eaten with chips. Volp prefers Fritos Scoops!. Heads-up from Volp: "This is a recipe people will love, so you better grab what you want because it'll go quick! The chili recipe yields more than you'll need for the dip, so serve it as is alongside—it's yummy!"

2 tablespoons olive oil

1 large onion, finely chopped

5 cloves garlic, minced

2 pounds ground beef (preferably 85% lean)

Sea salt and freshly ground black pepper

4 cups water

2 tablespoons chili powder

1½ teaspoons ground cinnamon

1 tablespoon ground paprika

1 tablespoon cocoa powder

½ teaspoon allspice

½ teaspoon ground cloves

1 teaspoon ground cumin

½ teaspoon celery seed

1 tablespoon Worcestershire sauce

2 tablespoons apple cider vinegar

1 (15-ounce) can crushed tomatoes

2 bay leaves

2 tablespoons chopped fresh oregano

Corn chips, for serving

Green onions for garnish

1. Sauté the onions in the oil in a skillet over medium-high until translucent, about 3 minutes. Add the garlic, and sauté gently, until fragrant and soft. (Be careful not to burn the garlic.)

2. Stir in the ground beef, and cook for about 3 minutes, stirring occasionally. Season with salt and pepper. Add the water, and simmer over medium-low, uncovered, for 30 minutes, stirring often, breaking up the meat to make a thin, pourable chili.

3. Add the chili powder, cinnamon, paprika, cocoa, allspice, cloves, cumin, celery seed, Worcestershire, vinegar, tomatoes, bay leaves, and oregano. Stir to combine. Reduce the heat to low, and simmer for about 2 hours, stirring often.

4. Remove from the heat, and let cool overnight. Skim off any fat that has collected on the top.

5. The next day, make the chili dip (see Friendly Fangating Tip below). Serve with corn chips.

FRIENDLY FANGATING TIP: To make the chili into a dip: Preheat the oven to 375°F. Lightly grease an 8- x 8-inch baking dish with cooking spray. Spread 10 ounces room-temperature cream cheese evenly into the bottom of the prepared dish. Spread 1½ cups of the chili evenly on top, and cover with 8 ounces shredded Cheddar. Bake for about 15 minutes, until the cheese is melted and the sides are bubbly.

BUFFALO CHICKEN DIP

CONTRIBUTOR: DON DAVIS | MAKES ABOUT **5 CUPS**

Two-time Super Bowl Champion Don Davis is one of the smoothest guys you'll ever meet. I first got to know him in 2012 when, along with some other extraordinary athletes you'll be introduced to in this book, we attended business school at George Washington University. Don oozes confidence and intelligence, and he is an incredible public speaker. Whenever he made a presentation to the class, he sounded like John Coltrane playing the saxophone. Were it not for his imposing physical appearance (Don is downright jacked), you'd probably never guess he spent 11 years of his life as an NFL defensive lineman for the Saints, the Bucs, the Rams, and ultimately the Patriots, with whom he earned his two Super Bowl rings. Don's more than just a leader on the field and in the classroom—he's a family man who knows his way around the kitchen.

2 1/2 cups shredded rotisserie chicken or 1 pound chicken breasts, cooked and chopped

12 ounces cream cheese, softened

3/4 cup store-bought Ranch dressing

1/2 cup red hot sauce

1/2 cup tangy Buffalo wing sauce (to make homemade, see page 169, but omit the oil)

1 cup shredded mild white Cheddar or mozzarella cheese

1 (10-ounce) bag Tostitos Scoops

1. Preheat the oven to 350°F.

2. Combine the chicken, cream cheese, Ranch dressing, hot sauce, and Buffalo wing sauce in a medium bowl, and mix well. Spoon into a baking dish, top with the cheese, and bake for 30 minutes.

3. Serve immediately with the Scoops.

Me with my grad-school classmates. From left to right: US Olympic rower Garrett Klugh, Super Bowl winner Don Davis, me, and professional baseball player Justin Humphries.

BACON HUMMUS (PICTURED ON PAGE 48)

MAKES ABOUT 1¾ CUPS

I know, I know. No need to tell me. Hummus is a Middle Eastern dish, and people from that part of the world don't necessarily embrace bacon like we do here in the States. Is it sacrilegious to add bacon to hummus? Maybe. If it is, I apologize. But my goodness, hummus—like so many other foods—really does taste better with bacon. If you decide to whip up this dip for your tailgate, don't fret if it's a bit grainy. That's the bacon flavor crystals parading around on your taste buds like it's Brazilian Carnival. You can serve this with crackers, cucumbers, celery, carrots, or other sliced veggies.

8 strips bacon

1 (15.5-ounce) can chickpeas, drained and rinsed

5 ice cubes

2 tablespoons extra-virgin olive oil

3 tablespoons fresh lemon juice

2 crushed cloves garlic

¹/₂ teaspoon sea salt

1 teaspoon freshly ground black pepper

1. Brown the bacon in a large skillet over medium-low for 15 minutes. Transfer the bacon to a paper towel–lined plate, and reserve the drippings in the skillet.

2. Purée the bacon and its drippings in a food processor until smooth, not grainy (or as minimally grainy as possible). Alternatively, purée 6 slices, and reserve 2 for garnish. Add the chickpeas, and blend well, adding in 1 ice cube at a time. (This helps to make it creamy.)

3. Add the oil, lemon juice, garlic, salt, and pepper, and blend again until smooth. Transfer to a serving bowl, and crumble the remaining 2 slices of bacon over the top.

Carrot Cilantro Hummus
and Bacon Hummus (page 47)

CARROT CILANTRO HUMMUS

MAKES ABOUT **2 CUPS**

I developed this recipe for March Madness a few years ago. I was playing on the word *dunk* and made up a couple of dip recipes (in which you could dunk food). Cheesy, I know. But I happened to really like how this recipe came out, so I went with it. You could also serve this at your next NBA All-Star Weekend party. To keep with the theme, I'd suggest serving it during the Dunk Contest. Da dun dun ching! Okay, now I'm just being silly...

1 cup chopped carrots

1 (15.5-ounce) can chickpeas, drained and rinsed

$1/4$ cup tahini

Zest of 1 lemon, finely chopped

$1/4$ cup fresh lemon juice

2 teaspoons honey

3 cloves garlic, minced or pressed

$1/3$ cup roughly chopped fresh cilantro, plus more for garnish

3 ice cubes

Sea salt

1. Place the carrots in a microwave-safe bowl with $1/4$ cup water, and microwave at HIGH for 3 minutes. Drain.

2. Place the carrots, chickpeas, tahini, lemon zest, lemon juice, honey, garlic, and cilantro in a blender or food processor. Purée until smooth, adding one ice cube at a time as you blend until you reach the desired texture.

3. Transfer to a serving bowl, add salt to taste, and garnish with more cilantro. Serve with sliced vegetables, crackers, or chips for dipping.

TWELFTH (MAN) LAYER DIP

MAKES **3 QUARTS**

I came up with this recipe right before the 2015 Super Bowl. It is my ode to the Twelfth Man, the name by which the amazing fans of the Seattle Seahawks are known. These people have my love and admiration. They have not only set world records for the incredible level of noise they create, they have literally caused earthquakes—actual seismic activity on the Richter scale. This dip is intentionally colorful, looks great in a parfait dish, and is comprised of the flavors you'd associate with Seattle and the Pacific Northwest. Beware: If you're not a seafood person, this dip is not for you. And do not let it stand for a long period of time; it should be served and enjoyed immediately!

1 cup crème fraîche

1 teaspoon coffee grounds

1 cup sour cream

2 ripe avocados, pitted and peeled

4 teaspoons fresh lemon juice

8 ounces cream cheese, softened

6 ounces smoked salmon, roughly chopped

1 cucumber, finely chopped

1 1/2 tablespoons finely chopped fresh dill

2 (3.75-ounce) cans smoked oysters

12 ounces lump crabmeat

4 ounces salmon roe

1 cup diced hearts of palm

7 1/2 ounces wild pink salmon, flaked

18 to 20 bagel chips, crumbled, and more for serving

1. This is essentially a 12-layer dip. First make all your layer components: Combine the crème fraîche and coffee grounds; combine the sour cream and fresh dill; and mash the avocados with the lemon juice.

2. Layer the ingredients in a 2½-quart round baking dish as follows (starting from the bottom and working your way up): cream cheese, smoked salmon, cucumbers, oysters, sour cream–dill mixture, crabmeat, salmon roe, hearts of palm, coffee–crème fraiche mixture, salmon, and mashed avocados. Top with the crumbled bagel chips. You can eat with more bagel chips, toasted baguette rounds, crackers, tortilla chips, regular chips, or whatever you'd like.

FRIENDLY FANGATING TIP: If making in advance, do not put the bagel chip crumbles on top until serving or they will get soggy. This dish could be prepared in the morning and served for the evening game, but I wouldn't leave it in the fridge for more than six hours. You can serve this dip chilled.

ITALIAN-STYLE SPINACH ARTICHOKE DIP

MAKES **2 QUARTS**

I know some people are weird about artichokes. I happen to love them, and I love them in dip. But typical spinach-artichoke dip (of which I can eat an entire bowl myself) is really, really bad for you. It's basically all cream, mayo, and cream cheese—fat upon fat upon fat. And for me, that takes away some of the fun of devouring it—even if it's my eat-whatever-I-want day. This version is much healthier and it's yummy. Win-win!

   I first made this dip to bring to my friend's NYC Marathon party in Brooklyn. Her apartment (and its quintessential stoop) happens to line up perfectly with the mile-eight marker along the route. It was a beautifully crisp fall day, and this warm dip was just perfect to munch on as we cheered the runners passing by. Both my friend and another guest at the party are judges on *Iron Chef America* and are famously picky. I watched them eat multiple servings of my dip, which left me feeling pretty good. Serve this yumminess with sliced baguette, crostini, or crackers. You can also serve it atop my Chicken Nachos on page 38.

1 head cauliflower, cut into florets

1 cup plain Greek yogurt

¹/₂ cup cream cheese, softened

2 tablespoons extra virgin olive oil

1 teaspoon sea salt

1 teaspoon freshly ground black pepper

1 tablespoon dried chopped or minced onions (I use McCormick's)

¹/₂ pound pancetta, cut into ¹/₄-inch cubes

1 (10-ounce) box frozen spinach, thawed and squeezed dry

1 (14-ounce) can artichoke hearts, drained and coarsely chopped

4 cloves garlic, minced

2 heaping tablespoons finely chopped fresh basil

¹/₄ cup finely chopped fresh Italian (flat-leaf) parsley

2 cups grated Parmesan cheese

1. Preheat the oven to 375°F.

2. Purée the cauliflower and the yogurt in a food processor. Midway through, add the cream cheese, olive oil, salt, ¹/₂ teaspoon of the pepper, and the onions, and continue pulsing until smooth. Set aside.

3. Sauté your pancetta (no oil needed as it's plenty fatty) in a skillet over medium-high until browned, about 8 minutes. (I like mine a little crispy to add extra texture to the dip.) Use a slotted spoon to drain off the excess fat before adding it to the dip.

4. Combine the cauliflower mixture and the pancetta in a large, oven-safe bowl. Add the spinach, artichokes, garlic, basil, parsley, Parmesan, and remaining ¹/₂ teaspoon pepper. Mix very well.

5. Bake for 35 minutes, until the cheese is melted, lightly browned, and piping hot.

BACON GUACAMOLE

MAKES ABOUT **3 CUPS**

I mean, be serious. Guacamole is one of the most delicious foods on the planet. But as I discovered while I was tinkering around in the kitchen in preparation for an afternoon of World Cup viewing, guac can be so much better with bacon! I like this rendition of my more classic guacamole recipe (page 247) because it's got great texture. Guacamole is a bit mushy, but when you add in the crispy bacon, there's so many more layers to enjoy. And I don't use just any bacon to make this recipe—it's thick cut all the way for chunks of crispy, porky goodness in every bite!

4 ripe avocados, pitted and peeled

4 small cloves garlic, minced, or to taste

2 tablespoons poblano pepper, minced (or more if you like it hot; you can also use a spicier pepper)

1 large shallot, minced

1 teaspoon kosher salt

$1/2$ teaspoon freshly ground black pepper

$1/4$ cup fresh chopped cilantro

Juice of 1 large lime

1 vine-ripened or heirloom tomato, seeded and diced

5 slices of thick-cut bacon, cooked crispy and chopped

Tortilla chips, for serving

1. Making this dish is über easy—a child could do it (minus the cooking the bacon part, which I like to do on a griddle).

2. Put the avocados into a large serving bowl, and smush to your preferred consistency with a fork, a large spoon, or even a potato masher.

3. Add the remaining ingredients and mix well. Serve with tortilla chips.

BACON TRUFFLE DIP

MAKES ABOUT **5 CUPS**

You don't often come across truffles in your typical game-day recipe. They're usually reserved for fancy special-occasion dinners where they're delicately shaved over your risotto or pasta. (If you ever meet me or my dad, be sure to ask us about the famous Falk truffle story featuring my lovely friend Diana. It's still funny years later.) In any case, I came across some truffle cream cheese (that was not crazy expensive like those special dinner truffles are), took one whiff of it, and knew I had to make it into a dip. Thus was born this delicious recipe, which can be served with chips, vegetable crudité, crackers, or toasted baguette rounds.

2 pounds bacon, cut into $1/2$-inch pieces

1 medium onion, sliced

16 ounces Urbani truffle cream cheese

2 cups plain Greek yogurt

2 teaspoons extra virgin olive oil, optional

$2/3$ cup finely chopped fresh chives, plus more for garnish

$1/2$ cup seeded and diced serrano chiles

Sea salt and freshly ground black pepper

1. Working in batches, sauté the bacon in a skillet or on a griddle over medium until it is brown and crispy, but not burnt, about 6 minutes. Transfer to a paper towel–lined plate. Discard all but 2 tablespoons of bacon fat.

2. Add the onions to the bacon fat in the skillet, and cook over medium until caramelized, about 10 minutes. Cool slightly, and then roughly chop.

3. Preheat the oven to 350°F.

4. Combine the cream cheese and yogurt in a medium bowl or stand mixer. Mix well, using olive oil to thin the dip, if necessary. Add the bacon, onions, $1/3$ cup of the chives, and the chiles. Season with salt and pepper, and spoon into a baking dish. Bake for 20 minutes.

5. Sprinkle with the remaining chive, and serve warm.

WATERMELON SALSA (PICTURED ON PAGE 56)

MAKES ABOUT 3½ CUPS

When I think of summertime, I envision picnicking and drinking cold lemonade (or beer if it's that kind of day) while sitting out on the lawn (aka the cheap seats) while watching America's favorite pastime—baseball. I recall many a warm North Carolina day catching a Durham Bulls game, or other times spent on the grassy patch outside Petco Park in San Diego following the innings on the Jumbotron. Certain summers offer World Cup tournaments or the Summer Olympic Games. All are great opportunities to kick back and fangate with friends in the sunshine.

Watermelon is probably my favorite summertime fruit—it's just so refreshing and simply tastes like summer. Summer is also when tomatoes are in season and, in my humble opinion, ripe tomatoes are probably the greatest thing on earth. I eat them like apples. This salsa recipe captures the effervescence of these two ingredients but still gives you the kick you'd expect from a salsa. This might just be my favorite salsa recipe.

2 cups watermelon, cut into ¼-inch cubes

1 cup quartered Kumato or other cherry tomatoes

2 tablespoons diced jalapeños

½ cup diced red onion

1 heaping tablespoon minced fresh cilantro

1 heaping tablespoon plus 1 teaspoon minced fresh mint

¼ cup coconut water

Juice of half a lime

1 teaspoon sea salt

Pinch of freshly ground black pepper

Tortilla chips, for serving

Place all ingredients into a medium serving bowl, and stir together. Serve with tortilla chips.

Black Bean Salsa and
Watermelon Salsa (page 55)

BLACK BEAN SALSA

CONTRIBUTOR: **MARK SCHLERETH** | MAKES ABOUT **3 CUPS**

If you're like me and watch ESPN regularly, then you know Mark Schlereth. In fact, that's where I met Mark—when I was up at the campus visiting. Mark's both a talented radio and TV sportscaster. And certainly it goes without saying, with an NFL career like his, he was a pretty good football player, too. During his 12 years in the NFL, he played in two Pro Bowls and won three Super Bowls—one with the Washington Redskins and two with the Denver Broncos.

This is Mark's black bean salsa recipe, which he recommends you serve with his Green Chile Eggs Benedict. You can find that recipe on page 165.

1 (14-ounce) can black beans, rinsed and drained

1 cup Homemade Salsa (see below)

$^1/_4$ cup chopped fresh cilantro

Juice and zest of 1 lime

Sea salt and freshly ground black pepper

Combine the black beans, salsa, cilantro, and lime juice, and zest ingredients in a bowl. Season with the salt and pepper, and stir well.

HOMEMADE SALSA (MAKES ABOUT 2 CUPS)

I read that salsa has overtaken ketchup as America's favorite condiment. I can't say I am all that surprised. It's so simple, so delicious, and I love the texture. I can demolish an entire jar myself without even thinking about it. Just give me some chips—or don't. I've been known to eat salsa with a spoon from time to time. Don't judge. You know you have, too (wink wink).

Here's a very simple recipe to make good, quality salsa at home, so you don't have to buy the packaged stuff at the store. I guarantee you'll get a boost to your game day street cred when your friends hear you made this yourself.

1 pint cherry tomatoes

2 jalapeños, roughly chopped, seeds included

$^1/_2$ cup fresh cilantro leaves

2 green onions, chopped

Juice of 1 lime

Sea salt and freshly ground black pepper

Combine all the ingredients in a food processor, including salt and pepper to taste, and pulse to your preferred consistency.

SOUPS, SALADS & FLATBREADS

This chapter is chock-full of some of my favorite recipes—and it's probably the most varied chapter in this book. I grouped soups, salads, and flatbreads because these recipes are not quite the finger food like those dishes featured in the last chapter, but they could suffice as a meal for an individual or very easily be shared at a fangating meal.

I happen to be a soup fiend. All kinds of soups—I simply love them. I eat them when it's cold or warm out. I don't discriminate. In the world of sportsfood, chili seems to be everyone's go-to, particularly once the weather starts to get cold. You can make it well in advance of your fangate, and the flavor only seems to improve as it sits and marinates in its own goodness. The same can be said for most, if not all, of the other soup recipes you'll find in this chapter. I encourage you to branch out and give some a try. They're hearty and flavorful and are good alternatives to the same bowl of chili over and over again.

Salad need not only consist of rabbit food—I like my salads to be meals unto themselves. They're generally easy to make in bulk and can be served in both an attractive serving bowl or in a large aluminum container, depending where you're eating or serving. And you don't have to be a health nut to enjoy them. I find that beyond their nutritional value, salads also add a lot of color to a plate otherwise stacked high with ribs, mac 'n' cheese, and other fangating favorites. They say you eat with your eyes, and my eyes happen to love a colorful dish.

And I threw flatbreads in here because they've been some of the most popular appetizers that I've served to friends. While they're not dissimilar to pizza—and I've got a couple "pizza" recipes in here, too—they don't always have to be simply cheese atop tomato sauce atop bread.

BAKED POTATO SOUP

SERVES **12**

My mom used to be a secret baked potato fiend. When I was a kid, we'd occasionally bring in dinner and she'd order a super-loaded baked potato. I'm talking butter, sour cream, chives, Cheddar cheese, and bacon. The works! It made her so very happy. You could see it all over her face. As an ode to my mom as well as all you baked potato lovers, I give you this soup. It's essentially a fully loaded baked potato in soup form. Serve it piping hot during those colder tailgating months. And if you're reheating it the next day, just add some milk or additional veggie broth, stir well, and zap it in the microwave. You're good to go.

5 russet or Yukon Gold potatoes

Olive oil

½ teaspoon sea salt, plus more for sprinkling on the potatoes

12 slices bacon, chopped

4 large cloves garlic, minced

¼ cup all-purpose flour

6 cups vegetable broth

¾ cup half-and-half

4 tablespoons butter

½ teaspoon freshly ground black pepper

¼ teaspoon red pepper flakes

⅓ cup green onions, thinly sliced, plus more for serving

1½ cups sharp Cheddar cheese, plus more for serving

½ cup crème fraîche, for serving

1. Preheat the oven to 450°F.

2. Clean each potato, leaving the skin on. Wrap the potatoes individually in aluminum foil. Place them all on a baking sheet, and bake for 1 hour. Remove from the oven, and increase the oven temperature to 500°F.

3. Unwrap the potatoes, brush them with some olive oil, and sprinkle with a touch of salt. Return the potatoes to the oven, and bake for 15 minutes.

4. Meanwhile, sauté the bacon in its own fat in a Dutch oven over medium, stirring often, until crispy, about 12 minutes. Transfer to paper towels to drain. Discard all but ¼ cup of the bacon fat, add the garlic, and sauté for 1 minute. Stir in the flour, and cook, stirring, for 1 to 2 minutes. Pour in the broth and half-and-half, and bring to a simmer. Remove from the heat.

5. Mash the potatoes with the butter, ½ teaspoon salt, and pepper in a large bowl.

6. Bring the broth mixture up to a simmer. Add the mashed potatoes, bacon, red pepper flakes, and green onions. Stir in the cheese until it melts.

7. Serve the soup with a dollop of crème fraîche on top, some of the shredded sharp Cheddar, and another sprinkle of green onions and black pepper.

PAPPA AL POMODORO WITH BACON

SERVES **12**

Pappa al pomodoro is a Tuscan dish I came to love when I was living and studying in Florence. It's basically peasant food—a bowl of reconstituted stale bread with garlic, onions, olive oil, tomatoes, and herbs—but it tastes so stinkin' good, I happen to adore the texture, and it really fills you up. I make this dish often for friends and family, mostly because I love to eat it (selfish perhaps, but it always goes over well). And when the weather turns colder, I especially love serving this at my fangate. It's so hearty and warm and cozy and awesome, giving you energy to cheer your head off. For the purposes of jazzing it up a bit for you tailgaters who love your bacon (as do I), I added some Italian bacon—also known as pancetta. It gives the dish a nice smokiness and saltiness—I like to think of it as snazzy little bacon flavor crystals to discover throughout your bowl. *Buonissimo!*

1 (1-pound) loaf stale bread, pulled into chunks

1 pound pancetta (Italian bacon), cut into bite-sized chunks

1 cup diced yellow onions

5 cloves garlic, minced

1¹/₂ teaspoons sea salt

1 teaspoon freshly ground black pepper

4 (26.46-ounce) boxes Pomì finely chopped tomatoes

¹/₄ cup finely chopped fresh basil, plus leaves for garnish

¹/₄ cup finely chopped fresh Italian (flat-leaf) parsley, plus more for garnish

¹/₄ cup extra virgin olive oil, plus more for serving

Grated Parmesan cheese, for serving

1. Soak the bread in water in a large bowl until it's soaked through, about 1 minute, and then wring it out as you would a towel. Put in another large bowl, and set aside.

2. Cook the pancetta in a large stockpot over medium for 10 minutes, stirring often, until it begins to crisp on the edges and the fat has rendered. Add the onions, and cook for 5 minutes, stirring often. Add the garlic, and cook for 1 minute; at this point the pancetta should be crispy and the onions and garlic tender. Add the salt, pepper, tomatoes, basil, and parsley. Stir in the bread, and bring to a boil, stirring often to prevent sticking; reduce the heat to medium-low, and cover. Cook for 30 minutes, stirring often. Stir in the olive oil, and reduce the heat to low. Cover and cook for 1 hour.

3. Place the covered pot into the Hungry Fan™ 3-in-1 Fangating™ Bag and let cook for 3 hours. Alternatively, continue simmering on the stovetop over low heat, covered, for 3 hours.

4. Serve in bowls, each topped with a drizzle of extra virgin olive oil and a sprinkling of Parmesan cheese plus chopped basil and parsley.

BROCCOLI-CHEDDAR SOUP

SERVES **4**

I've noticed that there are a lot of people who'd rather not eat broccoli. I think some people consider broccoli to be Brussels sprouts' equally unappealing cousin. (I happen to love both with unadulterated affection. But that's just me.) But you know what else I've noticed? If you melt Cheddar cheese on broccoli, people like it—even those who aren't broccoli lovers. That's essentially what this soup is: Broccoli covered in melty, gooey Cheddar cheese—just put it into the food processor to achieve a puréed soup consistency. Sure, there's a bit more to it than that, but not much more. And here's a fun tip: You can serve this recipe as more than just soup! Pour it onto some chicken breasts, and bake to make Broccoli-Cheddar Chicken. (It'll be the star of your next fangate!)

2 ½ cups chicken stock

1 cup half-and-half

4 tablespoons butter

1 medium yellow onion, chopped

¼ cup all-purpose flour

12 ounces broccoli florets

1 teaspoon sea salt

½ teaspoon freshly ground black pepper

1 ½ cups shredded sharp Cheddar cheese, plus more for garnish

Sour cream, for serving, optional

1. Microwave the chicken stock and half-and-half in a glass measuring pitcher at HIGH for 2 minutes.

2. Melt the butter in a large saucepan over medium. Add the onions, and sauté for 3 minutes, until softened. Stir in the flour, and cook, stirring constantly, for 1 minute. Stir in the hot stock mixture, and bring to a simmer for 2 minutes, until slightly thickened. Add the broccoli, salt, and pepper. Reduce the heat to low; cover and simmer for 30 minutes, stirring occasionally, until the broccoli is tender but still bright green.

3. Remove from the heat, and let cool a bit. Then transfer to a food processor, and purée. (I like my soup a little chunky, so I leave a few lumps.) Return the soup to the saucepan over low heat, and stir in the cheese until melted.

4. Top the soup with a dollop of sour cream, if desired, and a sprinkle of shredded Cheddar, and serve!

CHICKEN MOAMBÉ

CONTRIBUTOR: DIKEMBE MUTOMBO | SERVES **8**

There are so many great things that can be said about Dikembe Mutombo, it's hard to know where to start. Many of you know him as the finger-wagging 7-foot-2-plus NBA All-Star ("No-no-no"). Others may know him as an NBA Global Ambassador, philanthropist, and incredible humanitarian. He is all these things and more, with a personality and smile that light up a room. Dikembe hails from the Congo—as does this recipe—and it's one of his favorites. It's essentially a chicken, tomato, and peanut butter soup (the *moambé* in the title refers to the peanut butter). Just a note about making this recipe: You can swap in bone-in chicken breasts and even thighs to add a lot of additional flavor, which both Dikembe and I prefer to do. But you'll need to remove them before serving, or advise those who'll be eating the soup to be on the lookout.

5 tablespoons red palm or coconut oil

3 pounds boneless, skinless chicken breasts, cut up into chunks

2 large yellow or white onions, diced

1 red chile pepper, seeds and veins removed, minced

12 whole pieces of okra, chopped

3 cloves garlic, minced

2 green onions, chopped

Sea salt and freshly ground black pepper

Red pepper flakes to taste, optional

1 (26.46-ounce) box Pomì finely chopped tomatoes

6 ounces tomato paste

1 cup water

³/₄ cup smooth peanut butter

1. Heat 3 tablespoons of the oil in a Dutch oven over high. Add the chicken, in batches if necessary, and brown on all sides, about 11 minutes, but do not fully cook it. Remove from the Dutch oven, and set aside.

2. Add the remaining 2 tablespoons palm (or coconut) oil to the Dutch oven, and reduce the heat to medium-low. Add the onions, chile pepper, and okra, and sauté until the onions are caramelized, stirring to ensure nothing burns, about 4 minutes.

3. Stir in the garlic, green onions, salt, pepper, and red pepper flakes, if desired, along with the tomatoes, tomato paste, and water; cook for 5 to 7 minutes.

4. Return the chicken to the Dutch oven, stir again, and cook for another 3 minutes.

5. Increase the heat to bring the soup to a boil, then reduce the heat, cover, and simmer for 30 minutes.

6. Remove 1 cup of the soup, and whisk it in a medium bowl with the peanut butter until the two emulsify. Return this mixture to the soup, and stir it in to combine well. Let the stew cook for another 5 minutes, uncovered, over low. Serve!

I had the great fortune to make Dikembe's recipe with him, and it's caught on video. You can check it out on hungryfan.com

TASTE-OF-FALL SQUASH SOUP

SERVES **8 TO 10**

Fall is my favorite time of year. I love the crispness in the air, the smell of wood-burning fireplaces, and the return of NFL and college football. I also adore fall veggies—especially squash and pumpkin. It may be fair to say that this adoration has actually become a healthy obsession. (I am one of those people who drinks pumpkin spice beer, pumpkin spice chai and coffee... and am beside myself when they're no longer on the menu after Thanksgiving.) This soup tastes like everything I love about fall, and I'll often prepare it on Monday or Thursday nights—when I am in the midst of a work week and am ready to come home after a long day to eat din din and watch football. This is easy to store in Tupperware in the fridge, so all you have to do is heat it up and your picnic dinner in front of the TV is ready!

3 tablespoons extra virgin olive oil

2 cloves garlic, minced

1 medium yellow onion, diced

2 shallots, minced

1 1/2 teaspoons minced fresh ginger

3 Padrón peppers, seeded and minced

2 teaspoons sea salt

1 cup white wine (I like Chardonnay for this recipe)

4 cups vegetable broth

1 red kuri squash or small sugar pumpkin, peeled and cut into 1-inch pieces

1 butternut squash, peeled and cut into 1-inch pieces

1 acorn squash, peeled and cut into 1-inch pieces

1/2 teaspoon freshly grated nutmeg, or to taste

1/2 teaspoon ground cinnamon, or to taste

2 cups low-fat goat's milk or half-and-half, optional

2 medium shiitake mushrooms, sliced lengthwise

Handful of pecans, chopped

1/2 cup minced fresh chives

Freshly ground black pepper

1. Heat 2 tablespoons of the olive oil in a large Dutch oven over medium to medium-high heat. Once the oil is hot, sauté the garlic, onions, shallots, ginger, and peppers for 5 minutes, until the onion and shallot pieces become translucent. Stir in the salt, wine, broth, and squashes. Cover and bring to a boil over medium-high. Reduce the heat to medium, and simmer for 20 to 25 minutes, stirring occasionally, or until the squash is very tender.

2. Using an immersion blender, blend your soup until it's smooth. Sprinkle in the nutmeg and cinnamon, and blend into the soup. Simmer uncovered for 20 minutes. Stir in the milk, if desired.

3. When the soup is almost done cooking, add the remaining 1 tablespoon olive oil to a skillet, and heat over medium-high. Add the shiitakes and pecans, and sauté, stirring frequently, for about 5 minutes, until the shiitakes are browned and the pecans are toasted.

4. To serve, ladle the soup into bowls, making sure to clean off the sides if you spill. Top with some of the shiitake and pecan mixture, a sprinkle of chives, and some freshly ground black pepper.

FRIENDLY FANGATING TIP:

If you find the soup is still too lumpy for your taste, strain it before garnishing and serving. If you choose not to use goat's milk or any dairy, you may want to add more wine and/or broth to make the soup more liquidy.

CHEESEBURGER SOUP

SERVES **6**

This soup—to be quite frank and simple—is a cheeseburger in a bowl, minus the bread. (But if you serve it with toasted crostini... bam! Just like that, you've got all the cheeseburger components.) I really tried to think outside the box when developing this soup section, and I came up with this recipe idea while eating a cheeseburger at a sports bar. I thought to myself, all these ingredients are delicious. And they taste so great together. What if I just blended them and called it a soup? So I went home and tried it. Epic success... at least I think so. I hope you do, too!

$1^{1}/_{4}$ pounds ground beef

4 slices bacon

4 tablespoons butter

$^{1}/_{2}$ medium onion, chopped

3 stalks celery, diced

8 ounces sliced baby portobello mushrooms

2 cups tightly packed baby spinach

4 cups chicken broth

1 teaspoon sea salt

$^{1}/_{2}$ teaspoon freshly ground black pepper

1 teaspoon dried parsley, plus more for garnish

$^{1}/_{4}$ cup all-purpose flour

6 slices Monterey Jack cheese

$^{1}/_{4}$ cup ketchup (to make your own, see page 245)

1 cup half-and-half

$^{1}/_{4}$ cup sour cream, optional

1 ripe tomato, chopped, for garnish, optional

1. Cook the beef in a large Dutch oven over medium-high until it browns evenly, about 6 minutes. Drain and transfer to a plate.

2. Cook the bacon in the same Dutch oven over medium until it gets crispy, 5 to 7 minutes. Transfer to a cutting board to cool, and drain all but 2 tablespoons of the bacon fat from the pan. Chop the cooled bacon into small, crunchy bits, and set aside.

3. Using the same Dutch oven, add 1 tablespoon of the butter to the remaining bacon fat, and stir in the onions and celery. Sauté until the onions become translucent, about 4 minutes. Add the mushrooms, and cook for 5 to 6 minutes, until tender and lightly browned. Add the spinach. (It will start to wilt amid the hot veggies.) Pour in the broth; add the beef, salt, pepper, and parsley, and bring to a simmer. Cover and simmer for 15 minutes.

4. Meanwhile, melt the remaining 3 tablespoons butter in a small skillet over medium. Add the flour, and cook for 1 minute while stirring. The roux should start to bubble, signaling that it's ready.

5. Add the roux to the soup and bring to a boil for 3 to 4 minutes, stirring well to incorporate the roux. Reduce the heat, and simmer for another 10 minutes. Add the cheese, ketchup, reserved bacon, and half-and-half. Stir well, and simmer for another 5 minutes.

6. Remove the soup from the heat, let sit for 3 to 5 minutes, and then stir in the sour cream, if desired.

7. Serve with a little sprinkle of additional parsley and the chopped tomatoes for a little color, if you like.

CHILLED RED BELL PEPPER SOUP

SERVES 2

Soup doesn't always have to be hot. (Think gazpacho.) I happen to love soup and I eat it year-round. I first came up with this recipe when I was home one night watching pre-season NFL (Giants vs. Steelers). As it was August in New York, you can imagine that it was still quite hot and sticky outside (and given my apartment's limited air conditioning, inside as well). I took stock of what was in the fridge and whipped up this easy but flavorful chilled soup.

1 red bell pepper, seeded and roughly chopped

¹/₂ cup low-fat plain Greek yogurt

¹/₄ yellow onion, roughly chopped

2 tablespoons tomato paste

1 mini cucumber, roughly chopped

2 tablespoons rice vinegar

2 teaspoons Dijon mustard (to make your own, see page 246)

2 large cloves garlic

2 tablespoons extra virgin olive oil

¹/₂ teaspoon sea salt

Fresh Italian (flat-leaf) parsley, minced, for garnish

Salted pumpkin seeds, for garnish

Freshly ground black pepper, for serving

1. Purée all the ingredients (except the garnishes) in a blender. Chill for 1 hour.

2. Serve topped with some parsley and a sprinkle of pumpkin seeds.

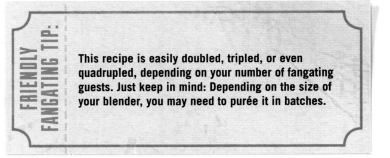

FRIENDLY FANGATING TIP: This recipe is easily doubled, tripled, or even quadrupled, depending on your number of fangating guests. Just keep in mind: Depending on the size of your blender, you may need to purée it in batches.

KENTUCKY TOMATO BOURBON SOUP

SERVES **4**

When I initially came up with this recipe, it was my go-to for the Kentucky Derby. But then the University of Kentucky Wildcats Men's Basketball Team went undefeated in the 2014–2015 regular season and made it all the way to the Final Four. To honor them, I debuted this recipe on ABC 7 (New York) in my March Madness segment. The soup went over really well with both anchors, especially Rob Nelson, who particularly enjoyed the Jim Beam component. He got a little silly, and needless to say, we all laughed quite a bit that day.

2 tablespoons butter

3 medium carrots, chopped

1 medium onion, chopped

3 cloves garlic, minced

¼ cup finely chopped fresh Italian (flat-leaf) parsley, plus more for serving

1 cup Pomì finely chopped tomatoes

2 cups Pomì tomato sauce

1 teaspoon sea salt

½ teaspoon freshly ground black pepper, plus more for serving

1 teaspoon brown sugar

¼ cup Kentucky bourbon

½ cup half-and-half

1. Melt the butter in a Dutch oven over medium. Add the carrots, onions, garlic, and parsley. Cook for 7 to 9 minutes, until the onions are translucent, being careful not to burn the garlic.

2. Stir in the tomatoes, tomato sauce, salt, pepper, brown sugar, and bourbon. Bring to a boil; reduce the heat to a simmer, cover, and cook for 30 minutes, stirring occasionally.

3. Stir in the half-and-half, and sprinkle with some more pepper and parsley. Enjoy!

ABC 7 New York anchor Rob Nelson and me making funny faces on set.

BACON BRUSSELS SPROUTS SOUP

SERVES **6**

This is another one of those recipes that disguises healthy veggies in a hearty—and in this case, bacon-y delicious—soup. I made this recipe with moms in mind. Can't get your kids to eat Brussels sprouts on game day (or ever)? Try this soup. It's delectable. And thanks to modern technological advancements in cooking tools, particularly in food processing, the kids won't even know it's got Brussels sprouts in it! For a creamy version of this soup, stir in 1 cup heavy cream at the end.

1 pound Brussels sprouts

1 tablespoon butter, melted

1 teaspoon finely ground Himalayan salt

1/2 teaspoon freshly ground black pepper

4 cups low-sodium chicken stock, plus more if needed

1 tablespoon extra virgin olive oil

1 pound bacon, cut into 1/4-inch cubes

4 large cloves garlic, finely chopped

1 medium yellow onion, finely chopped

2 medium russet potatoes, cut into 1/2-inch cubes

1/3 cup finely chopped fresh cilantro

1. Remove the bottoms and outer leaves of the Brussels sprouts. Halve lengthwise, and thinly slice almost to the root; discard the ends. Put the Brussels sprouts and enough water to cover by 1 to 2 inches in a large Dutch oven over medium-high and boil for 10 minutes, until they become very tender. (You need them to be quite tender or the purée will turn out lumpy.) Strain and then douse the Brussels sprouts with cold water to stop the cooking process; drain.

2. Transfer to a blender with the butter, salt, and pepper. Pulse while slowly pouring in the chicken stock and olive oil. Purée until you get a smooth texture. Set aside.

3. Heat the same pan over medium-high. Add the bacon, and cook, stirring frequently, until crisp, about 10 minutes. Using a slotted spoon, transfer the bacon to a paper towel–lined plate. Remove all but 2 tablespoons of the bacon fat.

4. Add the garlic and onions to the pan, and sauté until the onions are translucent, the garlic starts to brown, and there is little bacon fat left in the bottom of the pan, about 5 minutes. Add the Brussels sprouts purée, and bring to a simmer, stirring occasionally, about 6 minutes.

5. Add the potatoes, and simmer over medium-low, stirring occasionally, for 10 minutes, or until tender.

6. Stir in the cilantro and reserved bacon, and serve.

SUPER SPORTS SUNDAY SLOW-COOKED CHILI

SERVES **6**

Okay, I know I said an alternative to chili is a good thing—and it is. But I figured I couldn't write a game day cookbook without including a solid go-to chili recipe. There are so many things that are awesome about chili, but here are my top five: 1) Chili is incredibly hearty and, even though it's a soup, it can stand alone as a meal; 2) the texture is way more satisfying than most other soups—you don't have to just slurp it down, you can actually chew it; 3) if it's decent chili, it's got serious kick and tons of flavor; 4) it's perfect for late fall and winter fangating because it'll heat you up with both its temperature and spice quotient; and 5) it's easy to make ahead of time and tastes better the next day once the flavors and spices have had time to marinate in their own goodness. This chili recipe has it all—plus plenty of kick and even beer to get your tailgate going.

2 pounds ground beef

1 large yellow onion, diced, plus more for serving

2 cloves garlic, minced

1 (15-ounce) can pinto beans, drained

1 (26.46-ounce) box Pomì finely chopped tomatoes

½ habanero chile, seeded and very finely chopped (use less or more depending on your taste for spice)

1 (6-ounce) can or tube tomato paste

1 (4-ounce) can diced green chiles

¾ cup beer (I prefer dark beer such as Negra Modelo for a deeper flavor)

¼ cup chili powder

1 tablespoon dried oregano

1½ teaspoons ground cumin

¼ teaspoon cayenne pepper

1 teaspoon sea salt, plus more to taste

Sour cream or plain Greek yogurt, for serving

Shredded Cheddar cheese, for serving

Fresh cilantro, chopped, for serving

1 (10- to 11-ounce) bag tortilla chips, for serving

1. Cook the ground beef, onions, and garlic in a large Dutch oven over medium-high until no pink remains, about 6 minutes. Drain and return to the pan.

2. Add all the other ingredients except those for serving. Stir well, and then bring to a boil over high. Let boil for a couple minutes, then stir, cover, and reduce the heat to low; simmer for 15 minutes. Give the chili a good stir, cover again, and simmer for another 2 minutes.

3. Transfer the covered pan to the Hungry Fan™ 3-in-1 Fangating™ Bag, and seal well. Cook for 3 hours. Alternatively, continue to simmer over low, covered, for 3 hours, stirring occasionally. Season with salt.

4. Serve topped with your choice of fixings: sour cream (or Greek yogurt), shredded Cheddar, chopped cilantro, diced onions, and tortilla chips. (I like the chips crumbled on top.)

FRIENDLY FANGATING TIP:

I prefer to use organic grass-fed beef in my chili, and my friend, Will Witherspoon, sells great grass-fed beef from his farm at shiregatefarm.com. But this can easily be replaced with ground turkey, bison, venison, or even ostrich! Ask your butcher, or order online at fossilfarms.com

CHILLED AVOCADO SOUP

SERVES **2 TO 4**

My family has a beach house on Kiawah Island, South Carolina. One of the things that I love the most about Kiawah—aside from how beautiful and restful it is down there—is the food. Kiawah is just outside Charleston, which is an incredible foodie town. But in this case, I'm talking about the actual fresh produce and fish you can get on the island. I have a particular penchant for the fresh shrimp I've watched being brought in from local fishing boats along with the fresh fish. And no meal would be complete without some of the colorful produce that is sold at an adorable little roadside farmers' market just off the island. (They have the best butter beans.) Perhaps the only thing better is catching the fish yourself. On one fishing trip, we bartered the fish we had caught for some fresh blue crabs. Can't beat that freshness.

3 avocados, pitted and peeled

¹/₂ teaspoon sea salt

Freshly ground black pepper, to taste

¹/₄ cup extra virgin olive oil

¹/₃ cup roughly chopped fresh cilantro

¹/₂ yellow onion, roughly diced

1¹/₂ cups chicken, fish, or vegetable broth, plus more as needed

¹/₄ cup fresh lime juice, plus more to taste

1 cup lump crabmeat (from the claw)

Finely diced red onion, for garnish

1. Combine the avocados, salt, pepper to taste, olive oil, ¹/₄ cup of the cilantro, and the yellow onions in a blender. Pulse several times, and then blend (I like to use the "smoothie" setting) while pouring in the chicken broth and lime juice. Blend until the soup reaches a creamy consistency, adding more broth if necessary.

2. Combine the crabmeat and remaining cilantro in a separate bowl. Splash with some more lime juice and a sprinkle of pepper, and mix it all together.

3. Chill the avocado soup for at least 2 hours. To serve, top the soup with the crabmeat mixture and the red onion.

My dad and me—holding one of the soft-shell crabs my family and I bartered for on our Kiawah fishing trip.

50-MINUTE SEAFOOD GUMBO

CONTRIBUTOR: LANCE JOHNSTONE | SERVES **AT LEAST 12**

There are many things I find impressive about my friend Lance Johnstone. But perhaps most remarkable is that in his eleven NFL seasons, he only missed nine games. Nine! Maybe that's because he was living on his grandmother's gumbo. This recipe is a spin on her original Baldwin, Louisiana, recipe, which Lance first tried to make before giving it to me for this book. Lance explained that he and his wife took turns stirring the roux for hours and hours: "You gotta keep stirring it… all day! I need a break! More oil! More flour! More oil! More flour!" So Lance researched a roux replacement to make this recipe easier and less time-consuming. And it was a great success! Lance told me that this tastes just like his grandmother's gumbo. And then he laughed. Turns out as his grandmother got older, she started using the roux in a jar as well and didn't tell anyone. Sneaky! Lance warns that this recipe makes a lot of gumbo. He cooks it in a full-fledged Army pot. So unless you're feeding an army of fangaters, you can cut this recipe in half. Adding toasted French bread and a fresh salad makes this a complete meal.

1 pound fully cooked pork, beef, or turkey sausage links, sliced into rounds

1 cup chopped yellow onions

1 cup chopped green bell peppers

1/2 cup chopped celery

3 cloves garlic, finely chopped

1 (8-ounce) jar instant dry roux (see Tip)

3 1/2 cups cold water

1 (14.5-ounce) can diced tomatoes

2 tablespoons Cajun seasoning

1 teaspoon freshly ground black pepper

1/2 teaspoon dried thyme

1/2 teaspoon dried oregano

3 cups fresh or frozen okra

2 1/2 pounds medium shrimp, cleaned and deveined

1 pound lump crabmeat (from the claw)

2 pints shucked oysters, drained

1 tablespoon gumbo filé powder

12 cups cooked white or brown rice

Cayenne pepper, for serving

Tabasco sauce, for serving

(CONTINUED)

1. Make the stock (see opposite page): Combine the water, bouillon base, garlic powder, paprika, and bay leaves in a 6-quart pot. Bring to a boil over high; reduce the heat and simmer for 10 minutes. Remove the bay leaves. Reduce the heat to low, and keep the stock warm.

2. Add the sausage to a 12-quart pot, and cook over medium until browned, 6 to 8 minutes. Transfer to a plate. In the hot drippings, sauté the onions, peppers, celery, and garlic over medium to medium-high until the onions are translucent, about 10 minutes.

3. Combine the roux and cold water, and add to the large pot with the tomatoes, Cajun seasoning, pepper, thyme, and oregano. Cook, stirring constantly, for 5 minutes or until very thick. Gradually add the hot stock mixture while stirring constantly. Bring to a boil, stirring frequently, then lower the heat, and simmer for 10 minutes.

FRIENDLY FANGATING TIP: Dry roux in a jar may seem sacrilegious to some, but it saves you from having to make a roux from scratch, which is the longest and hardest part of making a gumbo. (In fact, it would be impossible to make gumbo in under an hour without it.)

(CONTINUED)

GUMBO STOCK

5 quarts water

¹/₃ cup Better Than Bouillon seafood and/or chicken base

2¹/₂ tablespoons garlic powder

1 teaspoon paprika

5 bay leaves

4. Stir in the okra and the reserved sausage, and simmer for another 10 minutes. Add the shrimp, crab, oysters, and filé powder, and cook over low for 10 minutes. Remove from the heat, cover, and let stand for 10 minutes.

5. Serve in deep soup bowls over white or brown rice with cayenne pepper and Tabasco sauce on the side for extra seasoning.

TOMATO BASIL SOUP

SERVES **2**

While tomato basil soup isn't the heartiest of fangating fare, it's great paired with a good old-fashioned grilled cheese sandwich. And it's also just great to warm up as football season progresses into the late fall and winter, when tailgating weather gets downright chilly. It's not as filling as a chili, per se, but it's just as warm and inviting! Sure, you could just go buy a can of it and heat it over a burner or grill. But I promise you, this isn't a tough recipe, and homemade just tastes so much better.

3 cloves garlic, minced

1 tablespoon extra virgin olive oil

1 (26.46-ounce) box Pomì chopped tomatoes

1 teaspoon sea salt, or more to taste

¹/₂ teaspoon freshly ground black pepper

2 tablespoons fresh basil, minced

¹/₄ cup heavy cream

Grated Parmesan cheese, for serving

BASIL OIL

¹/₂ cup tightly packed fresh basil leaves

¹/₄ cup extra virgin olive oil, plus more if desired

¹/₄ teaspoon sea salt

1. Make the basil oil: Purée all the ingredients in a food processor. To make it extra oily, add more olive oil until you reach the desired consistency. Strain through a fine-mesh sieve, and discard the solids.

2. Make the soup: Sauté the garlic in the olive oil in a medium soup pot over medium-low for 2 minutes.

3. Add the tomatoes, and stir in the salt, pepper, basil, and heavy cream. Heat over medium for 10 minutes, stirring occasionally.

4. Serve in bowls, each topped with a swirl of the basil oil and a sprinkling of Parmesan cheese.

GRILLED CAESAR SALAD

SERVES **8**

My sister and I are Caesar salad aficionados. In fact, Caesar salad was the first real dish I ever learned how to make. I found a basic recipe when I was in elementary school on the back of a bottle of Kraft Grated Parmesan Cheese. I took it upon myself to try it, and I have been perfecting my recipe ever since! I love all kinds of Caesar salads, but my favorite, hands down, is made with grilled lettuce. Such incredible texture! You'll want to make your dressing and croutons first so you can serve your salad as soon as the lettuce is ready to come off the grill.

4 tablespoons extra virgin olive oil

2 cups stale sourdough bread, cut into bite-sized pieces

1 teaspoon freshly ground black pepper, plus more for serving

$1/2$ cup grated Parmesan cheese

2 large heads romaine lettuce, quartered lengthwise

2 teaspoons sea salt

2 tablespoons chopped fresh Italian (flat-leaf) parsley

DRESSING

$1/2$ cup extra virgin olive oil

2 tablespoons Worcestershire sauce

2 teaspoons anchovy paste

Juice of 1 lemon

2 teaspoons grated Parmesan cheese

1 teaspoon garlic powder

$1/2$ teaspoon onion powder

1 teaspoon freshly ground black pepper

$1/2$ teaspoon sea salt

$1/4$ cup mayonnaise (to make your own, see page 250), optional

1. Preheat the grill to medium-high.

2. Make the dressing: Simply combine all the dressing ingredients in a mixing bowl, and whisk together until emulsified. (You will likely need to give it another quick whisk before plating.)

3. Make the croutons: Heat 2 tablespoons of the olive oil in a large nonstick skillet over medium. Throw in the stale bread cubes, season with $1/2$ teaspoon of the pepper, and sprinkle with 2 tablespoons of the Parmesan cheese. Stir frequently until the bread starts to toast and the Parmesan cheese melts into the croutons, 3 to 4 minutes. Set aside to cool.

4. Drizzle the lettuce with the remaining 2 tablespoons olive oil, and season with the remaining $1/2$ teaspoon pepper and the salt. Cook on the grill, cut side down, until you see grill marks, about 5 minutes. Turn the lettuce over, and grill for another 2 to 3 minutes on the second cut side.

5. To serve, place the grilled lettuce on a plate, and sprinkle with the croutons. (I like serving the whole lettuce stalks and letting my guests cut them up.) Next, evenly sprinkle with the remaining 6 tablespoons Parmesan cheese, and drizzle with the dressing (be sure not to drown the lettuce in it). Lastly, sprinkle with some freshly ground black pepper and the parsley, and serve.

BUFFALO CHICKEN SALAD

SERVES **2**

Need I mention again my obsession with Buffalo wings? Truth be told, my favorite way to eat Buffalo chicken is in the wing form—but chicken tenders are pretty awesome, too (such as those in my Buffalo Chicken Tacos recipe on page 169). A fun thing to do with these is to serve them atop a refreshing salad that nicely balances the sour, spicy tartness of the Buffalo sauce. Plus, it's on the healthier side, so you don't have to feel totally guilty about blowing your diet on game day.

6 chicken tenders

All-purpose flour or brown rice flour (if you're gluten-free), for dredging

2 tablespoons garlic chili oil

3 cups lettuce, kale, or baby spinach, or a combination

6 cherry tomatoes, quartered

$^1/_2$ Honeycrisp apple, sliced

$^1/_4$ cup crumbled blue cheese

$^1/_4$ cup microgreens

Freshly ground black pepper

BUFFALO SAUCE

2 tablespoons vegetable or olive oil

$1^1/_2$ tablespoons white vinegar

$^1/_4$ teaspoon cayenne pepper

$^1/_8$ teaspoon garlic powder

$^1/_2$ teaspoon Worcestershire sauce

2 teaspoons Tabasco sauce

$^1/_4$ teaspoon sea salt

6 tablespoons Louisiana hot sauce

DRESSING

2 tablespoons mayonnaise

1 tablespoon white balsamic vinegar

$^1/_2$ teaspoon fresh lemon juice

$^1/_4$ teaspoon freshly ground black pepper

1. Make the buffalo chicken sauce: Combine all the ingredients in a mixing bowl, and whisk well until emulsified.

2. Make the dressing: Whisk together all the dressing ingredients until emulsified.

3. Dredge the chicken tenders in flour, and then sauté them in the garlic chili oil in a large skillet until cooked through, about 3 minutes per side. Add $^1/_3$ cup of the Buffalo sauce and sauté until the sauce coats the chicken and starts to brown, about 2 minutes (watch the hot sauce fumes!). Remove from the heat, and drizzle additional sauce, as desired, over the chicken.

4. Combine the greens, tomatoes, apple slices, and blue cheese in a serving bowl. Drizzle with the dressing, and toss well. Top with the buffalo chicken, sprinkle with the microgreens and a couple grinds of pepper, and serve immediately.

SEEMINGLY FANCY
(BUT REALLY NOT) LENTIL SALAD

SERVES **4**

A very tasty lunch in Athens, Greece, inspired this dish. Prior to that trip, I can't say I ate a great deal of lentils. I've always liked them, but they just weren't a big part of my diet. Boy was I missing out! This salad is refreshing but also hearty, and I find it makes a great alternative to your normal lettuce-based fangating salad. It's also a good offering for your vegetarian or vegan friends—just hold the anchovies (unless they eat fish).

1 cup dried French lentils

$^1/_4$ cup extra virgin olive oil

2 tablespoons white wine vinegar

2 teaspoons fresh lemon juice

1 teaspoon lemon zest

2 teaspoons anchovy paste or 2 anchovies, minced

1 tablespoon chopped fresh oregano

$^1/_2$ cup roughly chopped fresh Italian (flat-leaf) parsley, plus more for garnish

$^1/_2$ teaspoon sea salt

$^1/_8$ teaspoon freshly ground black pepper

6 to 8 large cherry tomatoes, quartered

Shaved Pecorino-Romano cheese

1. Fill a medium saucepan about halfway with water, and add the lentils. Bring to a boil, then reduce the heat to a simmer, and cover. Cook for 25 minutes, until the lentils are soft; drain and cool to room temperature.

2. Combine the olive oil, vinegar, lemon juice and zest, anchovy paste, oregano, parsley, salt, and pepper in a blender. Blend until the parsley leaves are pretty well chopped and the dressing is emulsified.

3. Combine the tomatoes, the dressing, and the lentils in a bowl. Toss so the lentils are well coated.

4. Transfer the dressed lentils and tomatoes to plates, topping with some shaved Pecorino. Garnish with additional parsley, and serve chilled.

THE GREEN GODDESS SALAD

SERVES **6**

This famous salad originated at the Palace Hotel in San Francisco in 1923. It's named for the tint of its dressing, which predates Ranch dressing. For a very long time, this was the most popular salad dressing on the West Coast—and it's still quite popular today. I decided to share my rendition of the Green Goddess Salad for a segment I did in 2013 on the nationwide syndicated cable program *The Better Show*. It was my ode to the San Francisco 49ers, who faced off against (and lost to) the Baltimore Ravens in Super Bowl XLVII.

2 heads butter lettuce, leaves torn up

6 canned artichoke hearts, quartered

2 vine-ripened tomatoes, sliced into thin wedges (12 slices per tomato)

Freshly ground black pepper

DRESSING

2 green onions, cut into 1-inch pieces

3 tablespoons fresh lemon juice

4 anchovy fillets

1 large clove garlic, peeled

$1/4$ cup fresh tarragon leaves

2 teaspoons fresh chervil

$1/4$ cup fresh parsley leaves

Kosher salt and freshly ground black pepper

1 cup reduced-fat (2%) plain Greek yogurt*

*This recipe typically calls for sour cream or mayonnaise, but I substitute Greek yogurt to reduce the fat and calories.

1. Make the dressing: Place the green onions, lemon juice, anchovies, garlic, tarragon, chervil, and parsley in a blender. Season with salt and pepper, and blend until smooth. Add the yogurt, and process until just blended. Refrigerate for up to 1 week, if you like.

2. Combine the lettuce, artichoke hearts, and tomatoes in a serving bowl. Top with $3/4$ cup of the dressing. Sprinkle with an additional grind of pepper, toss, and serve.

Chopped Salad (page 84)
and Green Goddess Salad

CHOPPED SALAD (PICTURED ON PAGE 83)

CONTRIBUTOR: CHRIS DOLEMAN | SERVES **4 TO 6**

NFL Hall of Famer Chris Doleman is like my uncle. We often joke about it. When he's in New York, he often invites me to attend events with him, and when people ask me who I'm with, I'll say, "Oh, my Uncle Chris." Chris is immensely thoughtful and smart, and he enjoys food like I do. He was the first athlete to contribute a recipe to this book, and for that I'll always be grateful. I've since made this salad several times, and I'm guessing you'll enjoy it as much as I do. The secret to making it right—according to Chris—is to chop everything finely, which allows you to get a lot of flavor and texture in one bite!

1 pound large (24-count) shrimp

2 tablespoons olive oil

Sea salt and freshly ground black pepper

1 head romaine lettuce, finely chopped

$\frac{1}{2}$ head iceberg lettuce, finely chopped

$\frac{1}{4}$ cup minced fresh basil

$\frac{1}{4}$ cup minced fresh parsley

$\frac{1}{3}$ cup capers, sautéed in olive oil, or to taste

$\frac{1}{2}$ medium red onion, finely chopped

2 vine-ripened tomatoes, diced

1 cup pitted Kalamata olives, finely chopped

$\frac{3}{4}$ cup crumbled feta cheese

DRESSING

$\frac{1}{3}$ cup extra virgin olive oil

3 tablespoons champagne vinegar

1 tablespoon fresh lemon juice

$\frac{1}{2}$ teaspoon sea salt

$\frac{1}{4}$ teaspoon freshly ground black pepper

1. Heat the grill or a grill pan over medium-high. Toss the shrimp with the olive oil. Season with salt and pepper and toss again.

2. Grill the shrimp for 1 to 2 minutes per side, until slightly blackened. Let cool, and then roughly chop.

3. Combine the lettuces, herbs, capers, onions, tomatoes, olives, and feta with the shrimp in a large serving bowl. Set aside.

4. Combine all the dressing ingredients in a mixing bowl, and whisk until emulsified.

5. Pour the dressing over the salad, and sprinkle with freshly ground black pepper to taste. Toss together well, and serve.

TASTY TIDBITS

Chris Doleman is an eight-time NFL Pro Bowler, a three-time First-Team All-Pro, and was inducted into the NFL Hall of Fame in the class of 2012. During his fourteen-year NFL career, Chris played with three teams—the Minnesota Vikings, the Atlanta Falcons, and the San Francisco 49ers—after being selected fourth overall in the 1985 NFL Draft.

KALE QUINOA SALAD

SERVES **6**

Quinoa suddenly got big a few years ago. Like seemingly out of nowhere. I remember watching football in 2013—during a game the network aired a hilarious Bud Light ad about a tailgater who grilled (as he called it "Kwee-No") burgers on the grill, because his team always won when he did. (For the record, quinoa is pronounced "keen-wah.") The commercial was an ode to fans who will do whatever it takes to help their team win, even if it means eating (seemingly nasty) quinoa burgers. I assure you, not all quinoa is gross. I happen to love it and, from a nutritional perspective, it is a powerhouse, rocking tons of complete protein (especially compared to all other grains). I make this recipe for myself all the time—both for game day and non-game day consumption. The key to the flavor is the vinegar. And I happen to also enjoy digging through the quinoa to find the veggies and beans! It's kind of like a meal and an activity combined into one. This recipe is a cinch to make.

$1^1/_2$ cups quinoa

$^1/_3$ cup extra virgin olive oil, plus a dash for cooking quinoa

3 small shallots, minced

2 cups grape or cherry tomatoes, quartered

6 large kale leaves, stems removed, leaves finely chopped

1 (15-ounce) can organic black beans, drained and rinsed

$^1/_3$ cup red wine vinegar, or to taste

Sea salt and freshly ground black pepper

1. Cook the quinoa according to the package directions with a dash of extra virgin olive oil. Let cool slightly.

2. Transfer the quinoa to a large serving bowl with the shallots, tomatoes, kale, and black beans. Stir together well.

3. Add the remaining $^1/_3$ cup olive oil and the vinegar, amount dependent on your vinegar-flavor preference, and stir well. Season with salt and pepper, tasting and tossing until it's to your liking.

4. Serve warm, at room temperature, or chilled.

PANZANELLA SALAD

SERVES **4**

If you've never heard of a panzanella salad, don't sweat it: It's an Italian term that refers to a salad of stale bread (aka croutons) and tomatoes. It's super-easy and delicious, and you don't actually have to wait until your bread is stale to make it. You can easily toast bread to make croutons that are just as crunchy. Just be sure that when you make this salad—especially once it's dressed—you and your fellow fangaters eat it immediately. The salad dressing will make the bread soggy if you just let it sit (as with most croutons). If you plan to serve this at a tailgate, make the salad and dressing separately and wait until you're in the parking lot and about to eat before tossing them together.

2 cups rustic Italian bread, torn into bite-sized pieces

4 tablespoons extra virgin olive oil

1½ teaspoons sea salt

½ teaspoon freshly ground black pepper, plus more to taste

1 cup Tuscan kale, stemmed, leaves thinly sliced, plus more to taste

1 cup thinly sliced baby spinach

2 Kirby cucumbers, sliced lengthwise, then thinly sliced into half moons

¼ cup red onion, diced

¾ cup mozzarella cheese, cut into bite-sized pieces

5 slices Italian prosciutto, cut into bite-sized pieces

8 ounces cherry tomatoes, quartered

5 pepperoncinis, sliced into thin rounds

¼ cup finely chopped fresh basil

¼ cup finely chopped fresh Italian (flat-leaf) parsley

DRESSING

¼ cup plus 2 tablespoons extra virgin olive oil

2 tablespoons fig (or regular) balsamic vinegar

⅛ teaspoon freshly ground black pepper

¾ teaspoon dried oregano

1. Combine the bread with the olive oil, 1 teaspoon of the sea salt, and pepper in a skillet, and toast over medium-low until golden brown on both sides, about 10 minutes.

2. Combine the toasted bread, kale, spinach, cucumbers, red onion, mozzarella, prosciutto, tomatoes, remaining ½ teaspoon sea salt, and pepper to taste, and the pepperoncinis in a serving bowl.

3. Whisk the dressing ingredients together in a small bowl until emulsified. Drizzle over the salad, and toss well. Garnish with the fresh herbs, and serve immediately.

JOCELYN'S FAVORITE PASTA SALAD

SERVES 10 TO 15

My sister, Jocelyn, is a great eater and will eat just about anything I make. (I'd like to attribute that more to how delectable my cooking is than to how unpicky an eater she is, but I guess you'd just have to ask her to get to the bottom of it.) I'm pretty sure this is one of her favorites. I say that because she usually spends the 4th of July at the beach with her friends, and before one of their trips she actually emailed me asking for this recipe so they could make it. (Good job, me!) This is a very tasty take on a pasta salad, minus the mayo (which makes this recipe considerably more healthy, if that matters to you.) And it's easy to make in bulk so that you can feed a large group at your fangate. Served warm or cold, it's good no matter what.

Sea salt, plus more to taste

1 (16-ounce) box rotini pasta

5 cloves garlic, minced

1 large yellow onion, diced

2 tablespoons plus ¹/₂ cup extra-virgin olive oil, or more to taste

1 large broccoli crown, cut into individual florets

2 yellow bell peppers, diced

2 orange bell peppers, diced

Freshly ground black pepper, to taste

2 tablespoons Dijon mustard, or more to taste

2 tablespoons white wine vinegar

¹/₂ cup chopped fresh basil

2 cups organic cherry tomatoes, halved

³/₄ cup crumbled feta cheese

2 cage-free, organic chicken breasts, grilled and diced, optional

1. Fill a large Dutch oven with water and a large helping of sea salt. Bring to a rolling boil, then add the rotini, stirring the pasta immediately so it doesn't clump together. Cook until al dente, strain, and set aside, letting it cool to room temperature.

2. Sauté the garlic and onion in a large skillet over medium in 2 tablespoons oil until the onions are translucent, about 6 minutes. Quickly add the broccoli florets, the yellow and orange peppers, and a small pinch of salt and pepper. Cover and cook, stirring occasionally, until the broccoli becomes very green, about 4 minutes. Do not burn or caramelize the broccoli or peppers. Set aside, and let cool to room temperature.

3. Combine the remaining ¹/₂ cup olive oil, mustard, and vinegar in a mixing bowl. Whisk until emulsified. (Feel free to add more mustard or vinegar to taste.)

4. Combine the pasta, sautéed vegetables, basil, tomatoes, feta, and chicken, if desired, in a large serving bowl. Pour half of the dressing on top, and toss well; add more dressing, if desired. Sprinkle with a pinch of salt, and then top with a few grinds of pepper. Toss again, and serve.

FRIENDLY FANGATING TIP: My sister is gluten-free, so I typically make quinoa rotini pasta for her. I think it's the tastiest substitution for regular pasta, and it has great texture, too.

MEAT-LOVERS' FLATBREAD

CONTRIBUTOR: **MICHAEL JORDAN** | SERVES **8**

There probably isn't much I could say about the legendary basketball career of Michael Jordan that you don't already know. I've known MJ, as he is referred to in my house, since I was a baby—and I've had the pleasure of knowing his lovely wife, Yvette, for many years as well. I'm very glad I could include a recipe from them in this book. I've never had the opportunity to cook for MJ or Yvette, but I know MJ has enjoyed my chocolate chip cookies. I once made a big batch on a school night that my mom wouldn't let me eat because it was late. As I was heading up to bed, my dad and MJ walked into the kitchen. I said hello and goodnight, leaving my cookies covered in plastic wrap on the counter. The next morning, they were nowhere to be found. It doesn't take Sherlock Holmes to figure out what had happened. All I can say is that I hope my dad and MJ enjoyed them!

DOUGH

1 (.25-ounce) package active yeast

$^1/_2$ teaspoon sugar

$^1/_4$ cup warm water (100° to 110°F)

$1^3/_4$ cups all-purpose flour

1 teaspoon kosher salt

$^1/_2$ cup room-temperature water

1 teaspoon extra virgin olive oil, plus more for greasing

TOPPINGS

$^1/_2$ cup of your favorite low-sodium tomato sauce

4 ounces good salami or pepperoni

4 ounces mild Italian sausage, cooked and crumbled

3 slices thick-cut bacon, cooked and torn into pieces (I use house-smoked bacon from MJ's steakhouse)

3 thin slices good-quality deli ham

$1^1/_2$ cups shredded mozzarella cheese

$^1/_4$ cup Pecorino-Romano cheese, freshly grated

$^1/_4$ cup Parmesan cheese, freshly grated

Fresh basil leaves, torn

1. Make the dough: Combine the yeast, sugar, and warm water in a measuring cup; let sit for 5 minutes. Combine the bloomed yeast, flour, and salt in the bowl of a food processor. Pulse to combine. Add the room-temperature water in a steady stream, mixing until the dough begins to form a ball. Transfer to a floured countertop, and knead with the heel of your hand until the dough is smooth and elastic, about 5 minutes.

2. Coat a bowl with the olive oil. Place the dough in the bowl, and cover with a clean damp cloth. Put in a warm spot to rise until double in size, about 1 hour.

3. When the dough has doubled in size, punch the dough, scrape it onto the counter, and knead it lightly into a smooth ball. Cut into 8 pieces and, with a rolling pin, roll each one out to form a very flat 5- to 6-inch circle.

4. Preheat the grill to medium-high. Lightly oil. Place the bread rounds on the hot grill, and cook without touching until you see bubbles on the surface, about 2 minutes. Remove from the heat, and add the first 7 toppings. Reduce the heat to medium-low.

5. Return the flatbreads to the grill, close the lid, and cook for 3 minutes, until the cheese is melted and the bottoms are slightly charred.

6. Remove from the heat, and sprinkle with the freshly grated Parmesan and torn fresh basil leaves.

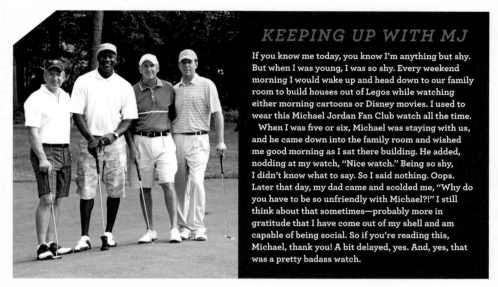

Michael Jordan and my dad (and two of my dad's friends) at a golf tournament in celebration of my dad's 60th birthday.

STUFFED-CRUST FLATBREAD

SERVES 8

A few years ago, while I was on a cleanse, a commercial for stuffed-crust pizza came on during a football game. Probably because I was starving, my eyes got huge: All I could think about for days was this stuffed-crust pizza. Once my cleanse was over, I still had stuffed-crust pizza on the mind. And then I thought, who says you can't make your own? If you get creative…like what about pita bread? It's got a pocket just aching to be stuffed with hot, melty cheese. Bingo! This'll be a hit at your next fangate.

2 store-bought (8-inch) pita rounds

4 ounces sharp provolone, shredded

4 ounces mozzarella, shredded

4 tablespoons Pomì marinara sauce

14 pepperoni slices

Fresh basil leaves, thinly sliced

Freshly ground black pepper

1. Preheat the oven to 500°F.

2. Cut a small slit into the top layer of each pita round, near the outside edge. As evenly as you can, stuff half of the provolone and a quarter of the mozzarella into each pita, and close the pita back up.

3. Spread 2 tablespoons of marinara sauce on each flatbread. Sprinkle the remaining mozzarella on top, dividing it evenly between the two flatbreads. Then add the pepperoni slices evenly.

4. Place the pitas on a baking sheet, and bake for 9 to 10 minutes—until the cheese on top is melted, the edges are browned, and the cheese on the inside is starting to ooze out.

5. Sprinkle with the basil and a grind or two of pepper. Slice into quarters or smaller bites, and serve.

MARGHERITA FLATBREAD

(PICTURED ON PAGE 94)

SERVES **6 TO 8**

This recipe is a cinch to make, and the flatbreads look gorgeous—like you spent forever making them. But the secret is that this recipe is basically a baby cheese pizza, and when served whole, it makes for a great appetizer to dish out at a fangating party at home. Or, cut up the flatbreads into small slices and pass them as hors d'oeuvres. *Mozzarella di bufala* is ridiculously yummy and can be found at proper cheese shops and often at gourmet grocery stores. If you can't find it, go ahead and use regular cow's milk mozzarella (the wetter the better).

2 (12-inch) homemade flatbreads (see Dough, page 90) or store-bought

4 tablespoons Pomì marinara sauce

2 plum tomatoes, cut lengthwise into 1/4-inch-thick slices

8 ounces mozzarella di bufala, cut into 1/4-inch-thick slices

Parsley-and-Kale Pesto (page 93), for drizzling, optional

Fresh basil leaves

Sea salt and freshly ground black pepper

1. Preheat the broiler to high.

2. Put the flatbreads on a baking sheet. Spread 2 tablespoons of the marinara sauce onto each flatbread. Arrange the tomato slices on top, and then add the mozzarella. Broil for 4 minutes, until the cheese is melted and the bottoms are slightly charred.

3. To serve, drizzle with some pesto, if you like, and top with fresh basil leaves (or slice the basil, and sprinkle over the pizza). Season with salt and pepper, slice into quarters or smaller bites, and serve!

FRIENDLY FANGATING TIP: If you want an equally easy way to make your own marinara sauce that's designed just for pizza, grab yourself a pouch of my Hungry Fan™ pizza-flavored spice blends. All you have to do is take 1 cup of plain tomato purée, and mix in 2 tablespoons, or more to taste, of my Hungry Fan™ Pizza Spice Blend. Stir and you're good to go!

ANDOUILLE-PESTO FLATBREAD

(PICTURED ON PAGE 94)

SERVES **10 TO 12**

This may just be my favorite flatbread recipe in this book. There's just so much flavor in one bite! You'll be very happy to let the look of these flatbreads fool your friends and fellow tailgaters—they look immensely complicated and gourmet, but I assure you, they're so easy. This recipe may leave you with more pesto than you need. I like to take the leftover sauce and toss it in pasta at another meal. Or just set it out and let your guests dip fresh bread into it.

1 teaspoon extra virgin olive oil

8 ounces andouille sausage, cut into bite-sized pieces

2 (12-inch) homemade flatbreads (see Dough, page 90) or store-bought

6 ounces yellow cherry tomatoes, halved

2 large leaves lacinato (Tuscan) kale, finely sliced

1/2 cup grated Romano cheese

PARSLEY-AND-KALE PESTO

2 1/2 cups tightly packed fresh basil leaves

2 cups tightly packed fresh Italian (flat-leaf) parsley leaves

1/2 cup grated Parmesan cheese

1/2 cup grated Romano cheese

1 1/4 teaspoons sea salt

1 teaspoon freshly ground black pepper

1/4 cup walnuts

1/4 cup pine nuts

8 large cloves garlic

2 large leaves lacinato (Tuscan) kale, ribs removed

1 1/2 cups extra virgin olive oil

1. Make the pesto: Combine all the ingredients except for the olive oil in a food processor, and purée. Slowly add the olive oil for a smoother consistency. Set aside.

2. Preheat the broiler to high.

3. Heat the olive oil in a skillet over medium. Add the sausage, and sauté until browned and the edges start to crisp up a bit, about 6 minutes, stirring often to brown evenly. Set aside.

4. Place the flatbreads on a baking sheet, and top each with 2 to 3 tablespoons of the pesto. Then generously scatter the sausage bites and tomato halves on the flatbreads. Finally sprinkle with the kale and cheese.

5. Broil the flatbreads for 4 minutes, until the bottoms are slightly charred. Slice as desired, serve, and enjoy.

From left to right: Andouille-Pesto Flatbread (page 93), Margherita Flatbread (page 92), Reuben Flatbread (page 97), and Fig-and-Prosciutto Flatbread (page 96)

FIG-AND-PROSCIUTTO FLATBREAD (PICTURED ON PAGE 95)

SERVES 10 TO 12

This fangate-friendly recipe is a spin on an incredible tart I had in a little café in Lyon, France, many years ago. A little savory, a little sweet—the combination of flavors on this flatbread seems to hit every taste bud on your tongue. If you're making this recipe when figs are in season, I highly recommend replacing the fig jam with real, sliced figs. This makes the flatbread so much tastier and fresh. In the absence of seasonal figs, the fig jam works great and yields a nice, sweet change-up from my savory flatbreads. Pair one of those flatbreads with this sweeter dish and you've got some great options that should please everyone!

2 (12-inch) homemade flatbreads (see Dough, page 90) or store-bought

$^1/_4$ cup fig jam

8 ounces goat cheese, crumbled by hand into small chunks*

4 ounces thinly sliced prosciutto di Parma

Freshly ground black pepper

*If goat cheese isn't your thing, no problem. Replace it with triple crème cheese or even a Brie.

1. Preheat the broiler to high.

2. Place the flatbreads on a baking sheet. Spread half the fig jam onto each flatbread. Top with the goat cheese and prosciutto. Sprinkle with the pepper.

3. Broil for 3$^1/_2$ minutes, until the bottoms are slightly charred. Serve.

REUBEN FLATBREAD (PICTURED ON PAGE 95)

SERVES 8 TO 10

If my memory serves me well, I ate my first Reuben sandwich at the Carnegie Deli in New York. My parents took me there—or maybe it was just my dad—when I was really young. I used to go to New York fairly often as a kid to watch the Knicks play and to visit my uncle. Now that I've officially been a New Yorker for several years, I try very hard to avoid touristy spots, such as the Carnegie Deli. But sometimes I cannot help it—the food there is just ridiculously good. The most recent time I was there was Mother's Day. We seriously chowed down and, as usual, I had my Reuben.

Here is my Reuben recipe. I like to serve it on flatbread to minimize the bread situation and instead devote my tasting experience to the salty yumminess of corned beef stacked high and topped with melty Swiss cheese. You'll see my recipe calls for a ton of corned beef. That's because I like a lot of it. Feel free to use less if you're not a piggy pig like me.

2 (12-inch) homemade flatbreads (see Dough, page 90) or store-bought

$^1/_2$ cup sauerkraut

$^1/_2$ pound sliced corned beef

4 ounces sliced Alpine Lace Swiss cheese

RUSSIAN DRESSING

$^1/_2$ cup mayonnaise

2 tablespoons ketchup (to make your own, see page 245)

$^1/_2$ teaspoon Louisiana hot sauce

2 teaspoons prepared white horseradish

2 teaspoons dried minced onions

1. Preheat the broiler to high.

2. Make the dressing: Combine all the ingredients in a food processor, and blend until smooth.

3. Place the flatbreads on a baking sheet. Spread $^1/_4$ cup of the Russian dressing on each flatbread, and then top with the sauerkraut. Layer on the corned beef, and top with the Swiss cheese.

4. Broil the flatbreads for about 3 minutes, or until the cheese is melted.

5. Slice as desired, serve, and enjoy.

SANDWICHES & BURGERS

I've been very fortunate in my life to get to travel quite a bit—some on my own and some with my family. For me, tasting different foods is an exceptional way to experience other cultures. I like to boast that I've eaten my way around the world—through six continents (all but Antarctica, which I will absolutely get to one day).

One of the things I love most about the United States is that with its great size comes such an array of cultures, cuisines, and traditions—you get to experience so much without leaving the country! You could argue that a sandwich is a sandwich is a sandwich. And I'd agree. A sandwich is most basically defined as something (usually meat or cheese but not always) encased in bread. But as you travel from tailgate to tailgate across America, sandwiches vary quite a bit, especially when you factor in burgers (which I consider, given their form, a type of sandwich).

This chapter focuses on a wide variety of meats and cheeses (and sometimes veggies and beans) sandwiched between two pieces of bread of some kind. I drew my inspiration from this country's many regional food cultures—the different ways Americans, those born here and those who have immigrated here, cook up something good.

LOBSTER ROLLS

SERVES **6**

The (tennis) US Open is played each August a short subway ride away from me in Flushing, Queens. I've been fortunate to cover it multiple times for local New York TV and my blog. I am a total tennis fan, but what I love just as much is the food served on the grounds. Those of you who have been to the US Open, nod your heads, because you and I both know that not only are the food and drink options at the Open delicious, they're so numerous they'll make your head spin. I've tasted pretty much everything offered both in the common areas and restricted VIP areas. One dish stands out as my favorite year after year—the lobster roll. It's the Open's signature dish—and a very commonplace New York one in the summertime, especially in the Hamptons. Here's my take on the classic, made with crème fraîche instead of the usual mayo (which you can certainly substitute).

4 (1¼-pound) live lobsters

2 stalks celery, chopped (I prefer the inner stalks as they are a bit less fibrous)

½ cup crème fraîche or mayonnaise (to make your own mayo, see page 250)

1 tablespoon fresh lemon juice

1½ tablespoons finely chopped fresh Italian (flat-leaf) parsley, plus more for garnish

½ tablespoon finely chopped fresh tarragon, plus more for garnish

Sea salt and freshly ground black pepper

4 hot dog buns or small sub rolls (or preferably, if you can find them, brioche buns), lightly toasted

¼ cup salted butter, melted

1. Bring a large stockpot filled halfway with salted water to a rolling boil. Working in 2 batches, plunge the lobsters head first into the boiling water and quickly cover the pot. When the water comes back to a boil, set a timer for 15 minutes. Transfer the lobsters to a work surface to cool slightly. Remove the lobster meat, which should be tender and opaque. Chill in the refrigerator for 1 hour.

2. Chop the lobster meat into bite-sized pieces, and place in a bowl. Add the celery, crème fraîche, lemon juice, parsley, tarragon, and a couple pinches of salt and pepper to taste. Stir together well.

3. While the rolls are still warm, brush them with the melted butter, making sure they're completely buttery. Fill each roll with equal servings of the lobster salad.

4. Garnish with an extra pinch of tarragon and parsley, and serve.

TASTY TIDBITS

You can attend the US Open—or at least most of the two-week tournament—without an actual ticket to a match. You could very easily and happily spend at least a couple of full days just wandering the grounds. And if you happen to be of my same mind, you'd spend at least a few days just tasting everything. Some of the concessions change each year, but in past years, there's been farm-to-table sandwiches and salads; an outpost of the famous Carnegie Deli; a wine bar featuring gourmet seafood, charcuterie, and cheeses; Hill Country Barbecue (one of my favorite BBQ spots in NYC); Champagne stands; a grilled cheese food truck; Grey Goose stands (with their Signature US Open cocktails); and even concessions from celebrity chefs including David Burke (think big, thick cuts of bacon to nibble on), Richard Sandoval, and Masaharu Morimoto (of *Iron Chef* fame).

BOLOGNESE CHEESESTEAK

SERVES **3**

What do you get when you combine the juicy deliciousness of a Philly cheesesteak sandwich with the hearty meatiness of a slow-cooked Bolognese sauce? Perfection on a hero. This sandwich doesn't need much more of an introduction. And, on the plus side, you'll have extra Bolognese sauce to pour over pasta for another meal.

BOLOGNESE SAUCE

$1/2$ **pound pancetta, diced**

$1^1/2$ **cups diced yellow onions**

$3/4$ **cup diced celery**

$3/4$ **cup diced carrots**

4 cloves garlic, minced

1 teaspoon sea salt

1 teaspoon freshly ground black pepper

3 fresh bay leaves (if you can't find fresh, use dried)

$1/2$ **teaspoon dried thyme**

1 teaspoon dried oregano

$1/2$ **teaspoon ground cinnamon**

$1/4$ **teaspoon ground nutmeg**

1 pound mix of ground beef and veal

1 pound spicy Italian sausages, removed from casings

$1/2$ **cup tomato paste**

1 cup red wine (go for something big like a Cabernet or Merlot)

1 (26.46-ounce) box Pomì chopped tomatoes

$3/4$ **cup beef broth**

2 teaspoons brown sugar

$1/4$ **cup heavy cream**

3 tablespoons finely chopped fresh Italian (flat-leaf) parsley

(CONTINUED)

1. Make the sauce: Heat a Dutch oven over medium. Once hot, brown the pancetta, stirring frequently, about 6 minutes. Before it begins to get crispy, add the onions, celery, and carrots, stirring frequently, until the onions get soft, another 6 minutes. Then add the garlic, salt, pepper, bay leaves, thyme, oregano, cinnamon, and nutmeg. Lower the heat, stir well, and simmer for 3 to 4 minutes. Stir in the meat and sausages, and cook for 8 minutes, stirring often to break them both up, until the meat is no longer pink.

2. Add the tomato paste, and give everything a good stir. Pour in the wine, stirring and scraping with a wooden spoon to ensure that it reaches the bottom of the Dutch oven to deglaze the bits stuck to the bottom. Then add the tomatoes, broth, and brown sugar, using the wooden spoon to remove whatever may be sticking to the bottom of the pot and mixing all the ingredients well. Reduce the heat to medium-low, cover, and let cook for 30 minutes.

3. Stir the cream and parsley into the sauce, cover the Dutch oven, and transfer it to a Hungry Fan™ 3-in-1 Fangating™ Bag to cook for 90 minutes. Alternatively, simmer the sauce on the stovetop, covered, for 90 minutes.

4. Meanwhile, bring the steak to room temperature, and preheat the broiler to high with the rack in the middle.

5. Season both sides of the steak with salt and pepper.

6. Heat a medium skillet over high. Add the ribeye, and brown it on both sides for 60 seconds on each. Then place the skillet 6 to 8 inches below the broiler, and cook for 4 minutes. (This will get the steak cooked but still a nice shade of reddish-pink on the inside. Cook longer if you prefer your steak well done.)

(CONTINUED)

2 pounds ribeye steak

Sea salt and freshly ground black pepper

3 (10-inch) hero buns

9 slices provolone cheese

7. Let the steak sit for 5 minutes before you slice it into very thin long strips.

8. Meanwhile, fill each hero bun with 3 slices of provolone, and lightly toast or grill the buns until you get nice grill marks and the cheese melts. Stuff several slices of ribeye in each. Last but not least, add $1/3$ to $1/2$ cup of the Bolognese sauce to each hero, so it's oozing out of the sandwiches (and as messy as you'd like). Serve immediately.

SWEET-AND-SAVORY PROSCIUTTO GRILLED CHEESE

(PICTURED ON PAGE 104)

SERVES **1**

This may be one of the weirder flavor combinations you'll find in this book. Pecorino and prosciutto are a brilliant yet unoriginal combination. But adding pumpkin butter to it? Yeah, that's a little different. The Pecorino and prosciutto are both so deliciously salty, and the sweetness of the pumpkin butter nicely cuts the saltiness. Give it a whirl and see what you think! Hopefully you'll agree with me that this is the perfect, seasonal, ooey, gooey salty version of a grilled cheese sandwich to serve for the start of football season (and, incidentally, the start of fall)!

2 slices bread (I like French wheat sourdough)

1 tablespoon butter, plus more for cooking, optional

1 tablespoon pumpkin butter (to make your own, see page 249)

Enough slices of Pecorino-Romano to fully cover an entire slice of bread

6 slices Italian prosciutto

1. Butter the top part of 1 piece of bread. Place in a nonstick skillet, butter side down, over medium for 1 minute, then flip over and toast on the other side for another minute. Repeat with the other bread slice.

2. Layer the grilled cheese as such: bread, pumpkin butter, cheese, prosciutto, and the top piece of bread (buttered side up). At this point, you can cook your sandwich over medium in a toaster oven, on a grill, or in melted butter on your griddle, being sure to brown both sides, 1 to 2 minutes per side, until crispy. Serve immediately.

Bacon-and-Jalapeño Grilled
Cheese (opposite) and
Sweet-and-Savory Prosciutto
Grilled Cheese (page 103)

BACON-AND-JALAPEÑO GRILLED CHEESE

SERVES **1**

Many years ago, I had lunch at Govind Armstrong's spot, Table 8, on Melrose Avenue in Los Angeles (before it became 8oz. Burger Bar). I had heard his short rib grilled cheese was ridiculous—and that it was Oprah's favorite. So I had to try it. Oh. Man. Ri-dic-u-lous. Here's my spin on that grilled cheese. I subbed bacon for short ribs—and it's best with thick-cut bacon. I like to serve it with tomato soup for dunking.

$1^1/_2$ **tablespoons salted butter, softened**

2 slices whole-grain pullman bread (or something similar)

$1/_4$ **cup shredded pepper Jack cheese**

$1/_4$ **cup shredded Cheddar cheese**

$1/_4$ **cup shredded Monterey Jack cheese**

2 slices bacon, cooked until crispy but not burnt, halved crosswise

$1/_2$ **jalapeño, sliced into thin rounds**

1. Use 1 tablespoon of the softened butter to butter both sides of each bread slice. Put the buttered bread in a nonstick skillet over medium, and toast on both sides until golden, 1 to 2 minutes per side. Remove the bread to a workspace but leave the skillet on the heat.

2. While the toast is still hot, top one piece with all three cheeses, the bacon halves, and jalapeño slices, and then top with the other piece of toast.

3. Reduce the heat to medium-low, and add the remaining $1/_2$ tablespoon butter to the skillet. As the butter melts, place the sandwich in the skillet, and use a spatula to press down on the top of the sandwich to help melt the cheese. (Another trick is to press down on the sandwich with a lid smaller than the skillet, which not only applies pressure but also retains the heat and melts the cheese faster.)

4. Once the cheese is melted, serve.

BITE-SIZED CUCUMBER SANDWICHES

SERVES **6**

Tennis was my sport growing up. I played on my high school team and on the Duke Women's Club Tennis Team in college. After my junior year, which I wrapped up in Paris studying (but mostly eating and enjoying *la vie Parisienne*), I stuck around for the French Open, and eventually my mom came out and joined me for a day of tennis. For better or worse, tennis is one of those posh sports in which etiquette and decorum always matter. Thus, I often associate the sport with bite-sized, light, gourmet eats and not the barbecue, pizza, or other heavy foods we often enjoy at a fangate. So, in honor of the French Open, I give you these little cucumber sandwiches. They're super easy to make and classy in presentation.

1 medium cucumber, thinly sliced into rounds

1/2 small bunch dill, finely chopped, plus 6 sprigs

1/4 teaspoon sea salt

1/2 teaspoon freshly ground black pepper

1 small bunch chives, minced

1 1/2 cups cream cheese (or stracchino cheese if you can find it)

1 (1-pound) loaf whole-wheat bread (or gluten-free bread if you prefer), thinly sliced

1. Lay the cucumber slices in a single layer atop paper towels. Top with another paper towel layer, and give them a couple of minutes to dry.

2. Combine the dill, salt, pepper, and the majority of the chives in a food processor, and pulse until they become a paste. Transfer to a mixing bowl, and stir in the cream cheese until well combined.

3. Cut the bread slices into squares just slightly larger than the diameter of the cucumber slices.

4. To assemble the sandwiches, spread some cheese mixture on a square of bread, and then top with 2 cucumber slices stacked atop each other. Repeat until you have a three-layered club. Place a tiny dollop of the cheese mixture in the center of the top square of bread, and top with a cucumber slice. Sprinkle with the reserved chives and a sprig of dill. Repeat until you have used up all your ingredients and have 6 little cuke sandwiches. Serve with a chilled glass of Champagne, and enjoy.

ROLAND GARROS 2004

The 2004 Roland Garros (aka French Open) was the scene of one of my most embarrassing athlete-related moments. My father hooked me up with an All-Access Pass to the players' family seating area in the stands, the players' cafeteria, and even the players' lounge, save for the Finals. I was a full-on tennis bum for nearly two weeks watching matches all day.

Paris in the summer is surprisingly hot. And the tennis facilities—particularly the courts—are encased in concrete, so you've got basically an open-air human pizza oven. There's a reason the tournament officials hand out free sunhats to fans each year.

One day, about halfway through the tournament, I got overheated. I knew I needed to get out of the sun and cool off a bit or I could potentially pass out. I made my way into the players' lounge and parked it on the end of this huge, brown leather couch. The coolness of the leather was so inviting, and the couch was terribly comfortable. Needless to say, I conked out. I don't remember how long I was asleep. What stands out in my mind—indelibly imprinted—was the mortification I felt upon waking up. Sitting on the couch next to me was American tennis star Andy Roddick. He was looking at me and down at the arm of the couch in utter disgust. You could see it all over his face. I looked down, and on the brown leather arm of the couch stood a puddle of drool. My drool. And attached to the puddle was this long strand of saliva still attached to my mouth. Oh yes. My proudest moment. So, Andy, if you happen to be reading this, please accept my most sincere apologies.

BACON CHICKEN SALAD MINI OPEN-FACED SAMMIES

SERVES **10**

When I was a little kid, I used to eat a lot of tuna fish sandwiches. The Falk family members are big tuna eaters in general. Then in my early twenties, I got diagnosed with mercury poisoning. That was not so fun. So instead of eating tuna pretty much every day, I started eating a lot of chicken salad. This recipe is what happens when you combine crunchy bacon with creamy chicken salad and then melt cheese over all that in the toaster oven. Can you say tasty? By slicing the ciabatta into four mini sandwiches, what you get are awesome, melty bites that can be easily shared. Just throw a bunch onto a platter and set them out. They won't last long. You have my word on that.

1 whole rotisserie chicken, skin removed, meat pulled apart into bite-sized chunks

4 slices thick-cut bacon, cooked until crispy but not burnt, cut into $^{1}/_{2}$-inch chunks

$^{1}/_{2}$ cup mayonnaise

2 teaspoons Dijon mustard

$1^{1}/_{2}$ teaspoons fresh tarragon, minced, plus more for garnish

$^{1}/_{4}$ teaspoon sea salt

$^{1}/_{2}$ teaspoon black pepper, plus more for garnish

$^{1}/_{4}$ teaspoon smoked paprika

1 (12-ounce) loaf ciabatta bread, halved lengthwise, each half cut into 10 slices

$^{1}/_{2}$ large yellow onion, cut into $^{1}/_{4}$-inch-thick slices, then quartered

10 slices Muenster or Gruyère cheese, halved

1. Preheat the oven to 425°F.

2. Combine the chicken and bacon. Add the mayo, Dijon, tarragon, salt, pepper, and paprika in a large mixing bowl. Mix well.

3. Top each slice of bread with onion pieces so that they lay flat but do not entirely cover each slice.

4. Lightly toast the onion-topped bread in the oven for 10 minutes. Top each slice of toast with $1^{1}/_{2}$ tablespoons of the bacon-chicken salad and a slice of cheese. Return the open-faced sandwiches to the oven, and lightly toast them again for 2 to 3 minutes, or until the cheese melts.

5. Let cool for 2 to 3 minutes. Top each sandwich with a tiny sprinkle of black pepper and some minced tarragon.

CHICKEN PARMESAN HEROES

SERVES **4**

Oh how I adore you, chicken Parmesan. The more mozzarella on top, the better. I make my chicken Parm on a toasted Italian hero, stuffed with lots of marinara sauce and extra slices of cheese. I want my sandwich to ooze yumminess when I take a bite. If it ends up on my chin, it's but a small price to pay for a great bite of food. If you're serving this sandwich at a tailgate, make the chicken Parm cutlets and the marinara ahead of time, package them up, and then heat them up in the parking lot. You can easily grill this sandwich, thereby melting the cheese as a finishing touch.

12 (¹/₄-inch-thick) slices mozzarella cheese, preferably buffalo milk

1 cup fine dried breadcrumbs

1 teaspoon dried oregano

1 teaspoon dried parsley

1 teaspoon dried basil

¹/₂ teaspoon sea salt

¹/₂ teaspoon freshly ground black pepper

2 large eggs, beaten

2 chicken breasts, butterflied and halved (making 4 fillets)

4 (8-inch) rustic Italian rolls

Extra virgin olive oil

Handful of fresh basil leaves

MARINARA SAUCE

5 large cloves garlic, minced

¹/₂ yellow onion, minced

2 tablespoons extra virgin olive oil

1 teaspoon sea salt

¹/₂ teaspoon freshly ground black pepper

1 (26.46-ounce) box Pomì finely chopped tomatoes

1 tablespoon tomato paste

2 heaping tablespoons minced fresh basil

1¹/₂ tablespoons minced fresh Italian (flat-leaf) parsley

1 tablespoon cane sugar

1. Preheat the oven to 425°F. Line a baking sheet with aluminum foil. Make sure the mozzarella is sitting out, as you want to bring it to room temperature.

2. Combine the breadcrumbs, oregano, parsley, basil, salt, and pepper in a large shallow bowl. Place the beaten eggs in another shallow bowl.

3. Coat each piece of chicken in the beaten egg, and then dredge in the breadcrumb mixture. Place on the prepared baking sheet, and bake for 15 minutes. Flip over, and bake for another 10 minutes.

4. Meanwhile, make the marinara sauce: Combine the garlic and onions with the olive oil in a large saucepan, and cook over medium-high for 4 minutes, until the onions become translucent. Watch your garlic; you don't want to burn it. Add the salt and pepper.

5. Reduce the heat to medium-low, and add the tomatoes and tomato paste. Stir for 5 minutes as they cook. Stir in the basil, parsley, and sugar, and simmer for 10 minutes.

6. Slice the rolls nearly in half lengthwise. Lightly toast in the oven during the last few minutes of baking the chicken.

7. For each sandwich, coat the top slice of bread with olive oil. Coat the bottom slice with ¹/₄ cup of the marinara sauce. Place the chicken (hot out of the oven) on the marinara sauce. Then top with 2 to 3 slices mozzarella, 2 to 4 fresh basil leaves, and ¹/₂ cup of the marinara sauce. The mozzarella should begin to melt quickly, sandwiched between the hot chicken and hot sauce. Serve immediately.

ITALIAN HERO SANDWICH
(AKA *IL MOSTRO*)

SERVES **2**

The classic Italian hero is probably my second favorite sandwich ever (second to a muffaletta). I love the saltiness of Italian deli meats—the mortadellas, prosciuttos, and salamis of the world. And when you stack them high, I'm in heaven. Add some crunch from a bell pepper and sour spiciness from pepperoncinis… ooooh boy. The only potential problem with this sandwich, which I have nicknamed *Il Mostro* (Italian for "The Monster"), is that it's so stinkin' big, it's hard to get everything in one bite. But it's worth every bite, even if the sandwich ends up all over your face.

$1/4$ cup extra virgin olive oil

$1/2$ teaspoon balsamic vinegar

$1/4$ teaspoon freshly ground black pepper

$1/2$ teaspoon dried oregano

4 ($1/2$-inch-thick) slices rustic Italian bread

4 thin slices green bell pepper

4 thin slices red onion

Baby spinach leaves

6 to 8 thin slices tomato

2 roasted red peppers, thinly sliced lengthwise

6 pepperoncinis, cut lengthwise, tops removed

4 slices provolone cheese

4 slices salami

4 slices cooked ham

4 slices prosciutto

4 slices mortadella

Baby dill pickles, optional

1. Combine the olive oil, balsamic vinegar, black pepper, and oregano in a small bowl. Whisk to emulsify, and then brush the vinaigrette on both sides of the bread slices.

2. Stack the ingredients high, starting with your veggies and working your way up to the cheese and then through the meats, divvying each ingredient up between 2 slices of bread. Close your sandwiches with the other 2 slices of bread, and enjoy.

HOT ITALIAN BEEF AU JUS SANDWICHES

SERVES **8 TO 10**

I'm often inspired by the concession food I eat at the many ballparks and arenas I visit over the course of each year. This particular sandwich was inspired by a dish that was specially offered at Fenway's Yawkey Way (right field concourse) during the 2013 World Series. The Series matchup was between the Boston Red Sox and the St. Louis Cardinals, and the Red Sox ceremoniously took the Series in 6 games (4 games to 2), marking the club's first World Series since 1918. Mama Falk is a big Red Sox fan (she's from Boston), so I had to include a Red Sox–inspired recipe in this book. This recipe requires a slow cooker, which makes it an easy dish to get going the morning of your fangate.

4 pounds chuck roast (preferably grass-fed)

Sea salt and freshly ground black pepper

1 tablespoon canola oil

1 small yellow onion, diced

5 cloves garlic, minced

2 tablespoons dried oregano

2 tablespoons dried basil

2 tablespoons dried Italian parsley

5 banana peppers, thinly sliced, or to taste

1 cup beef stock

8 to 10 whole-wheat buns

8 ounces fresh mozzarella cheese, thinly sliced

1. Season the beef with salt and pepper.

2. Heat the oil in a large skillet over high. Add the beef, and brown both sides quickly, about 2 minutes per side. Decrease the heat to medium, add the onion, and cook for 4 minutes, until softened. Add the garlic, and sauté for 1 minute.

3. Transfer to a 6-quart slow cooker, and add the oregano, basil, parsley, banana peppers, and stock. Add a couple healthy grinds of black pepper, and cover. Cook on low for 9 hours, or until the beef is soft and can be pulled apart with a fork.

4. Serve the beef hot on the buns, topped with a healthy slice of mozzarella, which will melt with the heat of the beef. Or put it under the broiler for 2 minutes to also lightly toast the tops of the buns. Serve with a small cup of the jus (the yummy juice left in the slow cooker) for dipping.

TASTY TIDBITS

Fenway Park, home of the Boston Red Sox, is the oldest ballpark in Major League Baseball (MLB). It was opened in 1912 and added to the National Register of Historic Places 100 years later on March 7, 2012.

SUMMER CHICKEN AND PEACH SANDWICHES

SERVES **4**

This was the third of three recipes I was ready to demonstrate in the *Today Show* kitchen a few years back, along with my Mediterranean Nachos (page 40). Unfortunately, as they so often do, the segment before mine ran long, squeezing my airtime and prohibiting me from debuting this recipe. Yet I happen to adore it—it's really refreshing on a hot, summer day. Although you can certainly make this any time of year, peaches are only in season during the summer months, and fresh peaches are what make this dish. Serve with a nice, cold and crisp rosé.

1 cup reduced-fat (2%), plain Greek yogurt

2 sprigs rosemary, finely chopped

1 tablespoon olive oil, plus more for brushing

Sea salt and freshly ground black pepper

4 skinless, boneless chicken breast fillets (or two large breasts, butterflied)

2 tablespoons Lawry's seasoned salt, or to taste (to make your own, see Tip)

2 teaspoons fresh lemon juice, or to taste

3 peaches, sliced lengthwise ¼ inch thick

4 burger buns (I prefer whole-wheat)

2 cups baby spinach

1. Preheat your grill to medium-high. Mix the Greek yogurt with the rosemary, olive oil, and a pinch each of salt and pepper in a bowl. Set aside.

2. Season both sides of the chicken fillets with the Lawry's and fresh pepper. Sprinkle with the lemon juice.

3. Place the peach slices in a pouch made out of aluminum foil. You don't need to seal it entirely, but be sure the sides of your pouch are high to prevent the peach juice from escaping as the peaches cook.

4. Grill the chicken fillets and peaches until the chicken is fully cooked (grill marks and all) and the peaches have become tender and released some juices, about 15 minutes.

5. Meanwhile, brush the insides of the buns with a little bit of the olive oil, and add them to the grill, oiled sides down, until crisp and golden brown, 2 to 4 minutes.

6. Build the burgers: Spread the yogurt aioli on the top and bottom of the buns. Sandwich a chicken breast, baby spinach, and peach slices between the buns. Repeat. Serve immediately.

FRIENDLY FANGATING TIP: To make your own seasoned salt, simply mix 1 tablespoon garlic powder, 1 tablespoon onion powder, ½ teaspoon ground turmeric, 1 teaspoon brown sugar, ½ teaspoon paprika, 1 teaspoon sweet smoked paprika, and 1 teaspoon sea salt. Keep in a tightly sealed container for up to 1 month.

BACON-WRAPPED HOT DOG WITH CHIPOTLE AIOLI

SERVES 1

I struggled a bit with where to put hot dogs in this book. When served alone, they'd be considered meats. But we never serve hot dogs alone. That's just silly. We couch them in buns, which I think therefore classifies them as sandwiches. In any case, you may have noticed a theme in this book: Bacon makes everything better (apologies, kosher friends). Wrapping a hot dog in bacon brings it to a new tier of scrumptiousness. And paired with a spicy chipotle aioli (a fancy word for flavored mayonnaise)— yes, yes and yes.

3 toothpicks

2 slices bacon

1 jumbo hot dog

1 tablespoon mayonnaise

1 teaspoon chipotle sauce

1 hot dog bun

1. Soak the toothpicks in water for about 15 minutes. Preheat the oven to 350°F, and line a baking sheet with aluminum foil.

2. Lightly cook the bacon over medium in a skillet or on a griddle until it's no longer raw but still very pliable, 4 minutes. Transfer to a paper towel–covered plate to cool.

3. Once the bacon has cooled, wrap the hot dog in the two slices of bacon so they overlap in the middle, and secure them with a toothpick. Secure both ends with toothpicks as well.

4. Place the hot dog on a roasting rack over the prepared baking sheet, and bake for 10 minutes.

5. Combine the mayonnaise and chipotle sauce in a small bowl.

6. Once the hot dog is cooked, remove the toothpicks, and place the dog in the bun. Top with the chipotle aioli, and serve immediately.

FRENCH TOAST SAVORY SAMMIES

SERVES **2**

A lot of games start early—like one o'clock in the afternoon. That means, if you're tailgating, it can still be breakfast time when you get started. Thus, I give you this sandwich—it's a breakfast sandwich that is deceptively un-sweet, especially given the ingredients. If you're a sweet breakfast meal person, top this with maple syrup and you're good to go!

2 large eggs, beaten

$1/3$ cup whole milk

$1/4$ teaspoon ground nutmeg

$1/2$ teaspoon ground cinnamon

$1/4$ teaspoon brown sugar

$1/4$ teaspoon sea salt

2 tablespoons butter, plus more if needed

4 slices peasant bread or brioche

3 tablespoons pumpkin butter (to make your own, see page 249)

1 (3.5-ounce) bar dark chocolate

3 ounces Brie cheese, sliced

Confectioners' sugar, for sprinkling

1. Combine the eggs, milk, nutmeg, cinnamon, brown sugar, and salt in a mixing bowl. Whisk together well.

2. Melt 1 tablespoon butter in a large skillet over medium. Dunk the bread in the egg mixture until fully coated, and cook in the skillet (no more than two slices at a time) for about 2 minutes on each side, until very lightly browned. Transfer to a large plate, and then repeat with the remaining bread and egg mixture, adding more butter for cooking as needed.

3. Slather one side of your toast with pumpkin butter. Then top with 2 to 4 dark chocolate squares and a few slices of Brie. Top with the other piece of toast, return to the skillet, and cook, adding more butter to the skillet if necessary, for 1 to 2 minutes per side, until the chocolate and Brie are melted and the bread is deep golden brown.

4. Sprinkle the sandwich with confectioners' sugar to taste, cut in half so the gooey insides start to ooze out, and serve.

CRACKER JACK CORN DOGS

SERVES **16**

I did my first big celebrity chef appearance at MetLife Stadium's Toyota Coaches Club in November 2014 when the New York Giants took on the Dallas Cowboys. For such a big game, I knew I had to serve something pretty awesome in the way of sportsfood. If you've never been inside the Coaches Club, it's enormous, and they serve pretty much every food you can think of, from sushi to fresh seafood to mac 'n' cheese to barbecue to pasta to farm-fresh salads. (I would know—I strategically used my break time to eat my way through the entire space.) So I came up with an idea to mash together some classic sportsfoods into one delectable dish: I give you my Cracker Jack Corn Dogs, which were a hit with the Giants' season ticket holders. They're corn dogs mixed with Cracker Jacks mixed with extra caramel and a hint of spice that ends up yielding a satisfying dish with a surprising depth of flavor.

---

2 (2-ounce) boxes Cracker Jacks

$^{1}/_{4}$ cup salted peanuts

8 tablespoons plus 2$^{1}/_{2}$ teaspoons brown sugar

1 cup fat-free milk

1 package active dry yeast

2 tablespoons extra virgin olive oil, plus more for greasing

1 cup fine yellow cornmeal

2 tablespoons plus 2$^{1}/_{2}$ teaspoons brown sugar

$^{1}/_{4}$ teaspoon baking soda

1$^{1}/_{4}$ cups all-purpose flour, plus more for dusting and kneading dough

1 teaspoon red pepper flakes

1 teaspoon sea salt

1 tablespoon dried chopped onions

$^{1}/_{4}$ cup heavy cream

16 hot dogs

1 large egg, beaten

1. Make the topping: Pulse the Cracker Jacks in a food processor once or twice, and then add the peanuts and 1 tablespoon of the brown sugar, and pulse again until roughly chopped. Transfer to a bowl, and set aside.

2. Make the corndog dough: Warm the milk in a saucepan until it's hot to the touch but won't burn your finger (about 110°F). Pour the milk into a medium mixing bowl, and sprinkle in the yeast. Let sit for 3 minutes until the yeast has dissolved into the milk. Then stir in the olive oil, cornmeal, and 2 tablespoons of the brown sugar. Add the baking soda, flour, red pepper flakes, salt, and dried onions. Mix well to form a sticky dough.

3. Flour a work surface, and turn the dough out on it. Using additional flour as needed, knead the dough until it's smooth but still a bit sticky. This should take about 5 minutes. Shape the dough into a ball.

4. Grease the insides of a large mixing bowl with olive oil. Put the dough in the bowl, cover with plastic wrap, and let rise for 1 hour until the dough has doubled in size.

5. Preheat the oven to 450°F. Line two baking sheets with aluminum foil.

6. Make the caramel: Combine 5 tablespoons of the brown sugar with the cream in a medium skillet, and melt over medium-low until it begins to bubble and get sticky, about 5 minutes. Remove from the heat and let cool for 3 minutes.

7. While the caramel is still warm, roll each hot dog in the caramel, thinly coating them on all sides. Quickly move on to the next step, but keep the caramel slightly warm.

8. Return the dough to a floured work surface. Divide the dough into 16 equal portions. Roll each portion into a rectangle about $1/4$ inch thick. Sprinkle $1/4$ teaspoon of the brown sugar on top. Then place a caramel-coated hot dog on one side, and roll until the dog is entirely wrapped. You don't want too much overlap, so use a knife to cut off additional dough. Brush the dough-wrapped hot dog on all sides with the beaten egg, and transfer to a foil-covered baking sheet. Repeat until you've wrapped all 16 hot dogs.

9. Bake for 15 minutes. Remove the corndogs from the oven, and let cool for 2 minutes. Top each corndog with an equal portion of the remaining caramel, and quickly sprinkle with the Cracker Jack topping. (It should stick to the melty, gooey caramel.) Serve and enjoy.

GIANTS VS. COWBOYS

That evening was probably one of the best football games I've ever seen—it was the game in which the Giants' Odell Beckham, Jr., made a ridiculous one-handed Spiderman catch—easily the best catch of the 2014–2015 NFL season.

New Jersey's MetLife Stadium is home to both of New York's NFL teams, the Giants and the Jets. The cost to build MetLife was approximately $1.6 billion, thereby making it the most expensive stadium ever built and the largest stadium in the NFL in terms of permanent seating capacity. Incidentally, the new Yankee Stadium cost $1.5 billion to build (including financing), making it the most expensive baseball stadium ever built and the second-most expensive stadium of any kind (second to MetLife).

I'm serving up my Cracker Jack Corn Dogs in the Coaches Club.

NEW YORK–STYLE SMOKED SALMON SANDWICH

SERVES **1**

The classic New York breakfast bagel is known by many as "lox and schmear" (pronounced "shmee-yah"). It's a bagel with cream cheese, (sometimes) capers, red onion, tomato, and smoked salmon. I happen to think it's utterly delectable. But it's not sportsfood, it's breakfast food. And yes, many people begin tailgating during what would be considered breakfast hours for an early afternoon game. I can't quite wrap my head around eating a bagel while tailgating. I can, however, process eating a sandwich with similar ingredients. This sandwich is super-duper simple, taking maybe five minutes to whip up. It's a rendition of the New York breakfast staple that I deem far more appropriate for game day.

2 tablespoons cream cheese (I like scallion cream cheese), softened

1 ciabatta bun, cut in half

1 teaspoon capers

$1/4$ cup baby spinach leaves

1 $1/4$-inch-thick slice red onion

1 $1/4$-inch-thick slice tomato

$1/4$ cup alfalfa sprouts

4 to 5 slices smoked salmon

1 half-sour pickle

1. Spread the cream cheese on the bottom slice of the bun. Top with the capers, then the spinach, onion, tomatoes, sprouts, salmon, and the top of the bun.

2. Serve with the pickle.

NEW ORLEANS MUFFALETTA SANDWICH

SERVES 4

At last. My favorite sandwich in the whole wide world. Thank you, thank you, New Orleans. You've given us so many great dishes, but none more special to me than the mouthwatering muffaletta. While New Orleans may, in fact, be a French city, this sandwich, which is one of New Orleans' most famous, is actually Sicilian in origin, brought over by Sicilian immigrants years and years ago. I first debuted this recipe on *Late Night with Seth Meyers*. In fact, I was the first person to use the new *Late Night* kitchen. I was like a kid in a candy store! Seth poked fun at the level of difficulty of this sandwich—in that it isn't difficult at all. I responded that it's not about the level of difficulty, it's about the level of awesomeness in your mouth, which is an 11 on a scale of 1 to 10. The sandwich that I made on the set was enormous and fed pretty much the entire crew after we wrapped. I got several enthusiastic thumbs ups. (A much-owed shout out here to my friend, Lisa, for helping me prepare everything for the show. I couldn't have done it without her.) So I'm pretty confident with this one—it's a winner.

¼ cup red wine vinegar

2 cloves garlic, minced

1 teaspoon dried oregano

⅓ cup olive oil

10 large pitted green olives, chopped

⅓ cup chopped kalamata olives

¼ cup chopped roasted red bell peppers

¼ cup chopped pepperoncinis

2 anchovy fillets, chopped

Sea salt and freshly ground black pepper

1 (1-pound) round bread loaf (about 7 inches in diameter and 3 inches high)

4 ounces thinly sliced ham

4 ounces thinly sliced mortadella

4 ounces thinly sliced salami

4 ounces sliced provolone cheese

1 medium red onion, thinly sliced

2 cups loosely packed arugula

1. Whisk together the vinegar, garlic, and oregano in a large bowl to blend. Gradually pour in the oil while continuing to whisk. Stir in the olives, roasted peppers, pepperoncinis, and anchovies. Season the vinaigrette with salt and pepper.

2. Cut the bread loaf in half. Hollow out the top and bottom halves of the bread. Spread half of the vinaigrette over the bottom half. Layer the meats and cheese next. Top with the onions and then the arugula. Spread the remaining vinaigrette on top, and carefully cover with the bread top.

3. Cut into 4 wedges, and serve immediately.

TASTY TIDBITS

The Mercedes-Benz Superdome is home to the NFL's New Orleans Saints. But because of the Superdome's large size and enviable location in one of the United States' most visited cities, it's also been home to many other sporting events besides regular season NFL. In fact, the Superdome has hosted seven Super Bowls—the most recent of which was the (infamous) 2013 game during which a power failure halted the game for 34 long minutes.

MINI CHICKEN AND WAFFLES

MAKES ABOUT **12**

I didn't really discover chicken and waffles until I went to college in the South. But once that first bite hit my taste buds, I was hooked. When seasoned right, this combo is the perfect interplay of salty and sweet and soft and crunchy all together in one dish! Usually chicken and waffles is more of an entrée—even a late-night bite (à la Roscoe's House of Chicken and Waffles, the late-night LA spot)—and not quite fitting for a fangating spread. So I say, just like sliders, make 'em mini—as in finger food—and problem solved! I add a little Brie and green apple on top to create a bit more flavor, but feel free to leave them off. There's nothing wrong with keeping this dish simple.

2 tablespoons molasses

1/2 cup balsamic vinegar

Sea salt

1 large egg, beaten

Splash of whole milk

4 chicken tenders

3 tablespoons olive or vegetable oil

1 tablespoon sesame oil

24 whole-wheat mini waffles

1 small Granny Smith apple, cored and thinly sliced into 12 bite-sized wedges

Brie cheese, cut into 12 bite-sized wedges

PANKO MIXTURE

1 cup panko breadcrumbs

1/4 teaspoon sea salt

1/4 to 1/2 teaspoon Lawry's seasoned salt, to taste

1/8 teaspoon chili powder

1/4 teaspoon freshly ground black pepper

1/8 teaspoon garlic powder

1. Combine the molasses, vinegar, and a pinch of salt in a small saucepan. Stir well, and then reduce over low for about 15 minutes, whisking frequently, until you have about 1/4 cup.

2. Meanwhile, combine all the ingredients for the panko mixture in a large shallow bowl, and mix well. Combine the egg and milk in another shallow bowl. Dunk each chicken tender in the egg mixture before coating them completely in the panko mixture.

3. Combine the oils in a large skillet over medium. Add the coated chicken tenders, and pan-fry them over medium to medium-high, making sure to flip them until both sides are browned and the chicken is cooked through, 6 to 8 minutes. Remove from the heat, and cut each tender into 12 chunks, roughly the size of the waffles.

4. Warm the waffles, preferably in a toaster oven or low oven so they're warm but still have a bit of texture.

5. Sandwich a piece of chicken between two waffles, top with a wedge of apple and a wedge of Brie, drizzle with the molasses-balsamic reduction, and serve.

FRIENDLY FANGATING TIP: I like the extra sweetness and nuttiness that whole-wheat waffles bring, and that they're a little healthier. You can also skip the molasses reduction entirely and just use maple syrup!

TEXAS TOAST BRISKET SANDWICHES

SERVES 6

This is a surprise new favorite. When I think of brisket—other than thinking it's my favorite dish that my maternal grandmother makes—I think of Austin, Texas (even though brisket there is usually smoked and my grandmother's is not). So when I was tinkering around in the kitchen trying to figure out what to do with this family brisket recipe, I thought, "Okay, Texas toast!" Winner, winner, chicken, errrr…brisket dinner, y'all! If you do have a smoker, feel free to smoke this instead of slow cooking it. I'll bet it'd also be quite tasty.

¹/₂ cup ketchup (to make your own, page 245)

¹/₂ cup chili sauce

2 teaspoons Louisiana hot sauce

¹/₂ cup red cooking wine

1 (1-ounce) package Lipton Onion Soup Mix

4 pounds beef brisket

1 cup baby carrots

1 small sweet onion, sliced into thin rings

2 tablespoons butter

¹/₄ teaspoon sea salt

¹/₄ teaspoon freshly ground black pepper

¹/₄ teaspoon dried parsley

2 cloves garlic, puréed

12 (1-inch-thick) slices white bread (I like Pullman)

6 slices Monterey Jack cheese

1. Preheat the oven to 325°F. Line a 9- x 13-inch baking dish with aluminum foil.

2. Mix the ketchup, chili sauce, hot sauce, wine, and soup mix in a bowl.

3. Place the brisket on the foil in the prepared baking dish, and cover with the sauce. Sprinkle the carrots and onions around the edge of the meat. Use a brush or the back of a spoon to coat the top of the meat with the sauce. (Note: Most, if not all, of the sauce will pool around the brisket, not on it.) Fold the foil up tightly so that the brisket is concealed inside.

4. Bake for 3¹/₂ hours, or until very tender. Transfer to a cutting board, and let cool for about 15 minutes. Slice the brisket into ¹/₄- to ¹/₂-inch slices.

5. Melt the butter in a small saucepan, and then add the salt, pepper, parsley, and garlic, stirring to combine. Brush the butter mixture onto all sides of the bread slices.

6. Grill or toast the bread in a skillet over medium, 1 minute per side, until lightly golden brown.

7. Cover 6 pieces of the toast with the 6 slices of cheese, and then top each with 2 slices of brisket, some of the carrots and onions, plenty of the sauce, and a second piece of toast. Serve and enjoy.

FRIENDLY FANGATING TIP: If you like your sauce a bit goopier, remove the carrots and onions from the baking dish with a slotted spoon, and then transfer the sauce to a skillet. Reduce over high, stirring constantly, for 10 to 15 minutes. Once it has reduced by half, it will goo-ify better as it cools.

Beer-Battered
Cajun-Style
Deep-Fried Okra
(page 206)

FRIENDLY FANGATING TIP:

Despite its name, pork butt is actually part of the shoulder. The shoulder is a hardworking part of the pig, and the meat is therefore pretty tough. Slow cooking is a great way to make it soft and succulent. That said, the best way to get the most out of your pork—since 5 pounds is a lot—is to cut it into smaller pieces.

SLOW-COOKED BBQ PULLED PORK SANDWICHES

SERVES **18**

This is a really easy-to-make but very flavorful sandwich. It's classically southern, if you ask me. It reminds me of my days eating Carolina barbecue down at Duke. And while I've devoted an entire portion of Chapter 4 to barbecue, I had to include this recipe here because I like pork best served as a sandwich. The toppings are simple—just some jalapeño and red onion slices. Some cilantro, too, if you like it. You really don't need a whole lot because the barbecue jus that you get from slow cooking this pork is so crazy flavorful. I like this dish served with my Asian Slaw (page 191) and some plain potato chips. (Sometimes I even put the potato chips on the sandwich to give it some crunch.) This recipe is perfect to prepare at home and then bring to a tailgate in my Hungry Fan™ 3-in-1 Fangating™ Bag.

5 pounds boneless pork butt, cut into 8 to 10 pieces

4 teaspoons sea salt

4 teaspoons freshly ground black pepper

$^1/_2$ teaspoon garlic powder

1 tablespoon dried minced onions

1 large shallot, finely minced

2 tablespoons salted butter

1 cup Pomì tomato sauce

1 cup apple cider vinegar

2 tablespoons tomato paste

$1^1/_2$ tablespoons yellow mustard

1 tablespoon Worcestershire sauce

1 teaspoon molasses

$^1/_3$ cup dark brown sugar

$^1/_2$ teaspoon cayenne pepper, or more to taste

1 teaspoon Smoulder or other smoky seasoning blend

FIXIN'S

36 thick-cut slices bread (I like sourdough) or 18 brioche buns

2 jalapeños, sliced into thin rounds

1 red onion, sliced into very thin rounds

Roughly chopped fresh cilantro, optional

1. Place the pork in a large Dutch oven, and season with 2 teaspoons of the salt and pepper, the garlic powder, and dried onions. Set aside.

2. Sauté the shallots in the butter in a skillet over medium until they begin to caramelize, about 4 minutes. Lower the heat to a simmer, and stir in the tomato sauce, vinegar, tomato paste, mustard, Worcestershire, molasses, brown sugar, cayenne pepper, and Smoulder. Season with the remaining 2 teaspoons salt and pepper, and simmer for 5 minutes.

3. Pour the sauce all over the pork. Cover the Dutch oven and boil over medium-high to high for 20 minutes, stirring occasionally to prevent the bottom from burning. (Steam will seep out of the pot so be sure to turn your vent on.) Reduce the heat to medium-low, and cook for another 40 minutes.

4. Transfer your lidded Dutch oven to your Hungry Fan™ 3-in-1 Fangating™ Bag, and cook for 7 to $7^1/_2$ hours. Alternatively, skip step 3, and pour the sauce over the pork in a 6-quart slow cooker; cook for 7 hours on low.

5. Remove the pot from the Fangating™ Bag, if using. Transfer the liquid to a saucepan (leaving the pork in the Dutch oven or slow cooker, covered), and reduce the sauce by half over medium-high, stirring frequently to avoid burning, for 18 minutes.

6. Using a fork, gently pull the pork apart until you have a pot full of pulled pork.

7. Make the sandwiches: Top a slice of bread with the reduced barbecue sauce. Add a healthy serving of pulled pork, 3 to 4 jalapeño rounds, some red onion slices, and a sprinkle of cilantro, if you like. Serve immediately.

DC-STYLE SPICY HALF SMOKES

CONTRIBUTOR: **JEFF GREEN** | SERVES **6**

Jeff Green is a fellow Marylander and such a great guy. He is one of my favorites of my dad's clients and also one of the first that was in college when I was. Jeff is a big food fan like I am, and when I asked him what his favorite sportsfood is, he quickly replied DC-style spicy half smokes served with potato salad and honey barbecue baked beans. (I think someone used to frequent the classic DC spot Ben's Chili Bowl.) Here you have Jeff's half smokes recipe. Per his advice, serve these with potato salad and my BBQ Baked Beans (page 203).

2 tablespoons extra virgin olive oil

4 cloves garlic, minced

¹/₂ large white onion, diced

1 Fresno chile pepper, minced

1 pound 80/20 ground chuck beef

1 tablespoon yellow mustard

1 teaspoon brown mustard seeds

¹/₂ teaspoon ground cumin

1 teaspoon sea salt

2 tablespoons chili powder

¹/₂ teaspoon cayenne pepper, or more for extra heat

2 tablespoons tomato paste

3 tablespoons apple cider vinegar

2 tablespoons salted butter

¹/₄ cup all-purpose flour

1¹/₂ cups chicken or beef broth

6 jumbo hot dogs

6 hot dog buns, lightly toasted

Hot mustard, optional

1 small red onion, diced

1. Heat the olive oil in a large skillet over medium-high. Add the garlic, onion, and chile, and sauté until the onions start to become translucent, about 5 minutes. Lower the heat to medium, and stir in the ground beef, mustard, mustard seeds, cumin, salt, 1 tablespoon of the chili powder, and cayenne pepper. Mix well, and cook for about 12 minutes, using a spoon to break up the clumps of meat.

2. Stir in the tomato paste, and cook for 4 minutes. Add the vinegar, and deglaze the skillet, stirring well and scraping up any browned bits from the bottom of the skillet, another 4 minutes.

3. Melt the butter in a separate medium skillet over medium. Add the flour and the remaining 1 tablespoon chili powder, and stir well. Slowly pour in the broth, whisking continuously to remove any clumps. Continue to cook, reducing the liquid by a quarter while continuously whisking, about 4 minutes.

4. Add the flour mixture to the chili and mix well to combine. Cook for 5 minutes over medium, continuing to stir.

5. Preheat your grill. Slice the hot dogs lengthwise about three-quarters of the way through, and then grill them, cut-sides down, for about 8 minutes. Spread mustard inside each bun, if desired. Place a hot dog in each, and top with a large scoop of chili. Sprinkle with some red onions.

From left to right: Jeff Green; Patrick Ewing, Jr.; me; and Greg Monroe at my dad's 60th birthday party.

TASTY TIDBITS

Jeff is a Georgetown Hoya and went on to be picked fifth overall in the 2007 NBA Draft. He has since played for the Oklahoma City Thunder, the Boston Celtics, and the Memphis Grizzlies.

POT ROAST SLIDERS

SERVES 12

These sliders were the hands-down hit of my 2015 Super Bowl spread. And with good reason—they are really, really tasty with mouth-pleasing texture. The combination of crunchy onion rings and juicy pickles combined with the meatiness of the pot roast and the softness of the bun—there is a lot going on in one single bite. I opt for potato buns in this recipe because they're on the sweeter side, which nicely offsets the saltiness of the pot roast jus and onion rings. Cook the pot roast well ahead of time, but don't make the onion rings until you're ready to serve. If you let rings sit, they get soggy. And potato buns get soggy, too. So put everything together, and then enjoy immediately.

2 tablespoons extra virgin olive oil

2^1/$_2$ pounds boneless beef chuck roast

Sea salt and freshly ground black pepper

^{1}/$_4$ cup all-purpose flour

1 packet Lipton Onion Soup Mix

1 cup beef broth

2 bay leaves

3 cloves garlic, minced

1^1/$_2$ cups water

2 tablespoons white horseradish

1 cup mayonnaise (to make your own, see page 250), plus more if needed

1 cup tempura batter mix

1 large egg

^{3}/$_4$ cup ice water

4 cups avocado or vegetable oil, or a combination

^{1}/$_2$ large onion, sliced into 24 (^{1}/$_4$-inch-thick) rings

12 potato slider buns

Thinly sliced pickle rounds, optional

1. Heat the olive oil in a large Dutch oven over medium-high.

2. Generously sprinkle both sides of the beef with salt and pepper, and then coat both sides in flour. Brown both sides in hot oil, turning the meat over as needed, about 8 minutes total.

3. Add the soup mix, broth, bay leaves, garlic, and 1½ cups water. Bring to a boil for 10 minutes, and then cover and reduce the heat to low. Cook for 30 minutes.

4. Transfer the covered Dutch oven to your Hungry Fan™ 3-in-1 Fangating™ Bag, and cook for 8 hours (or overnight). Alternatively, skip the boiling and bake the pot roast at 350°F for 3 hours, or until the meat is very tender.

5. Meanwhile, make the horseradish aioli: Stir together the horseradish and mayo, seasoning with black pepper and adding more mayo if needed. Keep in the fridge until serving time.

6. You will want to wait until just before the meat is done to make the onion rings. Combine the tempura mix, egg, and ice water in a medium bowl. Whisk well so the batter takes on the consistency of pancake batter.

7. Fill a large deep skillet or wide pot with 2 inches avocado oil, and heat to 365°F. Coat the onion rings well with the batter, and then fry a few rings at a time in the hot oil for 2 to 3 minutes, until crispy and golden brown. Transfer to a plate covered in a couple layers of paper towels to drain.

8. Once the meat is done, cut it into large pieces, removing fat as necessary. To assemble the sliders, lightly toast the buns in a toaster oven or low oven. Spoon some aioli on both the tops and bottoms, and then layer the sandwiches with pot roast, onion rings, and pickles, if desired. Serve immediately.

(VEGAN) LENTIL BURGERS

SERVES 6

I used to think that if I was going to eat a burger, I might as well go all out and eat a big, fat, juicy, beefy burger. But with all the sporting events I cover, the frequency with which I eat burgers has increased considerably in recent years. In an effort to mix up my burger selections, I've started trying to eat veggie burgers. Today's veggie burgers have seriously come a long way and are very enjoyable to eat. Not to toot my own horn (but I am going to a little), but this lentil burger is really, really good. Between the fatness of the patties and the delicious ingredients that go into them, I promise you won't feel like you're eating health food.

1 cup green lentils

3 cups low-sodium vegetable stock

2 to 3 tablespoons olive oil

2 Fresno chiles, minced

2 large cloves garlic, minced

1 large shallot, minced

1 cup baby spinach

1/4 cup finely chopped walnuts

Juice of 1 lemon

1/2 teaspoon freshly ground black pepper

1 teaspoon sea salt, preferably pink Himalayan

1 teaspoon cumin seeds

3/4 cup rolled oats, ground

6 white Cheddar cheese slices, optional

Whole-wheat or potato hamburger buns

3 cups loosely packed arugula

2 to 3 roasted red peppers, cut into strips

CILANTRO MAYONNAISE

1/2 cup vegan mayonnaise

1 tablespoon minced fresh cilantro

1. Cook the lentils in the vegetable stock in a medium pot over medium-low, until they are fully softened and the stock is absorbed, about 35 minutes. Transfer to a medium bowl, and mash them as you would potatoes. Set aside.

2. Heat 2 tablespoons olive oil in a skillet over medium. Add the chiles, garlic, and shallots, and sauté for 3 minutes. Add the spinach and walnuts, and cook until the shallots are golden brown, about 3 minutes more.

3. Transfer the spinach mixture to the lentils. Add the lemon juice, pepper, salt, and cumin seeds. Stir in the rolled oats. Transfer to a food processor, and pulse 4 times, or until the mixture begins to bind together.

4. Using your hands, form the lentil mixture into 6 patties, and grill or pan-fry them over medium (adding 1 tablespoon olive oil if pan frying), flipping after about 4 minutes and cooking the other side for another 4 minutes. If you'd like to top your burger with cheese, reduce the heat to low, add a slice of cheese, and cover the pan until the cheese melts, 2 to 3 minutes.

5. Meanwhile, mix together the cilantro mayonnaise ingredients in a small bowl. Spread the insides of the buns with the cilantro mayonnaise. Add the lentil burger with the arugula and roasted red pepper strips. Serve immediately.

FRIENDLY FANGATING TIP: I like my lentil burger with white Cheddar cheese. But if you're vegan, feel free to use vegan cheese or no cheese at all. Everything else about this recipe should comply with your dietary restrictions. And if you're gluten-free, be sure the rolled oats you use are gluten-free and serve your patty atop a gluten-free bun.

TASTY TIDBITS

If you visit Oriole Park at Camden Yards, home of the Baltimore Orioles, you'll notice that in a sea of dark green plastic seats, there are two orange ones. One can be found in the left field bleachers at Section 86, Row FF, Seat 10. This seat commemorates where Cal Ripken landed his 278th homerun on July 15, 1993, breaking Chicago Cubs legend Ernie Banks' record. Two years later, on September 6, 1995, Cal Ripken went on to break MLB legend Lou Gehrig's record of 2,130 consecutive games played. Interestingly, the second orange seat at Oriole Park, which can be found in right-center field at Section 96, Row 7, Seat 23, commemorates the spot where Eddie Murray hit his 500th career homerun—exactly one year to the day from when Ripken broke Gehrig's record.

FOOTBALL YARDS

CRAB CAKE BURGERS

SERVES **4**

I was born in Washington, D.C., but was raised in the great state of Maryland. I cannot tell you how many people I meet who have zero idea where Maryland is or that it's even a state. ("Oh yeah, Maryland. That's in D.C. right?" Umm. No, it's not.) If you've ever seen the movie "Wedding Crashers," you may recall the funny line said by Bradley Cooper's character. He exclaims, "Crab cakes and football. That's what Maryland does!" Indeed, all you Terps, Orioles, and Ravens fans will surely agree that the most quintessential Maryland dish is crab cakes. You can certainly serve them on a platter at your fangate. You can even make mini one-bite crab cakes and serve them as finger food. I like mine on a bun. Since I don't eat red meat super-duper often, I find that crab cakes make a nice substitution for the traditional ground chuck burger patty. Be sure to remember the Old Bay! In Maryland, it's basically sacrilegious to eat crab without it.

2 green onions, finely sliced

1 large egg, lightly beaten

¼ cup plain Greek yogurt

1 tablespoon Dijon mustard

Dash of hot sauce

2 teaspoons fresh lemon juice

1½ teaspoons Old Bay Seasoning

1 pound lump crabmeat, picked over and shredded

1 cup panko breadcrumbs

¼ teaspoon kosher salt

⅛ teaspoon freshly ground black pepper

2 tablespoons canola oil

4 hamburger buns

4 large romaine lettuce leaves

4 thin red onion slices

Tzatziki (page 244)

1. Whisk together the green onions, egg, yogurt, mustard, hot sauce, lemon juice, and Old Bay Seasoning in a bowl. Add the crab, and mix to combine. Then add in the panko breadcrumbs, salt, and pepper, and stir together.

2. Form the crab mixture with your hands into four 1-inch-thick round patties.

3. Heat the oil in a large skillet over medium. Fry the cakes on both sides until golden brown and crisp, 4 minutes per side.

4. Serve the patties on the buns with lettuce, red onion, and tzatziki, as you would a burger. (You can also serve them on lettuce without the bun for an almost carb-free crab cake burger.)

FRIENDLY FANGATING TIP:

Be very careful with the Old Bay if you have any open cuts on your hands or fingers—especially those from removing the meat from a crab. I'm 100% certain nothing hurts more—not even lemon—than Old Bay in an open wound. I speak from experience!

NACHOS BURGERS

SERVES **4**

You may have noticed a theme here. I love mashing together some of my favorite sportsfoods into one dish. See my Cracker Jack Corn Dogs (page 118) or Cheeseburger Soup (page 67). Who says you can't put nachos on a burger? Often, nachos are served with ground meat or carne asada on top. So why not reverse things a bit and put nachos on your burger patty? Nachos lend the burger a bit of much-wanted crunch. And the cheese, salsa, guac, and sour cream are just as great on a burger as they are on nachos. So here, you get it all! *Olé!*

1¹/₂ pounds 80/20 ground beef chuck

1 teaspoon sea salt

1 teaspoon freshly ground black pepper

2 tablespoons olive oil

14 yellow corn tortilla chips

¹/₃ cup shredded sharp Cheddar cheese

¹/₃ cup shredded pepper Jack cheese

¹/₂ jalapeño, thinly sliced into rounds

¹/₃ cup canned drained pinto beans

4 hamburger buns

¹/₄ cup sour cream or plain Greek yogurt

¹/₄ cup Salsa Roja (page 248) or Homemade Salsa (page 57)

¹/₂ cup Basic Guacamole (page 247)

1. Preheat the oven to 450°F. Line 2 baking sheets with aluminum foil.

2. Combine the beef, salt, and pepper in a bowl. Mix well with your hands, and then roll the meat into a large meatball. Flatten into 4 (1-inch-thick) patties, and then use your thumb to make an indentation in the middle of the patties.

3. Heat the olive oil in a large skillet over medium. Once the oil is warm, quickly brown both sides of the burgers, about 2 minutes per side. Transfer to a roasting rack set over one of the prepared baking sheets, and bake for 6 to 7 minutes for medium-rare or about 8 minutes for medium.

4. Preheat the broiler. Lay the tortilla chips in a single layer on the second prepared baking sheet. Evenly cover the chips with the cheeses, the jalapeño slices, and beans, and place them under the broiler for 3 minutes, until the cheese melts but doesn't burn.

5. Place 1 burger on the bottom half of 1 bun. Add 1 tablespoon each of the sour cream and salsa, some of the nachos, and finally 2 tablespoons guacamole. Add the top bun, doing your best to keep your burger together, repeat with the other burgers, and serve immediately.

FRIENDLY FANGATING TIP: In the United States, French fries are always served alongside a burger. In Greece, they're often served in a gyro. I figure, if they can do it, why can't we? If adding nachos to your burger patty isn't your thing, try adding fries and call it a French Fries Burger! Just be sure those are some crispy fries. You want a crunchy outside and warm and soft inside. Anything too soft will end up feeling like a lot of starchy mush.

SRIRACHA PORK BURGERS

SERVES **2**

Sriracha is seriously growing on me. For many of you, it may already be your favorite hot sauce, and I see why. The spice, the texture. So good. In my head, Sriracha always seems to accompany Asian flavors, and I decided to go with it in this dish, an Asian-inspired burger recipe using the other white meat (you need not always use turkey). There's a lot of flavor going on here, and a lot of spice. If spicy is your thing, this may just be your new favorite burger. This recipe is easily doubled, tripled, quadrupled…

12 ounces ground pork

$1/2$ teaspoon sea salt

$1/2$ teaspoon freshly ground black pepper

$1/4$ cup finely chopped green onions

$1^1/_2$ teaspoons Sriracha sauce, plus more for garnish

1 tablespoon extra virgin olive oil

2 tablespoons mayonnaise (to make your own, see page 250)

2 hamburger buns

$1/2$ jalapeño, thinly sliced

$3/4$ cup bean sprouts

2 tablespoons fresh cilantro leaves

$1/2$ cup shredded lettuce

1. Preheat the oven to 450°F. Line a baking sheet with aluminum foil.

2. Combine the pork, salt, pepper, green onions, and $1/2$ teaspoon of the Sriracha in a bowl. Mix well with your hands, and then roll into a large meatball. Flatten into two 1-inch-thick patties, and use your thumb to make indentations in the middles.

3. Heat the olive oil in a skillet over medium. Once the oil is shimmering, quickly brown the patties, about 2 minutes per side. Transfer to a roasting rack set over the prepared baking sheet, and bake for 20 minutes, until slightly pink in the center.

4. Meanwhile, combine the mayonnaise and the remaining 1 teaspoon Sriracha in a small bowl.

5. To build the burgers, place a pork patty on the bottom bun, and then top with a dollop of the Sriracha mayo and another $1/2$ to 1 teaspoon of Sriracha, depending on how much spice you can take. Add half the jalapeño slices, bean sprouts, cilantro, and lettuce. Top with the other half of the bun, repeat for your second burger, and serve immediately.

BBQ BACON CHEESEBURGERS WITH FRIED ONIONS

| CONTRIBUTOR: **GEOFF SCHWARTZ** | SERVES **4** |

If you're a New York fan, you may recognize Geoff from the New York Giants, for whom he played offensive guard. Duck fans may remember him from his time with the University of Oregon, where he started for three years at right tackle. He was selected by the Carolina Panthers in the 2008 NFL Draft and has also played with the Minnesota Vikings and the Kansas City Chiefs. Geoff and I share a couple of mutual friends, both of whom reached out to me to tell me all about him. "You have to meet Geoff! He's a big foodie like you!" So from one foodie to another to you, here's Geoff's cheeseburger recipe. Enjoy!

2 pounds 90/10 ground sirloin

$^1/_2$ teaspoon dried parsley

$^1/_4$ teaspoon garlic powder

Sea salt and freshly ground black pepper

8 slices thick-cut bacon

2 onions, sliced into $^1/_4$-inch-thick rings

2 cups buttermilk

2 cups all-purpose flour

Vegetable oil, for frying

Your favorite barbecue sauce

4 Cheddar or Colby Jack cheese slices

4 brioche buns

Mayonnaise, for serving, optional

1. Preheat your grill to 400°F or a grill pan over medium-high.

2. Mix together the ground sirloin, dried parsley, garlic powder, and salt and pepper to taste in a large bowl. Use your hands to form the ground meat mixture into 4 even patties.

3. Arrange the bacon on the grill rack. If using a charcoal grill, be sure to place the bacon around the edge of the grill so that the grease does not start a fire. If using a gas grill, place the bacon to one side over lower heat. After the fat has slowly dripped off, you can move the bacon toward the center of the grill to finish cooking, about 10 minutes. When the bacon is nice and crisp, but not burned, remove it from the grill, and set it aside.

4. Meanwhile, in a large shallow bowl, soak the onions in the buttermilk for 5 minutes.

5. Add the burgers to the grill. While they are cooking, place the flour in another large shallow bowl, and season with salt and pepper. Remove the onion rings from the buttermilk, and coat them in the seasoned flour.

6. Heat about 4 inches oil in a large Dutch oven over medium until it reaches 375°F on a deep-fry thermometer. Test the heat of the oil by adding a small onion ring. If it burns, your oil is too hot. Place the onions in the oil, and fry for 3 minutes, until golden brown. Using a slotted spoon, transfer them to a plate covered in paper towels.

7. Keeping an eye on the burgers, flip them after 5 minutes. When they are nearly cooked, after about 10 minutes total, brush the top with the barbecue sauce. Let sit for 1 minute, then flip again, brushing the other side with barbecue sauce. Add the cheese, and remove the burgers from the grill. Add the buns to the grill to quickly heat them.

8. To build the burgers, coat the bottom buns with more barbecue sauce, top with the cheeseburger, 2 slices of bacon, some fried onions, as well as any other desired condiments. (Geoff likes mayo.) Add the top bun, and enjoy.

PEANUT BUTTER AND BACON BURGERS

SERVES **2**

This burger is so ridiculously simple yet so stinkin' good. I first debuted this one on ABC 7 New York, and anchor Michelle Charlesworth loved it. If I remember correctly, she spent the better part of the segment eating her burger, so I did a lot of the talking. (My mom always says you know the food is good when no one's talking!) You may question combining the sweetness of peanut butter with the other, more normal burger components, but I promise it works. It works so, so well. For extra sweetness, add a healthy dab of your favorite BBQ sauce onto your burger buns for an almost PB&J-like taste!

2 slices thick-cut bacon

1 teaspoon brown sugar

12 ounces (80/20) ground beef chuck

$^1/_2$ teaspoon sea salt

$^1/_2$ teaspoon freshly ground black pepper

2 hamburger buns

2 heaping tablespoons all-natural smooth peanut butter

1. Preheat the oven to 450°F. Preheat a large skillet over high. Line a baking sheet with aluminum foil.

2. Sprinkle each slice of bacon on both sides with $^1/_2$ teaspoon brown sugar. Lay the bacon on the griddle, and cook both sides evenly until the bacon is just a little crispy, about 10 minutes in all. If the fatty oil starts to pop and spray everywhere, turn the heat down to medium-high. (You want the bacon to have bite but not be overcooked.) Cut each bacon slice in half, and set aside. Reserve 1 tablespoon of the bacon fat in the skillet to add extra bacon-y taste later.

3. Combine the beef, salt, and pepper in a bowl. Mix well with your hands, and roll into two equal meatballs. Flatten into two 1-inch-thick patties, and then use your thumb to make indentations in the middles.

4. Heat the reserved bacon fat in the same skillet over medium. Once the fat is warm, quickly brown both sides of the burgers, about 2 minutes per side. Transfer to a roasting rack set over the prepared baking sheet, and bake for 6 to 7 minutes for medium-rare and about 8 minutes for medium.

5. Place the patties on the bottom buns. Add the peanut butter and bacon, dividing it evenly, and finish with the top buns. Serve immediately.

TURKEY SLOPPERS

SERVES **2**

Thank you, people of Colorado, for giving us the "slopper." I think I speak for all of us when I say that I am eternally grateful. For those of you unfamiliar with a slopper, let me fill you in. The origin of the slopper is a bit controversial, but everyone agrees that over 40 years ago, Coloradoans created a dish featuring two open-faced cheeseburgers in a bowl smothered in green chili and raw onions. The slopper has taken on many variations since then—bun on top and then covered in chili, cheese on top of bun and then topped with chili, and so on and so forth. But the basics are always the same: a burger smothered in awesome chili sauce. My spin uses turkey simply because I usually find turkey burgers too dry. But when you smother even the driest of turkey patties in green chili, they're almost always delectable. Feel free to use a regular beef patty and whatever kind of green chile you like, though I like Stinkin' Good Chile Sauce from my buddy Mark Schlereth.

1¹/₂ cups sliced onions

4 tablespoons extra virgin olive oil

1 pound ground turkey

¹/₄ teaspoon garlic powder

¹/₄ teaspoon sea salt

¹/₂ teaspoon freshly ground black pepper

1 teaspoon ground cumin

1 large egg

¹/₄ cup salsa verde, plus more to taste

1 cup soft white breadcrumbs

4 Swiss or pepper Jack cheese slices

2 hamburger buns

2 slices tomato

1. Sauté the onions in 2 tablespoons of the olive oil in a nonstick skillet over medium until caramelized, about 15 minutes. Transfer to a plate, and keep warm. Reserve the skillet.

2. Mix together the turkey, garlic powder, salt, pepper, and cumin in a large mixing bowl. Mix in the egg, 2 tablespoons salsa verde, and the breadcrumbs. Mix well, and then form two 1-inch-thick patties.

3. Heat the remaining 2 tablespoons olive oil in the reserved skillet over medium-high. Add the patties, and cook for 5 to 6 minutes per side, until the internal temperature measures 165°F on a meat thermometer. (Only flip your patties once or they might lose their shape.)

4. Meanwhile, layer 2 slices of cheese on the bottom halves of each bun. Lightly toast in a toaster oven or low oven until the cheese is melted.

5. To serve, top each cheese-covered bottom bun with 1 turkey burger, 1 tomato slice, half the caramelized onions, and the remaining 2 tablespoons salsa verde or more, depending on how sloppy you want it.

TASTY TIDBITS

Denver is known as the Mile High City. But did you know that at Coors Field, home of the Colorado Rockies, the field sits only 5,176 feet 9.5 inches above sea level? The purple seats, however, are exactly 5,280 feet above sea level—a mile high.

BARBECUE & OTHER MAINS

This is probably the meatiest of all the chapters in this book—pun intended. Between all the barbecued meats and the different proteins featured in the wide array of entrées, this chapter is packed with plenty of rib-sticking, stomach-filling yumminess.

Grilling and fangating go together like peanuts and beer. In fact, according to the Hearth, Patio & Barbecue Association (HPBA), tailgating for football comprises 52% of tailgates (baseball makes up 7%). And what do we all love to do at tailgates? If you said barbecue, then we're on the same page. Perhaps not surprisingly then, the HPBA's 2011 industry report notes that charcoal grills are used at 76% of tailgates—likely because they're generally far easier to transport than their gas or electric counterparts.

So here are some great new recipes to make on your grill, whether you're at home or in the stadium parking lot. While there's nothing wrong with hot dogs and burgers (and I certainly encourage you to bust out the grill when cooking up those recipes in Chapter 3), sometimes it's good to mix it up a bit on game day. Try some new proteins, including fish, and certainly some different spins on your favorite flavors.

Many of the entrées you'll find in this chapter are likely far easier to make at home. That said, if you're tailgating on game day, there's nothing wrong with making these dishes ahead of time and bringing them still hot to the tailgate. (I encourage you to pick up a Hungry Fan™ Hot Bag to make this a breeze.) And if your game day fangate is at home, then you've got no worries—just cook and serve these dishes when your friends arrive to watch the game!

SMOKIN' BONES

CONTRIBUTOR: **DREW GOODEN** | SERVES **4**

Basketball fans, you probably know Drew Gooden as a much-fêted NBA journeyman. Coming off a 2002 Final Four Appearance with the Kansas Jayhawks, Drew was drafted fourth overall by the Memphis Grizzlies in the 2002 NBA Draft. Since then, he has played for a variety of teams—most currently the Washington Wizards. What you might not know about Drew is that he is a foodie and one hell of a smoke master. He clearly shares my love for wings, having opened up his own Wingstop in Florida. But for the purposes of this book, Drew wanted to share his barbecue-smoking know-how. Below is Drew's recipe for his famous St. Louis–style baby back ribs. You will need to let the ribs marinate the day before you intend to smoke and serve them.

3¹/₂ pounds baby back ribs

2 teaspoons liquid smoke

¹/₂ cup Memphis-Style Ribs BBQ Rub (page 147, or try my Hungry Fan™ Barbecue Spice Blend)

2 tablespoons dark brown sugar, or to taste

Hickory or mesquite wood chips, soaked for 30 minutes

BBQ sauce (page 250), or your choice

1. Place the slab of baby back ribs in a large oven-safe pan. Douse the ribs in liquid smoke. Let the smokiness settle into the ribs briefly, and then generously rub both sides of the ribs in your chosen BBQ seasoning. Finally, sprinkle both sides of the ribs with brown sugar (just enough for a little sweetness—you don't want too much).

2. Cover the ribs in aluminum foil, and place them in the fridge overnight.

3. Place the wood chips on the bottom of your preferred smoker (see Tip). Place the ribs in the smoker, and smoke for 3 to 3¹/₂ hours (depending on the amount of meat and kind of smoking device). The ribs are done when the bones are poking out—that means the meat is quite literally falling off the bone.

4. When the ribs are finished, use a brush to slather your preferred BBQ sauce on both sides. Serve hot.

FRIENDLY FANGATING TIP:

Drew specifies that to make this dish, you'll need a natural wood smoker or grill—or in their place, you can use a Green Egg or electric smoker. He likes using hickory or mesquite wood chips.

BARBECUE MARINATED RIBS

CONTRIBUTOR: **SCIPIO SPINKS** | MAKES ABOUT **2 CUPS**

If you were a fan of Major League Baseball in the late sixties and seventies, then you undoubtedly know of Scipio, or Scip as he's known to friends. Scip was drafted out of high school by the Houston Astros in 1966. In his six-year run with the Astros (including their AAA club), Scip set some impressive records, including one for striking out 20 batters in a single game. Scipio then finished his MLB career with the St. Louis Cardinals, both as a successful pitcher and a speedy pinch runner. After retiring from professional baseball in 1976, Scip ultimately returned to Houston, where he currently scouts for the Astros and cooks up yummy barbecue in his spare time. You will need to marinate the meat the day before you smoke or grill it.

3 cloves garlic, peeled

1 medium white or yellow onion, cut into chunks

1 to 2 red hot peppers, seeded, or to taste

1/2 green bell pepper, seeded and cut into chunks

1/2 yellow bell pepper, seeded and cut into chunks

2 teaspoons Lawry's seasoned salt

2 teaspoons Louisiana Cajun seasoning, optional

2 1/2 pounds baby back ribs

1. Combine the first 6 ingredients and the Cajun seasoning, if desired, in a blender, and purée until no lumps remain.

2. Pour the marinade over the ribs in a baking dish, cover with plastic wrap, and refrigerate overnight.

3. Smoke the ribs at 250° to 275°F for 3 1/2 hours (see opposite recipe for smoking instructions). Alternatively, you can grill them over a charcoal or gas grill.

FRIENDLY FANGATING TIP:

There's another super-easy way to make barbecue sauce. I specially crafted my Hungry Fan™ Barbecue Spice Blend after one of my own barbecue sauce recipes. To reconstitute the blend, stir together 2 tablespoons (or to taste) with 1 cup tomato sauce, 2 teaspoons Worcestershire sauce, and 1 to 2 teaspoons honey or brown sugar and you've got yourself some kickass homemade barbecue sauce!

MARCH MADNESS ATLANTA-INSPIRED BBQ PORK

SERVES **14**

I debuted this recipe in March of 2013 in celebration of the NCAA Final Four, which was held in Atlanta. In homage to the city, I incorporated some local flavors into my barbecue sauce. This recipe calls for you to slow cook the pork. By doing so, the pork will get so deliciously soft that you can easily pull it. If, however, you prefer to grill, I suggest that you marinate the pork in the barbecue sauce overnight (in a zip-top bag). You can then drench the barbecued pork in the marinade; just be sure to heat it up before serving. Regardless of how the pork is cooked, I like to serve mine topped with pickled red onions.

2 tablespoons butter

½ large yellow onion, finely chopped, plus ¼ cup diced

1 cup apple cider vinegar

2 cups Pomì tomato sauce

¼ cup brown sugar

¼ cup cola (see Tip)

1½ tablespoons yellow mustard

1 teaspoon liquid smoke, optional

1½ teaspoons sea salt, plus more for seasoning

1 teaspoon freshly ground black pepper, plus more for seasoning

½ teaspoon cayenne pepper

6 pounds boneless pork shoulder or butt roast, tied

Garlic powder, to taste

PICKLED RED ONIONS

½ cup apple cider vinegar

1 tablespoon sugar

1½ teaspoons kosher salt

1 red onion, thinly sliced

1. Melt the butter in a medium skillet over medium-low. Add the chopped onions, and sauté until lightly browned, about 10 minutes. Reduce the heat to a simmer, and stir in the vinegar, tomato sauce, brown sugar, cola, mustard, liquid smoke, if using, and the salt, pepper, and cayenne. Simmer over low heat for 15 to 20 minutes.

2. Season the pork with the salt, pepper, and garlic powder to taste. Place in a slow cooker with the diced onions and barbecue sauce, and cook on low for 9 hours, or until the meat can be picked apart easily with a fork.

3. Meanwhile, make the pickled onions: Combine the vinegar, sugar, and salt in a small bowl, whisking until the sugar and salt dissolve. Combine the vinegar mixture with the onion slices in a jar or container you can seal well, and let sit at room temperature for at least 1 hour. Drain and set aside.

4. Once the pork is done, transfer it to a large bowl, leaving the sauce in the pot. Using a fork, pull apart the pork.

5. Return the sauce to the skillet, and reduce by half over medium-high, about 10 minutes.

6. Pour the sauce into the bowl with the pork. Mix well, and serve either alongside or topped with the pickled red onions.

FRIENDLY FANGATING TIP:

Cola is my homage to Atlanta in this recipe, as Atlanta is the headquarters of Coca-Cola. I prefer to use cola that has been sweetened with cane syrup or natural sugars, as opposed to high fructose corn syrup. But please, by all means, use what you like best!

FRIENDLY FANGATING TIP: You will need 2 to 4 tablespoons of rub to smother each individual rack of ribs. (I like using the full 4 for really zesty flavor, but you can use less rub for less kick). Adjust the proportions according to your preference to ensure that you have enough rub to cover all the ribs you're making. This recipe makes 1¾ to 2 cups. What you don't use, you can store in an airtight container in your cabinet for up to 6 months.

MEMPHIS-STYLE RIBS

MAKES **4 SLABS OF RIBS**

I came up with this recipe in celebration of the 2014 Fantasy Football Draft. Not that I support eating as a way of managing stress, but the draft can be seriously tense, and there's nothing like meaty ribs to gnaw on while you go through the process (especially as Fantasy Drafts often overlap with dinnertime). These ribs are Memphis-style, which means they're done with a dry rub, rather than barbecue sauce. I find them just as delicious as sauced ribs and perhaps only slightly less messy. Be sure to serve these with a large roll of paper towels nonetheless, especially if you're eating them while you sit by your computer. You don't want dry rub all over your mouse and keyboard. Yuck.

This recipe utilizes smoking as a method of cooking the ribs. If you prefer not to smoke them, you can easily grill them or even bake them instead.

Hickory or mesquite wood chips

4 slabs beef baby back ribs (8 pounds), fat trimmed and membranes removed from backs of bones

BARBECUE RUB

$1/2$ cup paprika

2 tablespoons kosher salt

3 tablespoons freshly ground black pepper

$1\frac{1}{2}$ tablespoons dark brown sugar

$1/4$ cup garlic powder

3 tablespoons onion powder

2 teaspoons dry mustard

$1\frac{1}{2}$ tablespoons celery seeds

3 tablespoons mild chili powder

2 teaspoons cayenne pepper

1 tablespoon dried oregano

2 teaspoons ground cumin

1. Combine all the rub ingredients in a large bowl, and whisk thoroughly. Using your hands, rub the spice mixture onto both sides of each rack of ribs, using about $1/4$ cup per rack.

2. Brush and oil your grill, and place a drip pan in the center. I like to use a charcoal grill for this recipe, and add wood chips for a nice smoky flavor. Preheat the grill to medium (325° to 375°F). You can test the temperature with your hand—if you can hold your hand over the grill for 6 to 7 seconds before it feels like it will melt off, it's medium. If you're using a gas grill, you'll need a smoker box. Turn the gas to high. Once the wood chips start smoking, turn the heat down to medium.

3. Arrange the ribs in a single layer on the grate above the drip pan. Cover and cook for 75 minutes, until the meat is tender and pulling back from the tips of the bones. If they are not done, sprinkle the top of each rack with another 2 to 3 teaspoons of the spice rub and, if using a gas grill, continue to cook and check your ribs in 15-minute increments. (They will likely only need another 15 to 30 minutes.)

4. If using a charcoal grill, you'll need to add more charcoal (as at this point, the grill is losing heat and essentially just warming rather than cooking the ribs); you want to keep the temperature in the 325° to 375°F zone. Cook the ribs in 15-minute increments, and check so as not to overcook them.

5. Alternatively, you can use a charcoal smoker set at 250° to 275°F. Fill the water pan with water, and place the ribs, bone side down, on the top rack of the smoker. Smoke for 3 hours, until the meat is tender but still on the bone.

6. When the ribs are done cooking, wrap them in aluminum foil, and let them sit for 15 minutes before serving. (This will help make them even more tender.)

SLOW-COOKED BBQ PULLED PORK QUESADILLAS

MAKES **16**

I prefer to slow-cook meat in BBQ sauce because when it's done—especially after reducing the sauce—the sauce just sticks to the meat and the texture and taste are balanced between salty and sweet . . . oh man. Make this with pork butt because, when it is properly slow-cooked, it takes on this almost unreal tenderness that's hard to beat. So enough talking. Let's get to cooking, because the sooner we do, the sooner it's done, and the sooner we get to feast!

5 pounds boneless pork butt or tenderloin, cut into smaller pieces (see Tip, page 126)

Sea salt and freshly ground black pepper

2 tablespoons garlic powder

1 tablespoon dried minced onions

1 recipe BBQ Sauce (page 250)

16 (10-inch) flour tortillas (or corn tortillas if you're gluten-free)

8 ounces white Cheddar cheese, shredded

1 large bunch cilantro, roughly chopped

1 (15.5-ounce) can black beans, rinsed, drained, and cooked

1 (15-ounce) can whole kernel corn, drained, or kernels from 2 to 3 boiled ears of corn

8 ounces (2 sticks) salted butter

1 avocado, pitted, peeled, and thinly sliced lengthwise

1. Place the pork butt in a large Dutch oven or slow cooker, and season both sides generously with salt and pepper, the garlic powder, and dried onions.

2. Pour the BBQ Sauce all over the pork. Cover the Dutch oven, and boil over medium-high to high for 20 minutes, stirring occasionally to prevent the bottom from burning. (Steam will seep out of the pot, so be sure to turn your vent on). Leave the cover on, and reduce the heat from medium-low to low (but warmer than a simmer), and cook for another 40 minutes.

3. Transfer your lidded Dutch oven to your Hungry Fan™ 3-in-1 Fangating™ Bag, and cook for 7 to 8 hours. Alternatively, skip this step and simply pour the sauce over the pork in your slow cooker, and cook on low for 9 hours. Using a fork, gently pull your pork apart until you have a Dutch oven full of pulled pork.

4. Lay a tortilla on your workspace. On one half of the tortilla, layer several sprinkles of cheese, about $\frac{1}{2}$ cup of the pulled pork, 1 tablespoon of the cilantro, 2 tablespoons each black beans and corn kernels, and a few more sprinkles of cheese. Fold the other half of the tortilla over the filling to enclose it.

5. Melt 1 tablespoon of the butter in a large skillet over medium-low. Place your quesadilla in the skillet, raise the heat to medium-high, and brown both sides, flipping carefully, 1 to 2 minutes per side. Assemble and cook the remaining quesadillas in the same way.

6. Cut each quesadilla into triangular pieces, and serve with some avocado slices, a drizzle of barbecue sauce, and some additional cilantro sprinkled on top for good measure.

CAROLINA-STYLE BBQ CHICKEN

SERVES **6**

Carolina BBQ sauce has, in my humble opinion, the best balance of sweetness cut with acidity, provided mostly by vinegar and a little bit of mustard. Call me a barbecue snob if you'd like, but if the sauce is too sweet, I won't eat it. And most store-bought brands taste like bottles of straight goopy sugar to me. So I make my own and add in the acidity—or tartness—to ensure I don't get a mouthful of sugar. I've tested this recipe on friends, including those who, like me, have spent a large portion of their lives in the Carolinas. This got their seal of approval. I hope it gets yours, too!

1 large yellow onion, diced

2 tablespoons butter

$^2/_3$ cup yellow mustard

$^1/_2$ cup plus 1 tablespoon agave nectar or honey

$^1/_3$ cup distilled white vinegar

$^3/_4$ cup apple cider vinegar

1 teaspoon Worcestershire sauce

1 teaspoon soy sauce

$1^1/_2$ tablespoons garlic powder

1 tablespoon onion powder

1 teaspoon freshly ground black pepper

$^1/_2$ teaspoon cayenne pepper

$1^1/_2$ tablespoons chili powder

1 teaspoon Smoulder or smoky seasoning of your choice

6 bone-in chicken breasts (about $3^1/_2$ pounds)

1. Put the onions and butter in a large Dutch oven over high. Stir well and cook for 4 minutes, or until the onions soak up all the butter and start to become translucent.

2. Add the mustard, agave, both vinegars, Worcestershire and soy sauces, garlic and onion powders, black and cayenne peppers, chili powder, and smoky seasoning, and reduce the heat to medium-low. Stir everything together well for 3 to 4 minutes.

3. Place the chicken in a slow cooker, and pour the barbecue sauce on top. Cook on low for 6 hours.

4. Alternatively, add the chicken breasts to the barbecue sauce, basting with the liquid to ensure that each piece of chicken is covered in sauce. Cover the pot, increase the heat to high, and bring to a boil for 10 minutes. Transfer your lidded pot to a Hungry Fan™ 3-in-1 Fangating™ Bag, seal, and cook for 5 to 6 hours. (I have left chicken in the Fangater for up to 8 hours and it turned out great.)

5. You can serve the chicken whole, sliced, or pulled, as the long, slow cooking should allow for easy pulling.

FRIENDLY FANGATING TIP:

I've served this on top of tortilla chips with black beans, fresh cilantro, cheese (I like shredded cheddar and Monterey Jack), and corn kernels. It's also great on a potato bun with sandwich fixin's like red onions and thinly sliced jalapeños.

GRILLED SIRLOIN STEAK

CONTRIBUTOR: ADRIAN PETERSON | SERVES **2**

Adrian Peterson was drafted seventh overall in the 2007 NFL Draft by the Minnesota Vikings, and since then he has become their franchise player. It has been argued by many a sports publication that Adrian will go down as one of the greatest running backs in NFL history. The man has set so many NFL records, even after bouncing back from a torn ACL and MCL, it's tough not to be impressed. How does he do it? I can't speak to Adrian's diet, but I can say that the recipes he shared with me for this book are not only nutrient-dense but mighty tasty. Here's Adrian's take on a delicious steak. Serve with Adrian's Fresh Corn on the Cob (page 195) and Deep-Fried Okra and Potatoes (page 194).

2 (8-ounce) top sirloin steaks, fat trimmed

¹/₂ teaspoon cayenne pepper

¹/₂ cup Allegro Original Marinade

1. Sprinkle both sides of the steak with cayenne pepper.

2. Place the steak in a large (1-gallon or more) zip-top bag, add the marinade, and massage so it's evenly covered in marinade. Place in the refrigerator to marinate for 4 hours, turning occasionally.

3. Preheat your grill to medium. Grill the steaks for 1 to 3 minutes per side, or until cooked to your liking.

4. Let rest before serving.

TASTY TIDBITS

In his first NFL season, Adrian set an NFL record for most rushing yards in a single game (296 yards) and was named Offensive Rookie of the Year. Since then he was awarded MVP of the Pro Bowl; became one of five players in NFL history to rush more than 3,000 yards in his first two career seasons; set the record for most rushing yards in any eight-game period (1,322 yards); set the record for most 60-plus-yard touchdowns in a career (12 touchdowns) and the record for most 50-plus-yard runs in a single season (seven runs); and set several Viking franchise records, including most career rushing yards, most career carries, most rushing touchdowns in a single season, most rushing yards in a single season, and most career rushing touchdowns.

Adrian's Grilled Sirloin Steak, Fresh Corn on the Cob (page 195), and Deep-Fried Okra and Potatoes (page 194)

GRILLED FISH

CONTRIBUTORS: **JARED AND TOM JEFFRIES** | SERVES **2**

This recipe comes from my friend Jared Jeffries and his dad, Tom. Most of you probably know Jared as a former NBA player. What you might not know, unless you've seen Jared's angling show *Modern Fishing with Jared Jeffries* on the Outdoor Channel, is that he's also quite the fisherman. I'm told it runs in the Jeffries family. Thus, it's only fitting that Jared would give me a recipe for fish. While you may buy your fish for this recipe at the fishmonger or grocery store, I'm guessing Jared probably catches his.

1 (3-pound) whole striped bass or red snapper, scaled, gutted, and cleaned with head on

4 tablespoons olive oil

1¹/₂ tablespoons salt

1 teaspoon lemon pepper

1 teaspoon freshly ground black pepper

¹/₄ teaspoon red pepper flakes

1 teaspoon garlic powder

2 sprigs fresh rosemary

2 sprigs fresh thyme

2 sprigs fresh oregano

2 thin slices fresh lemon

3 thin slices onion

Several lemon wedges

1. Score both sides of the fish three times, and then brush with the olive oil.

2. Season the fish with the salt, lemon pepper, black pepper, red pepper flakes, and garlic powder.

3. Place the rosemary, thyme, oregano, lemon, and onion slices in the cavity of the fish.

4. Grease your grill. Preheat to medium-high (350°F). Place the fish on the grill, cooking for 12 minutes on each side. The fish is done when the meat is moist and flaky.

5. Squeeze lemon over the fish, and serve hot with additional lemon wedges on the side.

TASTY TIDBITS

Jared was the 11th overall pick out of Indiana in the 2002 NBA Draft by Washington after winning Big Ten Player of the Year. In the course of his 11-year basketball career, he also played for the likes of the Rockets, Knicks, and Trailblazers.

POMEGRANATE MAPLE SEA BASS

CONTRIBUTOR: **VICTORIA AZARENKA** | SERVES **2**

Victoria Azarenka, or Vika as she is known to her friends, is a tennis champion and a foodie—my kind of combination! Vika hails from Belarus and, with her two Australian Open singles titles in 2012 and 2013, she became the first Belarusian player to ever win a Grand Slam Singles title. Off the court, Vika is lots of fun, loves to cook, enjoys hosting friends for dinner, and trains arguably harder than most female tennis players (she can do Olympic dead lifts!). When I asked her for a contribution to this book, she sent me this delicious fish recipe. It's one of her favorites, and it's really flavorful but also wonderfully light. It's a great dish if you're looking for something on the healthier side to serve up!

3 tablespoons extra virgin olive oil

$^1/_2$ teaspoon sea salt

$^1/_2$ teaspoon freshly ground black pepper

$1^1/_2$ teaspoons finely chopped fresh rosemary

1 teaspoon maple syrup

2 Chilean sea bass fillets

2 tablespoons pomegranate seeds or dried cranberries (if pomegranates aren't in season)

1. Combine the olive oil, salt, pepper, rosemary, and maple syrup in a large bowl. Mix well, and add the fish to the bowl. Using a spoon, ladle the marinade all over the fish so it's evenly covered. Cover the bowl with plastic wrap, and marinate for 20 to 60 minutes in the refrigerator.

2. Preheat the oven to 350°F.

3. Remove the fish and marinade from the fridge, and transfer them to a large piece of aluminum foil. Top with the pomegranate seeds, and roll up each fillet so the pomegranate seeds are on the inside. Place the fish rolls, seam sides down, so they stay closed. Seal the foil to make a pouch.

4. Bake for about 25 minutes. Serve immediately.

TASTY TIDBITS

Vika has finished as runner-up in two US Open Championships, both of which she lost to Serena Williams, arguably her biggest rival in professional tennis. Once the number 1 player on the Women's Tennis Tour, Vika won a bronze medal in singles and a gold medal in mixed doubles at the 2012 Summer Olympics in London. She also won two mixed doubles Grand Slam titles in 2007 (US Open) and 2008 (French Open). Not too shabby.

SWEDISH MEATBALLS

CONTRIBUTOR: **BOOMER ESIASON** | SERVES **4 TO 6**

Most of you know Boomer Esiason from his prolific career both on and off the gridiron. But beyond his long list of noteworthy career successes, Boomer is simply the nicest guy and has a huge heart. He also happens to be my sister Jocelyn's godfather and was always kind enough to include me on his family's list of holiday gift recipients when we were growing up. (And if you've ever been lucky enough to receive a gift from Boomer and his lovely wife, Cheryl, you would have to agree that they have the best taste.) I also have Boomer to thank for my first NFL game—my dad took me to watch him and the Bengals take on the Redskins when I was itty-bitty (but old enough to remember). I've been hooked on football ever since. Serve Boomer's dish with your favorite beverage, and get ready for the big game.

1 cup finely chopped red onion

6 tablespoons butter

1 pound ground chuck

$^{1}/_{2}$ pound ground pork

$1^{1}/_{4}$ teaspoons sea salt

$^{1}/_{2}$ teaspoon freshly ground black pepper

$^{1}/_{4}$ teaspoon ground ginger

$^{1}/_{8}$ teaspoon ground nutmeg

1 cup plain Wonder Bread crumbs

$^{1}/_{2}$ cup whole milk

$^{3}/_{4}$ cup heavy cream

2 large egg yolks

$^{1}/_{2}$ cup all-purpose flour

$3^{1}/_{2}$ cups chicken broth

Handful of chopped fresh parsley

1. Sauté the onions in 1 tablespoon of the butter in a medium skillet over medium until soft, about 5 minutes. Let cool, and then transfer to a large bowl along with the ground chuck, pork, 1 teaspoon of the salt, the pepper, ginger, and nutmeg.

2. Combine the breadcrumbs, milk, and $^{1}/_{4}$ cup of the cream in a small bowl, and let sit until the breadcrumbs are soft. Add the breadcrumb mixture, and the egg yolks to the meat mixture and mix thoroughly. Roll the meatballs in your hands until smooth and round; they should be around the size of a half-dollar and you should get around 36. Set them aside on a large plate.

3. Heat 1 tablespoon of the butter in a large nonstick skillet over medium to medium-high until bubbly. Add half of the meatballs, and cook, turning them until the meatballs are browned on all sides, 6 to 8 minutes. Transfer to a plate and repeat.

4. Melt the remaining 3 tablespoons of the butter in a Dutch oven over medium. Add the flour, and cook, whisking, for about 1 minute. Whisk in the chicken broth a little at a time, and then cook, whisking constantly, until the sauce is thickened, bubbly, and smooth, 5 to 6 minutes.

5. Transfer to a large saucepan. Add the remaining $^{1}/_{4}$ teaspoon salt and $^{1}/_{2}$ cup cream. Bring to a gentle boil over medium-high, and then reduce the heat so that the sauce just simmers. Stir gently, and add in the meatballs. Cook, uncovered, for 30 minutes, stirring occasionally, until the meatballs are tender and the sauce is thick. Serve the meatballs sprinkled with the fresh parsley.

SHORT RIB POUTINE

SERVES **4**

This is a proper poutine recipe—French fries, meat, gravy, curds and all. It's hearty and the perfect dish for winter fangating action. In this recipe, I make the French fries from scratch, but feel free to use frozen fries and just cook them up in the oven. I like my fries crispy on the outside and soft on the inside. But cook yours as you like. I warn you now—this recipe is irresistibly delicious but hearty as heck, so don't be shocked if it feels like a meat-and-potatoes bomb in your belly. I like to think of that as the proper fuel for cheering at the game.

4 pounds beef short ribs

1$\frac{1}{2}$ teaspoons sea salt, plus more for seasoning

1$\frac{1}{2}$ teaspoons freshly ground black pepper, plus more for seasoning

2 tablespoons extra virgin olive oil

1 medium yellow onion, diced

6 cloves garlic, minced

3 carrots, diced

3 celery stalks, thinly sliced

4 sprigs savory or rosemary

8 sprigs thyme

2 cups dry red wine, such as Cabernet Sauvignon

$\frac{1}{3}$ cup balsamic vinegar

1 cup beef stock

$\frac{1}{3}$ cup tomato paste

2 tablespoons brown sugar

(CONTINUED)

1. Generously season both sides of the short ribs with salt and pepper.

2. Heat the olive oil in a large Dutch oven over medium-high. Once hot, brown all sides of the ribs, in batches if necessary, 3 to 4 minutes total per batch. Set the meat aside but keep the skillet over the heat. Add the onions and garlic, reduce the heat to medium-low, and sauté for 5 minutes, until the onions start to become translucent. Add the carrots, celery, and $\frac{1}{2}$ teaspoon each salt and pepper. Cook, stirring frequently, until the veggies start to brown (but don't let them burn), about 10 minutes.

3. Stir in the savory, thyme, another teaspoon each of salt and pepper, the red wine, balsamic vinegar, beef stock, tomato paste, and brown sugar, and bring to a boil for 10 minutes.

4. Reduce the heat to low, cover the pot, and simmer for 45 minutes. Transfer the lidded pot to your Hungry Fan 3-in-1 Fangating™ Bag, seal well, and let cook for 5 hours. Alternatively, skip the simmering, cover, and braise in a preheated 325°F oven for 3 hours, or until the short ribs are very tender.

5. When the meat is nearly done cooking, it's time to make the fries. Cut the potatoes into your desired fry shape, and dry well with paper towels.

(CONTINUED)

4 russet potatoes, cleaned but not peeled

2 quarts avocado or safflower oil, for frying (see Tip)

1 cup cheese curds, or to taste

6. Heat the oil in a deep fryer or large pot on your stovetop until it reaches 350°F on a deep-fry thermometer. Working in four batches, place the fries in the oil for 5 minutes, and then transfer to a paper towel–lined plate. Right before you plan to plate your poutine, throw the fries back in the oil, but increase the temperature to 375°F and fry until they are golden brown and crispy, about 5 minutes more. Transfer the fries to a fresh layer of paper towels, and lightly salt them.

7. To serve, fill a bowl with a healthy helping of French fries, top with the short ribs, veggies, sauce, and a generous sprinkling of cheese curds.

FRIENDLY FANGATING TIP: I like to make fries in a proper fryer with avocado oil, as it's far healthier and richer in nutrients than most other "frying" oils. If you like your short rib sauce a little thicker—more like a hearty gravy—simply transfer some to a medium skillet, and reduce over high, whisking constantly, until it reduces to your desired thickness.

SHORT RIB TACOS

MAKES **2**

If you have followed my recipe for Short Rib Poutine on page 156, here is a great use for any leftovers. Or simply go ahead and make the short ribs as you would for the poutine, but skip the potatoes and curds and just make these tacos!

¼ teaspoon prepared horseradish, or more to taste

1 heaping tablespoon plain Greek yogurt

2 (6-inch) flour or corn tortillas

1 cup shredded short ribs

2 tablespoons shredded romaine lettuce

Homemade Salsa (page 57), optional

2 teaspoons chopped fresh cilantro

Mix together the horseradish and yogurt in a bowl until smooth and fully emulsified. Spread half on each tortilla. Top with the shredded short ribs (be sure to drain the meat as much as possible to prevent the sauce from running all over the place). Sprinkle with the lettuce, drizzle any additional horseradish sauce on top if you like, dollop with salsa, if desired, and finally add the cilantro. Serve immediately.

MAMA FALK'S MEATLOAF

SERVES 6 TO 8

My mom used to make my sister and me meatloaf from time to time when we were kids, usually for a school-night dinner. Since leaving home and becoming a professional sports fan of sorts, I have continued to make her meatloaf—though I serve mine at fangates. The meatloaf is delicious on its own. I have also tried serving it between two slices of Texas toast, and even on a hero bun as a sub sandwich. Both are awesome options, and I highly recommend that you try them.

2 pounds ground sirloin, turkey, veal, chicken, or a combination

1 package Lipton Onion Soup Mix

2 large eggs, slightly beaten

1¹⁄₂ cups plain breadcrumbs

¹⁄₃ cup plus ¹⁄₂ cup ketchup
(to make your own, see page 245)

1 to 2 cups shredded sharp Cheddar cheese

1. Preheat the oven to 375°F.

2. Combine the meat, soup mix, eggs, breadcrumbs, and ¹⁄₃ cup of the ketchup in a bowl. Mix together well.

3. Place half the meat mixture in a 9- x 5-inch loaf pan. Sprinkle the cheese on top, and then add the rest of the meat mixture. Smooth the top with a spatula, and then evenly spread with the remaining ¹⁄₂ cup ketchup.

4. Bake for about 45 minutes. Let rest for 10 minutes, and serve however you like it.

FRIENDLY FANGATING TIP: You can easily turn a fork-and-knife-friendly slice of meatloaf into no-frills yumminess by making it into a sandwich. I like to serve meatloaf sandwiches on square ciabatta rolls (mimicking the shape of the meatloaf slice). Top the bread with some ketchup (or mayo—or both, if you prefer), throw on some arugula and a couple thick slices of red onion, and serve.

Italian String Bean "Spaghetti"
(page 207) and Mama Falk's Meatloaf

BUTTER-POACHED RIB CAP
WITH CREAMED CORN AND BRUSSELS SPROUTS

CONTRIBUTORS: **ANDRE AGASSI AND STEFFI GRAF** | SERVES **2 TO 4**

These recipes come from celebrity chef Michael Mina, who has won several awards from Michelin and the James Beard Foundation. In 2002, Andre Agassi first dined at Michael's restaurant in San Francisco, and during the course of that evening a great partnership was born. Together, they formed the Mina Group, which owns and operates restaurants in San Francisco, San Jose, Dana Point, Atlantic City, and Las Vegas, where Andre is from and resides today. Michael is Andre and Steffi's favorite chef, and if you ask them for their favorite dishes, they'll point you in his direction. (And for good reason—his food is insanely delicious.) Michael Mina noted to me, "It's very intimidating to cook a steak for Andre Agassi. He puts as much into his steak cookery as he would into a tennis match. So when cooking for him, I always have to be sure I'm on my best game!"

3 pounds unsalted butter, cut into small pieces

1 (20-ounce) bone-in rib cap steak, split vertically into 2 pieces, about $1^{1}/_{4}$ inches thick

Sea salt and freshly ground black pepper

8 sprigs thyme

3 shallots, coarsely chopped

3 cloves garlic, peeled and smashed

JALAPEÑO CREAMED CORN

5 ears of corn

1 tablespoon butter

Sea salt and freshly ground black pepper

$1^{1}/_{2}$ teaspoons jalapeño juice, or more to taste

$^{1}/_{2}$ jalapeño, minced, plus more for garnish

$^{1}/_{4}$ cup heavy cream

(CONTINUED)

1. First you must clarify the butter: Warm the butter in a heavy-bottomed pot over very low heat. Three things will happen: The milk solids will rise to the top as foam, the water in the butter will settle to the bottom, and in the middle will be what you want—the fat. When all the butter is melted, skim and discard the foam, and use a ladle to transfer the butter fat—the very yellow liquid—to a clean container. When the liquid you're ladling out of the pot starts to look much lighter in color, you're done.

2. Set a deep skillet just large enough to hold the steaks on top of a stockpot of simmering water. Add the clarified butter, and heat to 140° to 150°F, using the probe of an instant meat thermometer to measure the temperature. Keep the water at a gentle simmer throughout cooking, and regularly check the butter's temperature. (Don't let the probe touch the bottom of the pan, because that will give you a false reading.)

3. Meanwhile, season the steaks generously with salt and pepper.

4. Add the thyme, shallots, garlic, and steaks to the skillet. For every inch of thickness, poach the meat for 30 minutes, until the internal temperature reaches 120°F. (Note: If the butter doesn't totally cover the steaks, flip them halfway through poaching.)

5. While the steaks are poaching, make the creamed corn and Brussels sprouts (page 161). Scrape the ears of corn using a corn creamer. (What's a corn creamer? Visit peasandcornco.com.) Melt the butter in a large saucepan over low. Add the corn, and cook on medium to low, stirring constantly, until the corn has thickened and no longer has a raw taste, about 18 minutes. Season with salt, pepper, and the jalapeño juice. Stir in the minced jalapeno and heavy cream, and keep warm.

(CONTINUED)

SHAVED BRUSSELS SPROUTS

1 tablespoon butter

2 tablespoons diced bacon lardon (the fatty part)

$1/4$ cup peeled and diced apples

Sea salt and freshly ground black pepper

$1/2$ cup shaved Brussels sprouts (use a mandoline, or slice as thinly as possible)

6. Make the Brussels sprouts: Combine the butter and bacon in a medium pan set over medium. Cook for 2 minutes, occasionally scraping the bottom of the pan. Add the apples, season with salt and pepper, and cook for another 2 minutes, or until golden brown. Add the Brussels sprouts, and toss in the pan for a final 2 minutes, until softened. Serve hot.

7. Remove the steaks from the skillet, allowing the excess butter to drip back into the skillet. Season the steaks again with salt and pepper, and transfer them to a very hot cast-iron pan or grill. Sear on each side to develop a brown crust, about 2 minutes total.

8. Divide the creamed corn between two plates, and garnish with more jalapeño. Add the steak and Brussels sprouts and serve immediately.

POT ROAST AND POTATOES

CONTRIBUTORS: **MARIO AND MARY WILLIAMS** | SERVES **6**

When I was an undergrad at Duke, Mario Williams was tearing it up just down the road in Raleigh, North Carolina, as a member of the NC State Wolfpack. After his stellar college career, he went first overall in the 2006 NFL Draft to the Houston Texans. I'm never shocked when I meet NFL players who are good eaters. And Mario is no exception. Pot roast with potatoes is not only a delicious and hearty dish, but it happens to be Mario's favorite meal. This is his mother Mary's recipe.

1 (3- to 4-pound) boneless beef chuck roast

1 tablespoon garlic salt

2 teaspoons sea salt

2 teaspoons black pepper

2 teaspoons dried oregano

1 teaspoon dried basil

2 tablespoons canola oil

1 large onion, thinly sliced

1 cup beef broth

1 tablespoon gravy mix, like Kitchen Bouquet

3 bay leaves

2½ pounds russet potatoes, peeled and cut into 1½-inch pieces

1. Preheat the oven to 300°F.

2. Season the roast with the garlic salt, salt, pepper, oregano, and dried basil. Heat the oil in a large Dutch oven over medium-high until shimmering. Sear the roast on both sides until deep brown, about 4 minutes per side. Remove the roast to a plate, and add the onions to the Dutch oven. Stir to coat evenly in the oil, about 1 minute. Slowly pour in the broth, scraping up any browned bits. Stir in the gravy mix, and bring to a boil. Return the roast to the Dutch oven, add the bay leaves, cover with the lid, and roast in the oven for 1½ hours.

3. Remove from the oven and add the potatoes, arranging them around the roast and submerging them in the gravy. Return to the oven, for 1 hour. Remove the lid, and cook for another 30 minutes, until the potatoes are creamy and the meat is fork-tender.

4. Transfer the meat and potatoes to a platter. Strain the gravy through a fine-mesh strainer. Serve with the pot roast and potatoes.

QUICK RED BEANS AND RICE WITH HOT LINKS

CONTRIBUTORS: JAMES AND BEVERLY LOFTON | SERVES **6 TO 8**

There is a Nike ad from 1985 of James Lofton in his Green Bay Packers uniform jumping into the frame in the end zone of Lambeau Field. A copy of the ad hung in my parents' home for the longest time. I remember as a little kid associating the guy in the photo with someone who was a very big deal. Indeed, James Lofton was an incredible athlete and a big deal in football. James and his beautiful wife, Beverly, have remained family friends since his days in the NFL. They're always all smiles and the nicest couple to be around. Here's their recipe for a tasty game day fangating entrée. Keep in mind that hot links usually have enough spice to give the dish heat and seasoning. Taste as you cook, and add salt and pepper if needed.

1 to 1¹⁄₂ pounds beef, pork, turkey, or Andouille hot sausage links, thinly sliced

1 onion, finely chopped

1 green bell pepper, finely chopped, optional

3 cloves garlic, finely chopped

1 tablespoon chopped fresh thyme

4 (15.5-ounce) cans red or kidney beans, rinsed and drained

1 bay leaf

1 cup chicken broth, or more if you want a soupier dish

3 cups cooked rice

Cornbread, optional

1. Cook the sausage in a Dutch oven over medium for 6 minutes, or until browned.

2. Add the onion, green pepper, if desired, and garlic. Cook for 3 to 4 minutes, until the onions begin to sweat and become translucent. Add the thyme, beans, bay leaf, and chicken broth. Bring to a boil, and then reduce the heat to medium-low; cover and cook about 40 minutes, or until the sausage reaches your desired tenderness.

3. Serve over the rice in a bowl with a side of cornbread, if desired.

TASTY TIDBITS

You may not know that football wasn't James Lofton's only sport. He was also very accomplished in track and field and was an NCAA Champion long jumper (1978) at Stanford University. He then went on to enter the NFL as a wide receiver, the fourth overall first-round pick by the Green Bay Packers, where he played from 1978 to 1986. He also played for the Los Angeles Raiders (1987–1988), the Buffalo Bills (1989–1992), the Los Angeles Rams (1993), and the Philadelphia Eagles (1993). James is a member of the Pro Football Hall of Fame—no surprise given how many records he set. In his 16 seasons in the NFL, he became the first player to record 14,000 yards receiving; he was the second player (behind Drew Hill) to score a touchdown in the 1970s, 1980s, and 1990s; he played in seven Pro Bowls; he left Green Bay as the team's all-time leading receiver with 9,656 yards; and he became the oldest player to record 1,000 yards receiving in a season before the record was broken by Jerry Rice. James was also a wide receiver coach for both the San Diego Chargers and the Oakland Raiders.

GREEN CHILE EGGS BENEDICT

CONTRIBUTOR: **MARK SCHLERETH** | SERVES **4**

I introduced you to Mark Schlereth in Chapter 1, along with his Black Bean Salsa (page 57). Mark's nickname is Stink (but I won't tell you how he got it). He spent half his NFL career in Denver, home of their famous green chili. Together with his friend David Bloom, Mark launched Schlereth's "Stinkin Good" Green Chile Sauce in 2008. When I met up with Mark on ESPN's campus, he promised me he'd send me some, and he certainly did—one of every flavor. The chile sauce is good—and it reminds me of Colorado every time I eat it. When I asked Mark for a recipe for this book, it didn't surprise me that he'd include one with his chile sauce. Although this is a brunch recipe, it doesn't mean you can't serve it at your fangate on game day. In fact, many games start around lunchtime and, if you're like me, you arrive a few hours early so it's actually breakfast time. I say go crazy, make breakfast!

4 slices sourdough bread or English muffin halves, toasted and lightly buttered

1 tablespoon butter

1 pound fresh chorizo, removed from casings

4 large eggs

1 avocado, peeled, pitted, and sliced

1 tomato, sliced

1 to 2 (15-ounce) containers of your favorite Schlereth's Stinkin' Good Green Chile Sauce

1½ cups shredded pepper Jack cheese

Lime wedges, for serving

Mark Schlereth's Black Bean Salsa (page 57)

1. Preheat the broiler. Place the bread on a foil-lined baking sheet. Toast under the broiler for 1 minute, or until lightly golden brown. Lightly butter the warm toast. Set aside on the baking sheet; do not turn off the broiler.

2. Meanwhile, heat a large skillet over medium-high. Cook the sausage, stirring to break it into bite-sized pieces, for 8 to 10 minutes, until cooked through. Transfer to a paper towel–lined plate to drain.

3. Return the skillet to medium, and without wiping it, crack the eggs into the skillet, leaving space between each egg. Cook for 1 minute, and then carefully turn them over with a spatula and cook for 30 seconds more. Remove from the heat.

4. Top each piece of toast or English muffin half with a quarter of the avocado and tomato, about ¼ cup of the crumbled chorizo, and a fried egg. Pour ½ to 1 cup of Schlereth's Green Chile Sauce over the top, sprinkle with the cheese, and repeat for each serving. Place the baking sheet under the broiler for about 1 minute, or until the cheese melts and is lightly browned. Serve with the lime wedges and black bean salsa on the side.

FRIENDLY FANGATING TIP:
All of Mark's chile sauces are gluten-free and come in chicken and two pork flavors. He's also got a vegetarian version, and if you use that and omit the chorizo, you've got a tasty vegetarian entrée.

COACH'S FAMOUS LAMB CHOPS AND PASTA

CONTRIBUTOR: **AVERY JOHNSON** | SERVES **6**

I had met Avery Johnson, or Coach Avery as he likes to be called, a few times as a kid. I remember him as an NBA player—most especially as a standout player in the 1999 NBA Finals, when he made the championship-winning shot for the San Antonio Spurs with one minute and six seconds remaining in Game 5 against the New York Knicks. (It was a painful evening to be a Knicks fan.) But it wasn't until he and I were chatting in a lobby together a couple of summers ago that I got to know him a little bit. Turns out that the guy you probably know as a very successful NBA player (retired jersey and all) and as both an NBA and NCAA coach (he's currently the head coach of the Alabama Crimson Tide) loves to cook! Coach Avery and I chatted for a bit about wine and his favorite meals. He was very kind to lend me this recipe to share with you all and suggests serving it with a Napa Meritage wine.

6 lamb chops

2 teaspoons freshly ground black pepper, plus more for seasoning

2 teaspoons Lawry's seasoned salt

2 teaspoons onion powder

2 teaspoons garlic powder

1/2 red onion, diced

1/2 orange bell pepper, seeded and diced

1/2 green bell pepper, seeded and diced

1/2 yellow bell pepper, seeded and diced

2 cloves garlic, minced

1 (16-ounce) package fettuccine or spaghetti

Olive oil, for sautéing

1/4 cup red wine, preferably Pinot Noir

1. Season both sides of the lamb chops with the pepper, seasoned salt, onion powder, and garlic powder. Grind some extra pepper over the bones of all the chops. Set aside.

2. Combine the onions, bell peppers, and garlic in a bowl. Set aside.

3. Boil salted water in a large pot. Once the water comes to a boil, add the pasta, and cook until al dente, according to package instructions. Strain and set aside.

4. Meanwhile, cover the bottom of a large skillet with olive oil. Lightly heat over medium, and then add the mixed vegetables and sauté for 7 minutes. Add the lamb chops on top of the veggies, and cook for 5 minutes on each side for medium to medium-well, adding more olive oil as needed if the skillet starts to dry out.

5. Remove the chops to a platter, but keep the vegetables in the skillet over medium. Add the red wine, and sauté the veggies for about 1 minute more; and then add the pasta. Sauté for about 3 minutes. Return the lamb chops to the skillet, and cook for 5 minutes more. Serve immediately.

BUFFALO CHICKEN TACOS

SERVES **4**

These tacos were inspired by a dish served at Jay Z's 40/40 Club in Manhattan. I was there for an event with "Uncle" Chris Doleman. I was starving, so while Chris was talking with some people, I disappeared to quickly shove about five (or more) Buffalo chicken tacos in my mouth and then returned to be sociable. (I can only hope some of the greens weren't left stuck in my teeth.) Though I literally inhaled the tacos, I was still able to taste them, and they were really good. So I thought, I could make these. They used fried chicken in Buffalo sauce, but I prefer my chicken baked or pan sautéed. Either way, they're good. And they happen to travel well, though I would suggest bringing the individual ingredients wrapped separately and then assembling the tacos in the parking lot.

2 tablespoons mayonnaise

1 tablespoon chipotle sauce, or more to taste

1 pound chicken tenders

Sea salt and freshly ground black pepper

1 cup all-purpose flour or brown rice flour (if you're gluten-free)

1 tablespoon garlic chili oil, optional

1 tablespoon canola oil

4 (6-inch) flour tortillas (or corn tortillas if you're gluten-free)

1 plum tomato, diced

1 tablespoon minced fresh cilantro

$1/2$ cup microgreens

$1/2$ cup blue cheese crumbles

BUFFALO SAUCE

2 tablespoons vegetable or extra virgin olive oil

$1^1/_2$ tablespoons white vinegar

$1/4$ teaspoon cayenne pepper

$1/8$ teaspoon garlic powder

$1/2$ teaspoon Worcestershire sauce

2 teaspoons Tabasco sauce

$1/4$ teaspoon sea salt

6 tablespoons Louisiana hot sauce

1. Make the sauces: Combine all the ingredients for the Buffalo sauce in a small bowl. Combine the mayonnaise and chipotle sauce in another small bowl, and mix well.

2. Season the chicken tenders all over with salt and pepper, and dredge in the flour.

3. Sauté the chicken in the garlic chili oil and canola oil in a large skillet over medium-high until cooked through, about 8 minutes. Pour in the Buffalo sauce, and sauté until the sauce coats the chicken and starts to brown. Remove from the heat.

4. To make a taco, spread $1/2$ to 1 tablespoon of the chipotle mayo on a tortilla. Top with 2 chicken tenders plus a quarter of the tomatoes, cilantro, microgreens, and blue cheese. Repeat to make four tacos in all, and serve.

CORNFLAKE CHICKEN TENDERS WITH HONEY MUSTARD

SERVES **4**

Chicken tenders are classic sportsfood, found at stadiums and arenas all over North America. Normally they're dipped in batter and deep-fried. Don't get me wrong, I'd be lying if I didn't say I love them. Crispy, crunchy fried goodness? Umm, hello! But making them at home isn't always the easiest or healthiest method. So here is my spin on chicken tenders—baked but just as crunchy and flaky, thanks to the cornflake crust. I love my chicken tenders dunked in honey mustard, but feel free to serve these with ketchup, barbecue sauce, or even mayo.

2 cups crushed cornflakes

¹/₂ cup all-purpose flour

1 large egg, beaten

1 pound chicken tenders

1 teaspoon sea salt

¹/₂ teaspoon freshly ground black pepper

³/₄ teaspoon herbes de Provence (see Tip)

3 tablespoons Dijon mustard

3 tablespoons honey

1. Preheat the oven to 450°F. Spray a rack with cooking spray, and place it on a foil-lined baking sheet.

2. Put the cornflakes in a large zip-top bag, and crush until they become coarse crumbs. Transfer to a shallow bowl. Put the flour and egg in two separate shallow bowls.

3. Season the chicken tenders with the salt, pepper, and herbes de Provence. Dredge the chicken through the flour, egg, and cornflake crumbs, placing the coated chicken on the prepared pan.

4. Sprinkle any cornflake mixture remaining in the bag on top of the tenders. Bake the chicken for 15 minutes, until golden brown and cooked through.

5. Make the honey mustard: Stir the honey and mustard together. Serve immediately alongside the chicken tenders.

FRIENDLY FANGATING TIP:

To make your own herbes de Provence, combine 2 tablespoons each of dried rosemary, thyme, oregano, basil, and marjoram.

BAKED CHICKEN SPAGHETTI

CONTRIBUTOR: **ED MOSES** | SERVES **4**

Ed Moses has quite the impressive swimming resumé. In college, he swam for the University of Virginia, where he won the 100-meter and 200-meter breaststroke events at the 2000 NCAA Division I Championships and set a world record in each event. He then went on to the 2000 Summer Olympic trials, where he set another world record (see a pattern here?). Clearly, the trials went well as he went on to represent the U.S. at the Summer Olympics in Sydney, Australia, where he won both a silver and gold medal. Out of the pool, Ed is a big foodie, and I'm told by his close friends quite the cook as well. Here's Ed's recipe for baked chicken spaghetti—a perfect way to use leftover chicken. For cheese lovers, sprinkle in some more with your breadcrumb topping.

8 ounces spaghetti

$1/3$ cup butter

$1/2$ cup chopped onion

$1/4$ cup all-purpose flour

2 cups chicken stock

Sea salt and freshly ground black pepper

3 cups diced cooked chicken

1 (14.5-ounce) can stewed tomatoes, drained and chopped

$1/3$ pound Parmesan cheese, grated

$1/2$ cup fine dried breadcrumbs

1. Preheat the oven to 375°F. Grease a 2-quart baking dish with cooking spray.

2. Cook the spaghetti in a large pot of boiling salted water until al dente, checking the package instructions for timing. Drain and set aside.

3. Heat all but 1 tablespoon of the butter in a large skillet over medium. Add the onion, and sauté for about 6 minutes, or until translucent. Add the flour, and whisk well until blended. Cook for 1 minute.

4. Slowly add in the stock, whisking well. Bring to a simmer, whisking constantly, and cook for 3 minutes, or until the sauce is thick and smooth. Season with the salt and pepper. Stir in the chicken, tomatoes, and cheese. Set aside.

5. Melt the remaining tablespoon of butter in a small skillet over medium-low. Add the breadcrumbs and toast in the butter for 2 to 3 minutes. Remove from the heat.

6. Put the cooked spaghetti in the prepared baking dish. Add the chicken mixture, and then top with the buttered breadcrumbs.

7. Bake for 25 minutes. Serve immediately.

CHICKEN ROLLATINI

CONTRIBUTORS: KEVIN AND ROSALIE BOOTHE | SERVES **6**

Kevin Boothe is another NFLer friend of mine from grad school. Kevin—or KB as we call him—is a smarty-pants. He played college ball at Cornell and may have been the only Ivy Leaguer in our whole cohort. KB has two Super Bowl rings (one of which he let me wear one day in school!), both of which he won with the New York Giants (Super Bowls XLII and XLVI). What you might not know by looking at him is that KB is a giant teddy bear. Perhaps I shouldn't share that because offensive linemen are meant to be hulking, scary dudes on the gridiron. But off the field, Kevin is a wonderfully kind friend, a loving husband to Rosalie, and the sweetest dad. Here is a favorite dish of KB's and the Boothe household. Serve with spaghetti squash, linguine, or fettuccine.

3 tablespoons extra virgin olive oil, plus more for greasing

3 cloves garlic, minced

1 cup Italian seasoned breadcrumbs

12 chicken cutlets, pounded as thin as possible

Sea salt and freshly ground black pepper

8 ounces fresh mozzarella, cut into 12 thin slices

3 plum tomatoes, cut lengthwise into 12 slices

12 basil leaves, plus more for garnish

12 toothpicks

Lemon slices

1. Preheat the oven to 425°F. Grease a 13- x 9-inch baking dish with olive oil.

2. Heat the olive oil in a small skillet over medium. Add the garlic, and sauté for 1 minute. Transfer to a small bowl, and mix with the breadcrumbs. Set aside.

3. Season the chicken cutlets with salt and pepper. Sprinkle each with a small amount of breadcrumbs. Top with a slice of cheese, a piece of tomato, and a basil leaf.

4. Roll each of the cutlets up, securing them with a toothpick, and place in the prepared baking dish. Sprinkle with any remaining breadcrumbs, top with the lemon slices, and bake for 30 minutes, uncovered, until golden brown and cooked through.

LET'S MOVE! 2012

I was very honored to take part in First Lady Michelle Obama's Let's Move! campaign on May 3, 2012. At exactly 1:42 p.m. EST, students nationwide busted their best dance moves to Beyoncé's "Move Your Body." Joined together in gyms, on playgrounds, on basketball courts, on soccer fields, and wherever else could hold hordes of excited students, America's young people moved as one in a movement spearheaded by the First Lady to fight childhood obesity. I, along with my friends Kevin Boothe, Sean James, Jay Williams, and rapper Nikki D, danced it up with the kids of Harlem's PS 161. The kids were awesome (and had clearly practiced the choreography more than we had).

MICHAEL MINA'S WHOLE FRIED CHICKEN WITH ONION JUS

CONTRIBUTORS: **ANDRE AGASSI AND STEFFI GRAF** | SERVES **2**

In case the rib cap on page 160 wasn't delicious enough for you, Michael shared the recipe for Andre and Steffi's other favorite dish from his restaurant, Nobhill. I've already provided an overview of Andre's stellar tennis career. For this one, we'll focus on Steffi's, which as I'm sure you already know, is crazy impressive. According to many, including Billie Jean King (who knows a thing or two about tennis), Steffi Graf is the greatest female tennis player. And I am so happy to include one of her favorite dishes in this book, an upscale take on fried chicken that requires a few special ingredients. Take caution when frying the chicken, as the grease will spatter significantly.

2 to 4 quarts peanut oil (or 1 to 1½ gallons if not using duck fat)

2 quarts rendered duck fat, optional

1 (2- to 3-pound) whole chicken (preferably free-range), at room temperature

1 fresh black truffle, sliced paper thin (I use Urbani Truffles)

Kosher salt and freshly ground black pepper

3 tablespoons truffle butter, at room temperature

1 teaspoon minced fresh Italian (flat-leaf) parsley

1 teaspoon minced fresh chives

1 teaspoon minced thyme leaves

CARAMELIZED ONION SAUCE

2 tablespoons canola oil

4 yellow onions, sliced

1 cup dry white wine, such as Sauvignon Blanc

5 sprigs thyme

1 bay leaf

¼ teaspoon whole black peppercorns

3 cups chicken stock

(CONTINUED)

1. Make the caramelized onion sauce: Place a Dutch oven over medium and coat the bottom with canola oil. When the oil gets hazy, stir in the onions to coat, and sauté until softened and a deep caramel color, about 25 minutes. Add the wine, and deglaze the pan, scraping the bottom with a wooden spoon to loosen the brown bits. Simmer, stirring occasionally, until the wine has reduced and the liquid is almost totally evaporated, about 10 minutes. Stir in the thyme, bay leaf, and peppercorns. Add the chicken stock and demi-glace, and bring to a boil. Reduce the heat, and simmer until the sauce has a deep onion flavor and is reduced by half, about 30 minutes. Pour through a fine-mesh sieve into another small saucepan, pressing on the onions with a spatula to extract as much juice as possible. Discard the solids, place the sauce over medium-low, and stir in the butter. Lightly season with salt and pepper, and keep warm over low heat.

2. Fill a very large pot or deep fryer one-half to two-thirds full with the peanut oil and duck fat, if using. Place over medium-high and bring to 360°F on a deep-fry thermometer attached to the side of the pot.

3. Pat the chicken with paper towels so it's as dry as possible. Very gently lift up and peel back the skin from the chicken breast, taking care not to tear it. Slip the truffle slices under the skin without overlapping. Save any truffle scraps for garnish. Generously season both the exterior and the cavity of the chicken with salt and pepper.

4. Very carefully lower the chicken into the hot oil, placing a metal strainer on top to help keep it submerged, if necessary. The temperature of the oil will drop a bit; try to maintain 325° to 335°F, adjusting the heat level if necessary. Fry for 15 to 25 minutes (or 6 to 8 minutes per pound), until the chicken is cooked through. The chicken is done when the internal temperature reaches 165° to 170°F on an instant-read meat thermometer and the skin is a light golden brown. Carefully lift the chicken out of the hot oil, and transfer to a wire rack with a pan underneath. Be sure to drain the oil that collects inside the cavity. Let the chicken rest for 10 minutes, so the juices settle.

(CONTINUED)

2 tablespoons veal demi-glace

8 ounces (2 sticks) unsalted butter, cubed

Kosher salt and freshly ground black pepper

5. Mix the truffle butter, parsley, chives, and thyme in a small bowl. Using a pastry brush, coat the exterior of the fried chicken with the truffle and herb butter. Transfer the chicken to a cutting board, and pull each leg away from the body slightly in order to expose the joint. Using a sharp thin-bladed knife, remove the legs at the thigh joint, and transfer to a platter. You want to separate the thigh from the drumstick also. Repeat the same process with the wings. Carefully cut along each side of the breastbone, following the contour of the bone down to remove all the meat. Cut the breast meat into pieces, and transfer to the platter. Season all the chicken pieces with salt and pepper. Serve with the caramelized onion sauce.

TASTY TIDBITS

ANDRE AGASSI

Andre Agassi is perhaps one of the most charismatic men to ever play tennis, and as a former World Number 1, he dominated the sport from the early 1990s until the mid-2000s. He's been called many things, including one of the best service returners in the game, and even one of the greatest to ever play. His compilation of wins is impressive, to say the least. Andre racked up eight Grand Slam wins, an Olympic gold medal (Atlanta 1996), and finished as runner-up in seven other Grand Slams. Andre is one of only four Men's Singles players in the Open Era history of tennis to achieve the Career Grand Slam (winning all four Grand Slam Championships), and one of seven in overall tennis history—and the first of two Men's Singles players—to achieve the Career Golden Slam, which is the Career Grand Slam plus an Olympic gold medal. And to top it all off, Andre is the only man in history to win the Career Golden Slam and ATP Tour World Championships, which *Sports Illustrated* dubbed the "Career Super Slam" in 1990.

STEFFI GRAF

During her professional tennis career, Steffi Graf won a remarkable 22 Grand Slam singles titles, holding the Open Era record for most Grand Slam wins by any player, male or female. (She is second in wins in overall tennis history behind Margaret Court's 24 titles.) In 1988, Steffi became the first and only tennis player (among male and female players) to win the Calendar Year Golden Slam, winning all four Grand Slam singles titles and an Olympic gold medal all in the same calendar year. (She won her gold medal competing for West Germany at the Olympic Games in Seoul, South Korea. Incidentally, she also took home a bronze medal in doubles.) Steffi sat at World Number 1, as ranked by the Women's Tennis Association (WTA), for a record 377 weeks—the longest period any player (both male and female) has ever held the top spot since rankings began. In the span of her career, she won a total of 107 singles titles, placing third in WTA history (behind Martina Navratilova and Chris Evert).

TURKEY LASAGNA

CONTRIBUTORS: JUWAN AND JENINE HOWARD | SERVES **12**

I must say that Juwan is one of the friendliest basketball players I have ever met. His smile lights up a room and he's so incredibly kind. Juwan first made his name as part of the Fab Five at the University of Michigan—the famous Fab Five that reached the NCAA Finals in both 1992 and 1993. In 1994, Juwan was picked fifth overall in the NBA draft by the Washington Wizards, where he played for six-and-a-half seasons. I remember going to watch Juwan play quite a bit as a kid—the Wizards were my home team and Juwan was one of my dad's clients. In fact, during his time in D.C., Juwan used to come over for family dinners. Those are memories I'll always hang on to. Juwan and his fabulous wife, Jenine, were generous enough to share this recipe with me; their secret ingredient is the nutmeg.

12 whole-wheat lasagna noodles

1 tablespoon olive oil

$^1/_2$ cup chopped yellow onion

$^1/_2$ to 1 teaspoon red pepper flakes, to taste

2 cloves garlic, minced

1 teaspoon sea salt

1 teaspoon freshly ground black pepper

2 teaspoons Mrs. Dash seasoning

2 pounds ground turkey

1 (25-ounce) jar marinara sauce

3 cups part-skim ricotta cheese

3 cups part-skim shredded mozzarella cheese

1 cup grated Parmesan cheese

$^1/_4$ teaspoon freshly grated nutmeg

Fresh Italian (flat-leaf) parsley, for garnish

1. Preheat the oven to 350°F. Spray a 13- x 9-inch baking dish with cooking spray.

2. Fill a large pot three-quarters full with salted water, and bring to a boil. Add the noodles, and cook until al dente, 8 to 9 minutes. Drain, lay them out in a single layer on a baking sheet, and set aside.

3. Place the olive oil, onions, and seasonings in a large sauté pan over medium-high. Add the ground turkey, crumbling it with a wooden spoon, until cooked through, about 5 minutes.

4. Add the marinara sauce, and bring to a boil. Reduce the heat, and simmer, uncovered, for another 5 minutes.

5. Spread $^1/_2$ cup of the meat sauce in the bottom of the prepared dish. Top with 3 noodles, followed by another $1^1/_2$ cups meat sauce. Dollop with 1 cup of the ricotta, and sprinkle with $^1/_2$ cup of the mozzarella. Repeat twice, starting with the noodles and ending with the mozzarella. Top with the remaining 3 noodles, and sprinkle with the Parmesan and the remaining $1^1/_2$ cups mozzarella. Sprinkle with the nutmeg.

6. Cover with greased foil, and bake for 30 minutes. Uncover, and bake for another 30 minutes, until browned and bubbly.

7. Let the lasagna stand for 15 minutes before serving.

In 2013, the Miami Heat won the NBA Championships, and as a thank you to my dad, Juwan had a ring made for him, inscribed with his name on it. It's as badass as it sounds—the ring is huge and weighs a ton.

TASTY TIDBITS

By the close of his first year as a Washington Wizard, Juwan had already become a star. By the end of his second year, he was an All-Star, and soon thereafter, he became the first player in the history of the NBA to sign a $100-million contract. Not too shabby. Perhaps even more extraordinary, Juwan ultimately played 19 seasons in the NBA, made three NBA Finals appearances, and won two championships with the Miami Heat. He and Jenine live in Miami, where Juwan is an assistant coach for the Heat.

I HEART BACON: The inimitable, hilarious, and straight-up awesome "Spice" Adams in his quintessential shirt.

TASTY TIDBITS

"Spice" played defensive tackle for Penn State before he was drafted in 2003 by the San Francisco 49ers, where he played four seasons. He then went on to play another four seasons for the Chicago Bears. "Spice" announced his retirement in 2013.

APTLY NAMED SPICED TURKEY

CONTRIBUTOR: **ANTHONY "SPICE" ADAMS**	SERVES **6 TO 8**

If "Spice" Adams doesn't make you laugh, then I'd wager you probably have zero sense of humor because he is, hands down, one of the most clever people you'll ever meet. (If you don't follow him on social media, you're sorely missing out. His photos and video spoofs are like little gems that pop up in my newsfeed throughout the day, often providing much-needed giggles if not entire fits of laughter.) "Spice," also known as "Double A," is a former classmate of mine. We share a love for food—though he gets the award for biggest bacon fan. In fact, he likes to make this turkey dish and serve it wrapped in a bacon-weaved basket. You need to start this recipe two days ahead of serving, and it requires a smoker.

1 large turkey, fresh or frozen, thawed

2 tablespoons dark brown sugar

1 tablespoon onion powder

1 tablespoon garlic powder

2 tablespoons lemon pepper

1 (2.05-ounce) bottle Frontier Barbecue Seasoning

Hickory wood chips, soaked

1 1/2 pounds thick-cut bacon

BRINE

1 3/4 cups kosher salt

1/2 cup sugar

2 tablespoons Morton Tender Quick (a curing salt)

2 tablespoons onion powder

2 tablespoons garlic powder

2 tablespoons paprika

1 tablespoon white pepper

1 tablespoon ground ginger

1 teaspoon mustard powder

1 teaspoon ground sage

1 teaspoon ground nutmeg

2 gallons apple juice

1. Combine all the brine ingredients in a large pot over high. Bring to a boil, stirring, and then remove from heat, cover, and leave in the refrigerator overnight.

2. The following day, prep the turkey. Remove the neck and giblets from inside the turkey cavity. Remove excess fat from the skin, and separate the skin from the turkey breast. Submerge the turkey into the brine headfirst, and allow it to sit overnight in the fridge.

3. The next day, remove the turkey and season it on all sides with the brown sugar, onion powder, garlic powder, lemon pepper, and the entire bottle of barbecue seasoning.

4. Place the soaked hickory wood on top of the coals at the bottom of your smoker. Fill a water pan with water only, and heat your smoker to 300°F. Place the turkey on the top grate of the smoker, breast side up, and smoke for 4 hours, or until a meat thermometer measures 165°F when inserted into the thigh.

5. Meanwhile, preheat the oven to 350°F. Lightly grease a wire rack with cooking spray set over a rimmed baking sheet. Arrange 8 or 9 slices of bacon side-by-side parallel to the long sides of the rack. Interweave slices of bacon perpendicular to the first row of slices in an over-and-under fashion to form a basket-weave pattern, using 2 slices per row if needed to weave all the way across. Cover the bacon with aluminum foil, and bake for 30 minutes. Uncover and bake another 30 to 45 minutes or until bacon is almost crisp but still pliable. Remove from the oven, and cool slightly before gently transferring the entire sheet of woven bacon to parchment paper.

6. Wrap the sheet of woven bacon around the turkey during the last 30 to 45 minutes of smoking. This bacon-wrapped turkey will look super pretty when done. Either serve whole, or present it whole before slicing.

QUESADILLA CASSEROLE

CONTRIBUTORS: REBECCA AND ROBERT GRIFFIN III | SERVES **8 TO 10**

This recipe comes from NFL star Robert Griffin III (known as RG3) and his lovely wife, Rebecca. The two were kind enough to take time out of their schedule (which included gearing up for their first child together) to share this recipe with me. This is a great dish—sort of a Mexican spin on Italian lasagna—that's perfect for sharing at your fangate. You can easily divide it into as many servings as needed for everyone's taste bud pleasure.

1 teaspoon olive oil

1 pound ground turkey

¹/₂ onion, chopped

1 (15-ounce) can tomato sauce

1 (15-ounce) can black beans, drained and rinsed

1 (15-ounce) can yellow corn, undrained

1 teaspoon minced garlic

2 teaspoons chili powder

1 teaspoon ground cumin

¹/₂ teaspoon dried oregano

¹/₂ teaspoon crushed red pepper

6 (10-inch) flour or corn tortillas

1 to 2 cups shredded Mexican cheese blend

1. Preheat the oven to 350°F. Lightly grease a 13- x 9-inch baking dish with cooking spray.

2. Heat the oil in a large skillet over medium. Add the turkey, and cook, stirring frequently, for about 4 minutes. Add the onion, and cook for 3 minutes more, stirring often. Add the tomato sauce along with the black beans, corn, garlic, chili powder, cumin, oregano, and crushed red pepper. Stir well, and bring to a boil. Reduce the heat to low, and simmer until the ground turkey filling thickens, about 4 minutes.

3. Spread a third of the ground turkey filling across the bottom of the prepared casserole dish. Cover with tortillas (you may have to tear them to fit and form a layer). Add another third of the filling, and then sprinkle a thin layer of cheese on top (as much or little as you like), and cover with another layer of tortillas.

4. For the final layer, add the remaining ground turkey filling, and sprinkle with another layer of cheese.

5. Bake for 15 to 20 minutes, until the cheese is bubbling on top. Let cool for 5 minutes before serving.

TASTY TIDBITS

College football fans, you probably remember RG3 from his standout career at Baylor, where he not only met Rebecca, his college sweetheart, but also won the Heisman Trophy in 2011. RG3 went on to be selected by the Washington Redskins second overall in the 2012 NFL Draft and to win the NFL Offensive Rookie of the Year Award that same year.

ANDOUILLE JAMBALAYA

CONTRIBUTOR: **WILL WITHERSPOON** | SERVES **6 TO 8**

I introduced you to my friend Will Witherspoon's cooking prowess on page 11 where he shares his stuffed dates. Now he's back with another recipe for your taste buds' pleasure—jambalaya, which again features his farm's andouille sausage. If you can't find it in stores or don't feel like ordering it online, that's fine. But I'll be straight up with you and let you know that I have never tasted andouille sausage as good as Will's. If you opt to skip it, that's cool, no hard feelings. But you're missing out!

3 tablespoons olive oil

1 pound chicken breast and thigh, diced

6 ounces ham, diced

8 ounces andouille sausage, sliced into rounds (I use Shire Gate Farm brand)

1 cup chopped fresh tomatoes

1 1/2 tablespoons Redfish Magic Cajun Seasoning

1/2 cup chopped onion

1/2 cup chopped green bell pepper

1/2 cup chopped celery

3 tablespoons finely chopped garlic

4 bay leaves

1 1/2 teaspoons Worcestershire sauce

1 1/2 teaspoons hot sauce

1 1/2 cups rice

3 1/2 cups chicken stock, plus more if needed

3/4 cup seafood or shrimp stock

1 pound medium shrimp, peeled and deveined

Sea salt and freshly ground black pepper

1. Heat the olive oil in a large saucepan over medium to medium-high. Add the chicken, and cook until browned, about 7 minutes. Add the ham and sausage, and cook for 3 minutes. Add the tomatoes, and brown slightly, another 3 minutes. Add the Cajun seasoning, onions, bell peppers, and celery, and cook over medium for 10 minutes, stirring often to ensure that nothing sticks to the bottom of the pot.

2. Add the garlic, bay leaves, Worcestershire, hot sauce, rice, and both stocks, bring to a boil, and then reduce the heat and simmer for 15 minutes, or until the rice is almost tender. Add the shrimp, and cook for 10 minutes more, stirring occasionally and adding additional stock if needed, until the rice has absorbed all the liquid and the shrimp is cooked. Season with salt and pepper, and serve.

Will Witherspoon and me at Media Day at Superbowl XLVI, 2012.

SHRIMP WITH HOT PEPPER–RASPBERRY CHIPOTLE SAUCE

CONTRIBUTORS: ROY AND PADDY HIBBERT | SERVES **4**

Here is Roy Hibbert and his mother Paddy's second contribution to this book. This recipe calls for a hot pepper–raspberry chipotle sauce, which you can easily find in your grocer's aisle or online (I ordered one by Robert Rothschild Farm on Amazon). But I'm giving you a recipe for a homemade version below. Mrs. Hibbert suggests serving this dish with your favorite coleslaw (see mine on page 191).

1½ pounds large shrimp, peeled and deveined

Sea salt and freshly ground black pepper

A few sprinkles of Mrs. Dash seasoning

Juice of ½ lemon, or to taste

3 tablespoons olive oil

1 red bell pepper, cut into ¼-inch-thick slices

1 green bell pepper, cut into ¼-inch-thick slices

6 cloves garlic, minced

1 medium shallot, thinly sliced

3 tablespoons Hot Pepper–Raspberry Chipotle Sauce

1½ tablespoons chopped fresh chives

HOT PEPPER–RASPBERRY CHIPOTLE SAUCE

2 tablespoons red pepper jelly

1 tablespoon raspberry preserves

1 tablespoon chopped chipotles in adobo

1 tablespoon fresh lemon juice

1. Make the hot pepper–raspberry chipotle sauce: Stir together all the ingredients in a small bowl.

2. Season the shrimp lightly with salt and pepper, the Mrs. Dash, and the lemon juice. Set aside.

3. Heat the oil in large nonstick skillet over medium-high. Lightly sauté the red and green peppers, garlic, and shallots for 3 to 4 minutes, stirring from time to time.

4. Add the seasoned shrimp, and cook for at least 3 minutes. Add the chipotle sauce, and stir well until all the ingredients are well coated and the sauce is warm.

5. Transfer to plates, garnish with the chives, and serve.

SHRIMP CURRY

CONTRIBUTORS: **PATRICK EWING AND SHARON BANKS** | SERVES **4**

Call me biased, but I think Patrick Ewing is one of the best basketball players to ever play. He certainly is one of—if not my all-time—favorites of all the clients my father has ever had. It was because of him that I was the biggest Knicks fan (until I would argue they unceremoniously traded him to Seattle at the tail end of his career). Patrick has always been incredibly kind to me, calling to wish me happy birthday, sometimes sending flowers, and just generally being a super-thoughtful human being. And I must add that, according to my dad, Patrick is the most famous Jamaican-American. So it's only fitting that Patrick, with the help of his personal chef, Sharon, should share this Jamaican-inspired dish.

1 pound medium shrimp, peeled and deveined

2 tablespoons cornstarch

Sea salt and freshly ground black pepper

2 tablespoons olive oil

$1/4$ red or yellow bell pepper, diced

$1/4$ cup finely chopped onion

3 cloves garlic, finely chopped

1 medium Yukon Gold potato, peeled, cooked, and diced

1 medium carrot, peeled, cooked, and diced

$1/8$ teaspoon minced habanero chile

1 teaspoon Thai curry powder or 2 tablespoons Thai red curry paste

$1/2$ cup water

Leaves of 2 to 3 sprigs thyme or cilantro

1. Place the shrimp, cornstarch, and a pinch each of salt and pepper in a large zip-top bag, and shake to coat the shrimp.

2. Heat the olive oil in a large nonstick skillet over medium-high. Add the shrimp, and cook for 2 to 3 minutes, or until lightly golden brown on the outside. Stir in the red peppers, onions, and garlic, and cook for another minute. Add the potato, carrot, habanero, curry, a pinch of salt, and the water, stirring well to combine. Cook for 1 to 2 minutes, or until the sauce thickens slightly. Adjust the seasonings, sprinkle with the thyme, and serve immediately.

TASTY TIDBITS

Again, I may be biased, but I'd argue that Patrick needs little introduction. His accolades are long, but I'll share a few. Patrick was one of the most successful college basketball players in history, making it to the NCAA Finals three of his four years as a Georgetown Hoya and winning the title in the 1983–84 season. ESPN named Patrick the 16th greatest college player of all time. He went on to become the number 1 pick in the 1985 NBA Draft by the New York Knicks, for whom he played the bulk of his career. (His number 33 jersey has been retired at Madison Square Garden.)

He won multiple gold medals as a member of the 1984 and 1992 United States Men's Olympic Basketball Teams. He has been selected as one of the 50 Greatest Players in NBA History. And he is a two-time inductee at the Basketball Hall of Fame in Springfield, Massachusetts (once for his individual career and once as a member of the '92 Dream Team). I am proud to say I was there in 2008 for his individual induction.

SHRIMP PASTA

CONTRIBUTORS: **GREG AND NORMA MONROE** | SERVES **6**

You probably know the NBA's Greg Monroe (he was a star at Georgetown, Big East Rookie of the Year, and the seventh overall pick in the 2010 NBA Draft). You may know he hails from Louisiana. But what you probably don't know is that Greg's mother, Norma, is a sensational cook—famous among NBA moms (and the league in general) for her standout southern cooking. When I first told my dad about this cookbook, he immediately told me to ask Greg for a recipe from his mother. So I asked Greg for his favorite, and he responded with Norma's shrimp pasta. (I got a very effusive nod of affirmation from his cousin, who was with us.) So here it is for all of you to enjoy, straight from Harvey, Louisiana! Greg's mother suggests that if you want to eat like Greg, serve this with hot fried fish, corn, and garlic bread.

1 pound fettuccine

2 sticks butter

1 stalk celery, diced

1 pound Velveeta cheese, at room temperature

8 ounces jalapeño Velveeta cheese, at room temperature

2 cups heavy cream

1$\frac{1}{2}$ teaspoons Tony Chachere's Creole seasoning, or to taste

1 pound large shrimp, peeled and deveined

Handful of chopped fresh parsley, for garnish

1. Preheat the oven to 350°F. Grease with cooking spray a 13- x 9-inch baking dish.

2. Cook the fettuccine in a large pot of boiling salted water according to package instructions. Drain and set aside.

3. Melt the butter in a large Dutch oven over medium heat, add the celery and sauté until almost tender, about 5 minutes. Add the Velveeta cheeses, cream, and seasoning salt to taste. Stir well until completely blended and smooth, 5 more minutes.

4. Add the shrimp and pasta; toss to combine. Pour into the prepared baking dish and bake for 30 minutes, or until bubbly throughout and lightly browned.

5. Remove from the oven, sprinkle with parsley, and serve.

FRIED FISH AND "CHIPS"

SERVES **4**

This is another recipe that was inspired by Fenway's special 2013 World Series menu. The ballpark's take on fish and chips (fish and French fries) was available at Yawkey Way's Fish Shack. My version, detailed below, varies a little bit. I like to think mine's a little healthier, as I use a combination of panko crumbs and cornflakes as breading, and I opt to serve mine with kettle chips, rather than French fries. My mom is the biggest fan of Cape Cod–style kettle chips and they truly convey an image of New England in my mind, which I think is quite fitting for a BoSox recipe. That said, you'll find a great recipe for French fries on page 196. Feel free to use that in lieu of the kettle chips!

1 cup panko breadcrumbs, or more as needed

1 cup cornflakes, smashed, or more as needed

Sea salt and freshly ground black pepper

2 large eggs

4 (6-ounce) cod or haddock fillets, gently patted dry with a paper towel

Avocado or vegetable oil

Your favorite brand of Cape Cod–style (kettle) potato chips

1. Combine the panko breadcrumbs and cornflakes in a large shallow bowl. Sprinkle with about $1/2$ teaspoon salt and a couple grinds of black pepper.

2. Crack the eggs into a bowl, and scramble them with a fork.

3. Take a fish fillet and dip it in the egg so that it's entirely coated. Then dip it in the panko–cornflake mixture, again entirely coating it. Repeat this for all 4 fillets. (You may need more panko crumbs and cornflakes to coat your fish—it depends on how large your fillets are. Just repeat the seasoning process as you add more crumbs and flakes.)

4. Add enough oil to a large skillet to evenly coat the bottom of the pan. Heat over medium to medium-high for 1 to 2 minutes. If the oil starts to smoke, turn down the heat a little; you want the oil very hot but not smoking. Gently add the fillets, and use a spatula to flatten the fish so it sizzles and really gets down into that oil. Cook for 2 to 4 minutes per side, or until the fillets are cooked through and beautifully browned on both sides, but not burned.

5. Once the fillets are done, top with another grind of fresh black pepper, and serve next to a nice helping of potato chips.

PREGAME HONEY-LIME SRIRACHA SALMON

CONTRIBUTOR: LEBRON JAMES | SERVES **2**

LeBron James requires no introduction. I'm fairly certain that the entire world knows who LeBron is. And rightly so—he has won two NBA Championships, four NBA Most Valuable Player Awards, two NBA Finals MVP Awards, two Olympic gold medals, an NBA scoring title, and the NBA Rookie of the Year Award. He's also incredibly charitable and is featured in many international advertising campaigns by multiple brands and in feature films. (I think he was the best part of the movie *Trainwreck*.) He's even hosted *Saturday Night Live*—and was funny! (If you missed it, go Google "LeBron James Solid Gold SNL" right now.) I asked LeBron (thank you, Maverick) to share his favorite game day meal, and he sent me this recipe for seared salmon over coconut quinoa with steamed broccoli, topped with a Sriracha-cilantro-lime drizzle and shredded coconut. It's not only a tasty, colorful dish to serve at your fangate, but it's also a fantastic dish to eat if you're an athlete fueling up for game day. Enjoy!

1 cup quinoa

1 teaspoon coconut oil

2 cups coconut milk

1 teaspoon sea salt, plus more for seasoning

2 cups broccoli florets

2 to 3 tablespoons olive oil, as needed

1/2 teaspoon minced garlic

Juice of 1/2 lime

Freshly ground black pepper

2 tablespoons shredded coconut

1 side fresh salmon, skinned and filleted into 2 (8-ounce) pieces

Garlic powder

Lime wedges

HONEY-LIME SRIRACHA SAUCE

Juice of 3 limes

1 teaspoon chopped fresh cilantro

1 teaspoon honey

1 tablespoon Sriracha sauce

1 teaspoon olive oil

Sea salt and freshly ground black pepper

1. Rinse the quinoa with cold running water. Heat a saucepan over medium to medium-high. Add the coconut oil, and when it's hot, add the quinoa and toast for 4 minutes, or until you get a nutty aroma. Pour in the coconut milk and 1 teaspoon salt, and bring to a boil. Reduce the heat and simmer, covered, for 20 minutes or until all the liquid is absorbed. Let it sit, covered, off the heat, for 10 minutes. Fluff with a fork.

2. Meanwhile, make the Honey-Lime Sriracha sauce: Whisk together all the ingredients in a small bowl, being sure to season with salt and pepper.

3. To cook the broccoli, bring a pot of water to a boil. Add the broccoli, and cook until tender, about 4 minutes. Drain and set aside.

4. Heat 1 tablespoon of the olive oil in a sauté pan over medium to medium-high. Add the garlic, and sauté for 1 minute. Add the cooked broccoli, lime juice, and salt and pepper to taste. Cook for about 3 minutes, careful not to burn the broccoli or garlic.

5. Transfer the broccoli and garlic mixture to a bowl, and add the shredded coconut to the pan. Stir frequently until the coconut flakes brown, about 1 minute. Remove from the heat.

6. Season both sides of the salmon with salt, pepper, and garlic powder to taste. Heat a cast-iron skillet over medium. Add 1 to 2 tablespoons of the olive oil, and sear the salmon for about 2 minutes per side, until browned on the outsides and just cooked through.

7. To assemble, divide the quinoa between two plates. Top each with half the broccoli mixture and 1 piece of salmon. Drizzle the sauce over everything, and garnish with the toasted coconut. Serve with a lime wedge.

FISH TACOS WITH ASIAN SLAW

SERVES **8**

I am super picky when it comes to fish tacos. I can't tell you how many times—at both restaurants and ballparks—I've been served dried fish or sometimes all breading and no fish at all! So I came up with this recipe on the fly one day when I had a weird craving for Mexican and Asian food—and fish. It was during the NFL Playoffs, so I figured I'd make a picnic in front of the TV. My little experiment came out so well that now I make these all the time, especially for game day picnicking.

$1/4$ cup red miso paste

1 tablespoon dark sesame oil

1 tablespoon honey

1 tablespoon rice vinegar

1 tablespoon soy sauce

3 fillets wild halibut, cod, or snapper (about $1^1/2$ pounds)

8 (6-inch) flour or corn tortillas

1 avocado, peeled, pitted, and thinly sliced lengthwise

Peanuts, pulsed into small bits in a food processor, optional

ASIAN SLAW

2 cups shredded cabbage

$1/2$ cup shredded carrots

5 radishes (or 4 large ones), thinly sliced

$1/4$ cup thinly sliced green onions, plus more for garnish

2 cayenne peppers, seeded and minced

1 teaspoon sesame oil

3 tablespoons ponzu sauce

1 tablespoon soy sauce

$1/4$ cup plus 1 teaspoon mayonnaise

1 tablespoon rice wine vinegar

1 teaspoon Louisiana hot sauce

$1/2$ teaspoon freshly ground black pepper

$1/4$ cup finely chopped fresh cilantro, plus more for garnish

1. Preheat the oven to 425°F. Line a baking sheet with parchment paper.

2. Whisk together the miso paste, sesame oil, honey, vinegar, and soy sauce in a small bowl.

3. Rinse the fish clean, and pat dry. Brush with the miso glaze so the entire fish fillets are coated. Place on the prepared baking sheet and bake for 15 minutes, or until flaky and cooked through.

4. Meanwhile, make the slaw: Combine the cabbage, carrots, and radishes in a large bowl, and set aside.

5. Combine the green onions, peppers, sesame oil, ponzu and soy sauces, mayonnaise, vinegar, hot sauce, black pepper, and cilantro in a medium bowl. Whisk together to emulsify. Pour over the veggies, and mix well.

6. To assemble a taco, place a healthy portion of fish on a tortilla, top with $1/2$ cup of the slaw, avocado slices, additional green onions, cilantro, and peanuts, if using. Repeat to make 7 more tacos.

FRIENDLY FANGATING TIP: I'm not sure these would be great for the parking lot, as I don't think they'd travel so well. My best advice is to stick with making these for your watch parties at home. If you're serving a bunch of people, make a taco bar—lay out each of the finished ingredients (the fish, the Asian slaw, the tortillas, the avocado slices, and the garnishes), and let your friends build their own tacos. It's fun, interactive, and yummy!

SIDES

Something's gotta go on your plate next to your sandwich, burger, or your chicken or steak. Certainly a side salad is always nice and optimally healthy. But sometimes you want something salty and crunchy, or creamy and cheesy, or even sweet and hearty. That's what sides are for!

You'll find this chapter chock-full of tasty side dishes. Yes, I acknowledge there's a lot of mac and cheese, and that's for a couple reasons. First, I happen to love mac and cheese. And second, apparently I am not the only one. When I spoke to athletes about their favorite recipes, mac and cheese came up a lot. I think that says something about our culture—it seems every American family has a recipe for the cheesy pasta dish that they like to pass down through the generations. And why not? It's just so good!

This chapter, like those that precede it, also highlights a lot of different food cultures that you'll find as you travel throughout the United States. There's some Italian flavor sprinkled in, some Southern and French influences, a little Mexican street food, and even a bit of Bermudian panache. For me, these flavors encapsulate what it means to fangate across the United States. There's so much to experience and taste! So enjoy mixing and matching—find out what you like and have fun with it! I don't doubt your taste buds will.

DEEP-FRIED OKRA AND POTATOES (PICTURED ON PAGE 151)

CONTRIBUTOR: **ADRIAN PETERSON** | SERVES **4 TO 6**

NFL running back Adrian Peterson hails from Palestine, Texas, which is roughly 100 miles from the Louisiana border. I'd guess that might explain his choice of veggies and flavors for this dish. While growing up in Palestine, Adrian was certainly a football standout. But what you may not know is that he also excelled in track and field, very much following in the footsteps of his college track star mother, Bonita Jackson. She won the Texas 3A State Championship in the triple jump, the long jump, and the 100-meter and the 200-meter dashes in 1983. Adrian once noted in an interview with *Sports Illustrated Kids* that he ran the 400-meter dash in 47.6 seconds and that his best 100-meter time was 10.19 seconds.

1¹⁄₂ **cups buttermilk**

1 large egg

2 tablespoons Tony Chachere's Original Creole Seasoning

1 package Louisiana Seasoned Fish Fry Mix

Vegetable oil, for frying

12 to 15 whole pieces of okra

2 Yukon Gold potatoes, thinly sliced

1 white onion, thinly sliced

1. Whisk together the buttermilk, egg, and Tony Chachere's seasoning in a medium bowl. Pour the package of fish fry mix into a separate medium bowl.

2. Heat 1¹⁄₂ to 2 inches oil in a large stockpot over medium until it reaches 360°F on a deep-fry thermometer.

3. Dip the okra pieces in the buttermilk mixture, and then dredge them in the fish fry mix. Fry the okra pieces in batches until crispy and golden brown, placing them on a paper towel–lined baking sheet to absorb excess oil. Keep warm.

4. Check that the oil is still at 360°F. Fry the potato slices next, dipping them in the buttermilk mixture first, and then dredging them in the fish fry mix before frying them in batches until crispy and golden brown. Keep warm.

5. Double check that the oil is at 360°F. Lastly, place the onions in the buttermilk mixture, and then in the fish fry mix, and fry them until crispy and golden brown. Serve immediately.

FRESH CORN ON THE COB

(PICTURED ON PAGE 151)

CONTRIBUTOR: **ADRIAN PETERSON** | SERVES **4**

Corn on the cob can be prepared simply—merely boiled or grilled and served with butter and salt—or it can be paired with fancy marinades or dressings. However you choose to make it, it's certainly an American classic. Here is Adrian's buttery oven-roasted take on the traditional American side. He likes to serve this dish, along with the okra and potatoes opposite, with his Grilled Sirloin Steak (page 150).

4 corn cobs, husks removed

Sea salt and freshly ground black pepper

8 tablespoons (1 stick) salted butter, melted

1. Preheat the oven to 450°F.

2. Cut each corn cob in half crosswise, and place in a large zip-top bag. Season with the salt and pepper. Add the melted butter to the bag, shaking the bag to coat the corn with the butter, seal it, and then place the bag in the freezer for 2 to 3 minutes, until the butter solidifies on the cobs.

3. Remove the corn from the bag, and wrap each piece individually in foil (or put them all into an oven bag).

4. Roast for 20 to 25 minutes. Serve.

FRENCH FRIES AND SWEET POTATO FRIES

SERVES 2

I couldn't possibly dare to write a sportsfood cookbook without including a recipe for fries. I happen to prefer sweet potato fries to French fries almost any day of the week. But they're both solid, go-to sides that aren't as tough to make as you may think. This recipe is for straight-up, no-frills fries. Feel free to go crazy and dress them up however you'd like. You could sprinkle them with any of my savory Hungry Fan spices for something truly different (pizza fries, what?!); top them with grated Parmesan cheese, some fresh parsley, and even shaved truffles; or sprinkle on some minced fresh garlic for garlic fries. The fangate is your oyster. Have fun with it! You could certainly bake these in the oven on a baking sheet, or fry them in an air fryer for a healthier spin. Or you can just fry them, which I find yields the best, crispiest results.

3 sweet potatoes, baking potatoes, or a combination, scrubbed but not peeled

Sea salt

Avocado oil, for frying

1. Slice the spuds into French fry shapes of equal thickness and length. The more uniform the fries, the more evenly they'll cook.

2. Place the sliced spuds on a work surface covered in a layer or two of paper towels to drain them. Use additional paper towels to dab the taters. (You want them as dry as possible.) Once sufficiently dry, lightly salt the potatoes.

3. Heat about 3 inches of oil in a large pot or in a deep fryer over high until it reaches 375°F on a deep-fry thermometer. Add the potatoes, and cook until golden brown and crispy (I like mine crispy on the outside and warm and soft on the inside), 5 to 6 minutes. Transfer to paper towels to drain.

4. Feel free to lightly salt the fries again. Serve immediately.

FRIENDLY FANGATING TIP: I've had truffle Parmesan fries at a couple of stadiums, and they're so good it's flat-out ridiculous. To make them at home, simply drizzle your fries with Urbani White Truffle Oil, and sprinkle with coarse salt, black pepper, and some freshly grated Parmigiano-Reggiano. For extra credit, add some minced fresh Italian parsley or chives for color. Urbani also makes my favorite Truffle Ketchup.

CASSAVA PIE

CONTRIBUTOR: **KATURA HORTON-PERINCHIEF** | SERVES **10 TO 12**

Katura is one of my bestiest besties, and she is a rock star—a historical figure—in the Olympic world. During the 2004 Summer Olympic Games in Athens, Greece, Katura represented her home country of Bermuda and became the first black woman to compete in Olympic diving—she broke a 52-year-long streak during which Bermuda did not even compete in the sport! When I asked Katura for a recipe, she gave me this one, saying that this is not meant for dessert. For those of you unfamiliar with cassava, it's a starchy root vegetable similar to yucca, but it does need to be prepared exactly as instructed or else it can be poisonous. Don't fret, this recipe is worth the effort. If you're short on time, though, substitute yucca.

4 pounds cassava

2 pounds skinless, bone-in chicken breasts

12 sprigs thyme

1 Oxo chicken stock cube

About 10 cups water

1 tablespoon plus ¹/₂ teaspoon sea salt

12 ounces (3 sticks) butter, at room temperature

2 cups sugar

1 dozen large eggs, well beaten

Freshly grated nutmeg, to taste

1 teaspoon vanilla extract

1. Cut the ends off the cassava, cut in half crosswise, and peel. Place in a bowl with enough cold water to cover, and refrigerate for 24 hours. The next day, drain the cassava, and then grate on the large holes of a box grater. Spread the grated cassava on several layers of paper towels, and squeeze the starch out with additional paper towels. Set the cassava aside. (If using yucca, you can skip the soaking. Just peel until only the white flesh remains—the peel contains poisonous compounds, so peel well—and grate the flesh, discarding the fibrous center.)

2. Combine the chicken, thyme, stock cube, enough water to cover the chicken by 2 inches, and ¹/₂ teaspoon of the salt in a large pot, and bring to a boil. Reduce the heat to a simmer, and cook until the chicken is tender, about 30 minutes. Let the chicken cool completely in the broth for about 1 hour. Transfer the chicken to a cutting board, and remove the meat from the bones. Reserve 1 cup of the stock.

3. Preheat the oven to 300°F. Grease a deep 9- x 13-inch baking dish with cooking spray.

4. Cream the butter and sugar together in a medium bowl using an electric mixer until light and fluffy. Add the beaten eggs and grated cassava a little at a time, alternating between the two. Then stir in the nutmeg, vanilla, and remaining 1 tablespoon salt, mixing together well.

5. Fill the prepared baking dish with about three-quarters of the cassava mixture. Place the poached chicken on top, and cover with the remaining cassava. Spoon the reserved chicken broth over all. Place the baking dish on a baking sheet, and bake for 3 hours, or until deeply brown on the top and edges.

Katura and me in grad school.

FIVE-CHEESE MAC AND CHEESE

SERVES **6 TO 8**

This is my go-to mac and cheese recipe. Why five-cheese? That's easy—because I like all these cheeses and couldn't choose just one or two, so I went with 'em all! The flavors work well together, and all five cheeses lend texture to the ooey-gooey goodness you expect with mac and cheese! If you're gluten-free, substitute brown rice flour and whatever kind of gluten-free pasta and breadcrumbs you prefer. (I adore quinoa pasta and find it has the closest texture to non-gluten-free pasta.)

12 ounces elbow pasta

3 tablespoons salted butter

$^1/_4$ cup breadcrumbs

2 cups whole milk

2 tablespoons all-purpose flour

$^1/_2$ teaspoon sea salt

$^1/_2$ teaspoon freshly ground black pepper

1 cup shredded sharp Cheddar cheese

$^1/_2$ cup fontina cheese

$^1/_4$ cup freshly grated Parmigiano-Reggiano cheese

$^1/_4$ cup shredded Monterey Jack cheese

$^1/_4$ cup finely shredded aged pecorino cheese

1. Preheat the oven to 400°F. Grease an 8- x 8-inch baking dish with cooking spray.

2. Fill a large pot with water, and heavily salt it. Bring the water to a rolling boil, and then throw in the pasta. Stir immediately (especially if using gluten-free pasta, which has a tendency to clump quickly). Boil for approximately 7 minutes, or until the pasta is al dente. Drain in a colander, rinse with cold water, and set aside.

3. Meanwhile, melt 1 tablespoon of the butter in a medium skillet over medium. Add the breadcrumbs, and toss until they are coated with butter. Toast until golden brown, and then set aside off the heat.

4. Heat the milk in a saucepan over low or in a microwave-safe bowl at HIGH for 1$^1/_2$ minutes.

5. In the pot used to cook the pasta, melt the remaining 2 tablespoons butter over low. Whisk in the flour, raise the heat to medium-low, and slowly start to whisk in the warmed milk. Whisk continuously for about 5 minutes, or until the mixture has thickened. Stir in the salt and pepper.

6. Gradually add $^1/_2$ cup of the Cheddar, the fontina, Parmigiano-Reggiano, and Monterey Jack cheeses, stirring after each addition. Stir again to ensure that all the cheeses are melted and incorporated into the sauce. Then lower the heat, and stir in the pasta to thoroughly coat.

7. Gently pour the mac and cheese into the prepared baking dish. Use a spatula to evenly spread it. Sprinkle the remaining $^1/_2$ cup Cheddar evenly over the top, and then the toasted breadcrumbs, and finally the pecorino.

8. Bake for 20 minutes, until the mac is bubbling around the edges. Alternatively, if you prefer gooier mac and cheese, do not bake it. Simply place it under a broiler, preheated to high, for about 5 minutes to get the top golden brown but keep the rest as ooey-gooey as it is in the pot.

MOMMA'S REAL RONI AND CHEESE

CONTRIBUTOR: **GREG JENNINGS** | SERVES **6 TO 8**

If you ask the Miami Dolphins' wide receiver Greg Jennings what his favorite dish was growing up, he'd tell you it was his momma's "real roni and cheese." And I am so pleased that Greg shared this recipe with me so I could share it with you all! This is hearty and delicious—a great meal to fuel an NFLer in the making (or to feed your hungry friends at your fangate). I can't make any promises that by eating this dish your kid will grow up to be a successful NFLer, but Greg certainly did well.

12 ounces elbow pasta

1½ cups evaporated milk

16 ounces Velveeta cheese, cut into cubes

4 ounces pepper Jack cheese (or any cheese with a kick)

1¼ teaspoons Lawry's seasoned salt (or use my homemade version, page 34)

¾ teaspoon sea salt

¼ teaspoon freshly ground black pepper

1. Preheat the broiler to medium. Grease an 8-inch baking dish with cooking spray.

2. Cook the pasta in a large pot of salted boiling water over high according to package directions until tender. Drain.

3. Meanwhile, heat the milk in a large saucepan until simmering. Add both cheeses in batches, stirring to melt after each addition. Sprinkle in the seasoned salt, ¾ teaspoon salt, and ¼ teaspoon pepper. Mix well.

4. Pour the pasta into the saucepan, and gently stir it into the sauce. Pour into the prepared baking dish. Broil for 2 to 3 minutes, depending on how browned you like the top.

5. Let cool for 5 to 10 minutes before serving.

TASTY TIDBITS

Greg Jennings made the 2006 NFL All-Rookie Team, was a member of the NFL Championship Team in 2010, co-led the NFC in touchdowns received in 2010, played in two Pro Bowls in 2010 and 2011, and was ranked (by his NFL peers) as number 56 in the Top 100 Players in 2012. Did I mention that he and his Green Bay Packers won the Super Bowl (XLV) in 2011?

AUNT SARAH'S MACARONI AND CHEESE

CONTRIBUTOR: RALPH SAMPSON | SERVES **10**

Ralph Sampson, like Dikembe Mutombo or Patrick Ewing, is a tough guy not to spot in a crowd. Towering over us all at 7 feet, 4 inches, it's no shock he was a basketball phenom. I ran into Ralph when I first got the deal to do this cookbook. I mentioned it to him and he got really excited, raving about his Aunt's mac and cheese. He then emailed me two delicious-looking photos of the ooey-gooey cheesy dish in the days that followed. Including his favorite comfort food in this book was a must! So without further ado, here is a recipe that I'm sure you'll enjoy.

1 pound elbow pasta

1¼ cups whole milk

1 large egg

1 teaspoon sea salt

½ teaspoon freshly ground black pepper

3 tablespoons butter, plus more for greasing

3 cups grated extra-sharp Cheddar cheese

About half a 13.7-ounce box of Ritz crackers, pounded or processed to crumbs

1. Preheat the oven to 350°F. Grease a 2½-quart round baking dish well with butter or cooking spray.

2. Fill a large pot with salted water, and bring to a boil. Add the pasta, and cook according to package directions.

3. Meanwhile, whisk together the milk, egg, salt, and pepper in a small bowl.

4. Drain the noodles, and return them to the pot. Add the butter and melt over low, stirring to distribute it evenly. Stir in the milk mixture and the cheese until the cheese is melted. Remove from the heat.

5. Line the prepared baking dish with one layer of cheesy pasta. Top with ½ cup cracker crumbs. Then repeat, adding another layer of pasta and sprinkling with ½ cup cracker crumbs until you've used up all the pasta and cracker crumbs.

6. Bake the mac and cheese for about 15 minutes, until the top is golden brown. Serve hot.

TASTY TIDBITS

At the University of Virginia, where his number 50 jersey has been retired, Ralph was a three-time Naismith Award winner as College Player of the Year, and he went on to become the number 1 pick in the 1983 NBA Draft by the Houston Rockets. In the NBA, Ralph made the All-Rookie First Team in 1984 and played in four NBA All-Star Games in 1984–87, earning the MVP title in the 1985 game.

BBQ BAKED BEANS

SERVES 6

I'm fairly certain it would be a crime to publish a game day cookbook and not include a recipe for **BBQ** baked beans. They're pretty much a staple in any southern, barbecue, or comfort food–themed game day meal. Sure, you could always go buy a can of ready-made. But they're super easy to prepare and always taste better when you make them yourself. I promise. (And again, as in making anything at home versus buying store-bought, you're sparing yourself from a lot of preservatives and chemicals you don't want to ingest.) Plus, this recipe calls for actual bacon—bacon-flavor crystals, if you will—that you just can't get from a can. I find I have a tough time restraining myself when making this recipe for others; I can't help but sample as I cook because these beans are really, really good. I'm lucky to have anything to serve at all by the time I'm done cooking (wink wink).

8 slices bacon

$^1/_2$ cup diced onions

2 cloves garlic, peeled

1 red bell pepper, seeded and diced

2 (15-ounce) cans navy beans, drained and rinsed

1 tablespoon yellow mustard

3 tablespoons Worcestershire sauce

1 cup Pomì tomato sauce

$^1/_4$ cup maple syrup

3 tablespoons brown sugar

2 teaspoons onion powder

1 teaspoon freshly ground black pepper

1 teaspoon hot sauce

$^1/_4$ cup apple cider vinegar

2 teaspoons soy sauce

Smoulder or other smoky seasoning blend, optional

1. Preheat the oven to 375°F. Lightly grease an 8-inch baking dish with cooking spray.

2. Cook the bacon until brown and crispy in a large skillet over medium, about 10 minutes. Transfer the bacon to a paper towel–lined plate, and reserve $^1/_4$ cup bacon fat in the pan. Roughly chop the bacon.

3. Sauté the onions, garlic, and red pepper in the bacon fat over medium until the onions are translucent and soft, about 5 minutes.

4. Add the beans, and reduce the heat to medium-low. Stir in the reserved bacon, the mustard, Worcestershire sauce, tomato sauce, maple syrup, brown sugar, onion powder, black pepper, hot sauce, vinegar, and soy sauce, and smoky seasoning, if using, until well combined.

5. Transfer the bean mixture into the prepared baking dish, and bake for 40 minutes.

6. Alternatively, you can bake these beans in the Hungry Fan™ 3-in-1 Fangating™ Bag. If doing so, simmer the bean mixture for 15 minutes to reach the right temperature, and then bake in your Fangating Bag™ for 2 to 3 hours.

MEXICORN CUPS

SERVES 6

This is essentially Mexican street food that happens to make an awesome side dish for any fangate. Serve it in a big bowl or in individual 8.5-ounce cups. It's delicious and sure to please your friends and fellow fangaters!

3 ears corn, husks removed

$^1/_2$ cup mayonnaise

1 tablespoon chipotle sauce (I prefer the Cholula brand)

$^1/_2$ teaspoon smoky seasoning blend (I use the Smoulder brand)

$^1/_4$ cup finely grated Cotija cheese

$^1/_2$ poblano or 2 Fresno chile peppers, deveined and seeded, finely minced

1 heaping tablespoon minced fresh Italian (flat-leaf) parsley

1 lime

Freshly ground black pepper

1. Boil a pot of unsalted water over high. (Be sure not to salt your water as it will actually harden the corn. You can, however, add some sugar to the water if you'd like.) Add the corn, cover, and boil for 3 to 4 minutes. Remove the corn before it overcooks, and let it cool.

2. Hold the corn upright and, using a sharp knife, cut down the sides of the corn, removing the kernels from the cob. Set aside.

3. Combine the corn with the mayonnaise, chipotle sauce, smoky seasoning, Cotija cheese, chile peppers, and parsley in a large bowl. Mix well. Divide the spicy corn mixture among individual cups, sprinkle with a squeeze of fresh lime and some pepper, and serve.

BEER-BATTERED CAJUN-STYLE DEEP-FRIED OKRA (PICTURED ON PAGE 126)

SERVES **10**

I don't think okra gets as much love as it should. It's pretty popular in the South—particularly in Cajun cuisine. It's really quite delicious and can provide a good alternative to French fries, especially when fried. You can certainly serve this recipe with Will Witherspoon's Andouille Jambalaya (page 181), but I also suggest pairing it with a BBQ sandwich or even a burger.

1 to 2 quarts avocado or peanut oil, depending on size of fryer

¹/₂ cup all-purpose flour

¹/₂ cup yellow cornmeal

¹/₄ cup whole milk

³/₄ cup beer (preferably dark)

1 teaspoon Cajun seasoning, or more to taste

¹/₂ teaspoon Lawry's seasoned salt (or use my homemade version, page 34)

¹/₂ teaspoon sea salt, plus more for seasoning

¹/₄ teaspoon cayenne pepper

2 large eggs, beaten

25 okras, cut in half lengthwise

1. Heat the oil in a large saucepan or deep fryer over high until it reaches 350°F on a deep-fry thermometer.

2. Whisk together the flour, cornmeal, milk, beer, Cajun seasoning, both salts, cayenne, and eggs in a large bowl. Dunk the okra halves into the batter, coat well, and then remove, using a strainer to drain any excess batter. (Try giving your strainer a little shake to help ease off the excess.)

3. Working in four batches, deep-fry the okra in the hot oil until they're golden brown, about 2 minutes. Transfer to a paper towel–lined plate to drain excess oil. Sprinkle while hot with sea salt, if desired, and serve immediately.

FRIENDLY FANGATING TIP: I prefer to fry with avocado oil, because it's significantly higher in monounsaturated fat (the "good for you" fat that lowers your "bad" or LDL cholesterol), has an extremely high smoke point (520°F), is rich in nutrients such as vitamin E, and has comparatively high levels of protein and potassium (compared to other fruits). Most importantly, I like the taste!

ITALIAN STRING BEAN "SPAGHETTI" (PICTURED ON PAGE 159)

SERVES 4

Sportsfood can be very heavy, and let's face it, super unhealthy sometimes. And that's okay. If you're a healthy eater six days a week, then you should feel okay about indulging a little on game day. That said, I have a thing about getting my greens in every day. So I came up with this recipe: It feels hearty, is really delicious, and pairs well with many game day entrées—but it's also quite healthy and fulfills my personal daily "greens quota." Talk about a win-win!

8 ounces haricots verts, trimmed

4 tablespoons extra virgin olive oil

1/2 cup finely chopped onion

3 cloves garlic, minced

3/4 teaspoon sea salt

1/4 teaspoon freshly ground black pepper

1/2 teaspoon dried oregano

1 cup Pomì finely chopped tomatoes

1. Bring a pot of heavily salted water to a boil over high. Throw the string beans in for 2 minutes, and then scoop them out with a strainer and quickly transfer them to a bowl of ice water. Drain.

2. Heat 2 tablespoons of the olive oil in a medium skillet over medium. Add the onions and garlic, and sauté until the onions are translucent, 4 to 5 minutes. Add the remaining 2 tablespoons olive oil, salt, pepper, oregano, drained string beans, and chopped tomatoes. Cover and cook for an additional 10 minutes over medium-low. Serve.

ZUCCHINI TEMPURA FRIES

SERVES **6 TO 8**

I have this repeating flashback from time to time of an unbelievable meal I had in Positano, Italy, years and years ago that included the lightest, most delicious zucchini string fries. (My memory may be spotty, hit-or-miss even, but I always remember every detail of a good meal!) So I thought, "Okay, I recently bought myself a French fry cutter—what if I stuck a zucchini through that?" Well what do you know? You can certainly fry up zucchini at this size, or you can cut the zucchini pieces in half or even quarters (depending on your knife skills) to make zucchini fries that are more similar to shoestring fries. I like these with a side of Lemon Parsley Mayo, but you can always serve them plain, with plain mayo, or even ketchup. In any case, these are nice and crunchy, making for good munchies, and munchies are always good during a game!

³/₄ cup cornstarch

3 medium zucchini, cut into fries

1 cup all-purpose flour (or brown rice flour for gluten-free fries)

1 large egg, beaten

¹/₂ cup ice water

1 cup chilled sparkling water

1 teaspoon sea salt, plus more for seasoning

¹/₂ teaspoon freshly ground black pepper

Avocado or safflower oil, for frying

LEMON PARSLEY MAYO

2 large egg yolks

2 teaspoons Champagne vinegar

1 tablespoon fresh lemon juice

1 teaspoon sea salt

2 teaspoons dried parsley

¹/₂ cup avocado oil

1. Make the lemon parsley mayo: Whisk together all the ingredients except for the avocado oil in a medium bowl until well blended, about 1 minute. (I like to use a handheld mixer.) Continue to whisk as you slowly (slowly!) pour in the oil, a little at a time. (You won't get the creamy mayo texture right if you pour in too much oil at once.) You will notice the color of the mayo change and the consistency get fluffier. Once it has reached a consistency you like, you're done!

2. Make the zucchini fries: Place the cornstarch in a large zip-top plastic bag. Add the zucchini fries, and shake to coat.

3. Combine the flour, egg, ice water, chilled sparkling water, salt, and pepper in a medium bowl. Mix well with a whisk to make the batter.

4. Heat the oil in a large pot or deep fryer over high until it reaches 375°F on a deep-fry thermometer.

5. Meanwhile, just before frying, dip the zucchini sticks in the batter to coat completely. Place the zucchini sticks, a handful at a time, into the hot oil, and fry until brown and crispy, about 3 minutes. Transfer to a paper towel–lined plate to remove excess oil. Sprinkle lightly with salt. Serve hot with the Lemon Parsley Mayo.

FRIENDLY FANGATING TIP:
I find a store-bought French fry cutter is the easiest tool to use when making any type of fries (because I can be lazy). If you prefer to use sweet potatoes or even regular potatoes instead of zucchini in this recipe, go for it. Just try to use an equivalent amount of potatoes so you have enough batter!

DESSERTS

I used to think my sweet tooth was my entire set of teeth. If you put a sweet treat in front of me, even if I was stuffed to the gills already, I'd eat it. I'm fairly certain that's the result of a super-cool evolutionary advancement I somehow achieved wherein I actually formed two stomachs—one for all food and drinks and one solely reserved for dessert. I have since learned to curb my sugar consumption a bit, but that's not to say that I don't still love dessert. I do. If it's chocolate anything, I still struggle to control myself.

Desserts for fangating can be tricky. Take chocolate for example: It melts like nobody's business when left out in the sun or in a hot car. I'd suggest you be thoughtful about your desserts, especially if you're heading to the stadium parking lot to get your pregame on. A cooler (or the Hungry Fan™ 3-in-1 Fangating™ Bag) is your friend when it comes to most, if not all, desserts in this chapter. If you're fangating at home, dessert is epically easier, as you have access to a fridge and freezer. But you know what? If your cookies get a little warm, is it really that tragic? So they become ooey and gooey as if they're fresh out of the oven. In my book, that's a good thing! (I'd say the same logic won't hold so well for my Beer Sno-Cones, my Peanut Butter Banana Chocolates, or my Superfood Chocolate Nuggets, but you get the idea.) In any case, what follows is a selection of my favorite, easy-to-make dessert recipes. Enjoy!

PB B C'S
(PEANUT BUTTER BANANA CHOCOLATES)

MAKES **20**

Truth be told, I'm not a huge dessert person when it comes to game day. I'd so much rather fill up on ribs or nachos or Buffalo wings—and plenty of cold beer. But as I'm sure you may have experienced, after eating lots of salty food (like the majority of game day food), I find myself craving a little something sweet. Given that I'm a full-blown dark chocoholic, my cravings are for chocolate. These little suckers hit the spot for me. They're crunchy and salty and sweet all at the same time. I can pop one, and I'm so good.

2 bananas

¹/₃ cup crunchy peanut butter

8 ounces bittersweet dark chocolate, chopped

Large sea salt (I use Himalayan salt crystals), optional

1. Slice the bananas into 40 (¹/₄-inch-thick) rounds.

2. Using a spoon, top 20 of the banana rounds with a small dollop of peanut butter. Top each with another banana slice to make 20 banana peanut butter sandwiches.

3. Freeze for a minimum of 2 hours. (You can easily leave these overnight and resume making them the following day.)

4. When the banana–peanut butter sandwiches are frozen, microwave the chocolate in a small glass bowl at HIGH for 1 to 2 minutes, stirring every 30 seconds, or until melted and smooth.

5. Using a fork, dip the banana sandwiches into the chocolate, coating them on all sides. Set them on a parchment paper–lined baking sheet, and top each chocolate piece with a salt crystal, if desired.

6. Immediately return to the freezer. Serve frozen.

Crumbly Lemon Crème Bars
(page 216)

Go-To Game Day
Cookies

GO-TO GAME DAY COOKIES

CONTRIBUTOR: ISABELLA BERTOLD | MAKES **4 TO 5 DOZEN**

Isabella hails from Vancouver, British Columbia, easily one of the most beautiful cities in the world if you ask me. She has been sailing since she was five. At age 13, Isabella qualified for both the junior and senior Canadian national sailing teams, the youngest person to ever do so in the sport of sailing. Representing Canada, she has her eyes set on the 2016 Summer Olympics. And when it comes to food, Isabella is a woman after my own heart (her favorite food is chocolate). Here is her recipe for delicious chocolate chip cookies. I am particularly partial to her addition of peanut butter, nuts, and seeds. These aren't just any old chocolate chip cookies, folks.

1 cup creamy peanut butter

4 tablespoons unsalted butter, at room temperature

3/4 cup granulated sugar

3/4 cup brown sugar

2 large eggs

1 teaspoon pure vanilla extract

1 1/4 teaspoons baking soda

3 cups old-fashioned rolled oats

1 cup chocolate chips (or however much chocolate you want)

1/2 cup toasted sunflower seeds, optional

1/2 cup toasted chopped walnuts, optional

1/2 cup toasted chopped pecans, optional

1. Preheat the oven to 350°F.

2. Combine the peanut butter, butter, and both sugars in a large bowl, and beat with an electric mixer until creamy and well blended. Add the eggs, vanilla, and baking soda, and mix well.

3. Stir in the oats, chocolate chips, and seeds and nuts, if desired. Scoop out the dough in small balls (roughly a heaping tablespoon's worth), and arrange on a baking sheet, leaving about 2 inches of space around each cookie. (You can cover your baking sheet in parchment paper for easier cleanup, if desired.)

4. Bake for 10 to 12 minutes, until the edges are golden brown. Cool on the pan for 5 minutes, and then transfer to a wire rack. Serve warm, or cool completely.

FRIENDLY FANGATING TIP:

Make this recipe gluten-free by using gluten-free rolled oats. Isabella uses half dark chocolate and half milk chocolate chips for her cookies, but feel free to use your favorite kind.

CRUMBLY LEMON CRÈME BARS (PICTURED ON PAGE 214)

CONTRIBUTOR: LAUREN GIBBEMEYER | MAKES **8**

I was introduced to Lauren through a friend, who told me I simply had to meet the nicest volleyball player who also happens to have some great recipes. Indeed, Lauren is a sweetheart, and her volleyball career has been quite impressive. A member of the United States Women's Volleyball Team since 2011, Lauren won a bronze medal at the 2011 Pan American Games and two gold medals at the 2012 and 2013 Pan American Cups. Keep your eyes open for her in Rio in 2016! And in the meantime, please enjoy her scrumptious lemon crème bars!

1¼ cups all-purpose flour

1¼ cups old-fashioned rolled oats

¼ teaspoon sea salt

½ teaspoon baking soda

½ cup granulated sugar

½ cup packed light brown sugar

1 teaspoon pure vanilla extract

12 tablespoons (1½ sticks) unsalted butter, melted

1 (14-ounce) can sweetened condensed milk

1 tablespoon finely grated lemon zest

⅓ cup fresh lemon juice

2 large egg yolks

1 teaspoon cornstarch

1. Preheat the oven to 350°F. Grease an 8- x 8-inch baking pan with butter.

2. Whisk together the flour, oats, salt, and baking soda. Stir in both sugars, and mix until no clumps remain.

3. Stir the vanilla into the melted butter, and pour it over the dry ingredients. Using a wooden spoon, stir until you have evenly moistened crumbs. Sprinkle half of the crumb mixture into the bottom of the prepared baking dish, and gently press into an even layer.

4. Bake for 15 minutes. Remove from the oven and set aside. Leave the oven on.

5. Whisk together the condensed milk, lemon zest, lemon juice, egg yolks, and cornstarch in a medium bowl. Pour the lemony filling over the warm crumb crust, and spread into an even layer. Sprinkle evenly with the remaining crumb mixture.

6. Bake for 25 to 30 minutes, until lightly golden. Remove from the oven, and let cool at room temperature, about 1 hour. Once cool, cover and refrigerate for another hour, and then cut into squares and serve.

SUPERFOOD CHOCOLATE NUGGETS

MAKES **12**

I am a very healthy eater…when it isn't game day. It's my way of rationalizing eating my face off at least one day a week at a fangate. I figure if I'm good six days a week, I can let myself go one day and it'll balance out. (Besides, I am fairly certain there is an invisible calorie force field outside any given stadium on game day, and once you cross it, you can eat all you want but your body won't absorb any calories. It isn't highly scientific, but I'm pretty sure it's true.) I came up with this recipe as a way of incorporating good-for-you, healthy antioxidants and nutrients into a bite-sized sweet treat for me and my friends. They're jam-packed with goodness but they taste like dessert. It's a total win-win.

12 fresh raspberries, washed and patted dry

2 tablespoons pure honey, preferably Manuka

Goji berry powder, optional

3¹⁄₂ ounces dark chocolate, chopped

1 teaspoon coconut water powder, optional

1¹⁄₂ teaspoons pink peppercorns, crushed

1. Dunk the raspberries one by one in the honey. Then cover or roll in goji berry powder, if desired, and set on a plate covered in parchment paper. Cover the plate loosely with plastic wrap, and put into the freezer for a minimum of 2 hours. (Feel free to freeze overnight if making these in advance.)

2. When the coated raspberries are frozen, melt the chocolate with the coconut powder, if desired, in a small glass bowl in the microwave at HIGH for 1 to 1¹⁄₂ minutes, stirring every 30 seconds.

3. Using a toothpick, dunk the coated raspberries in the melted chocolate, covering them on all sides, and set on a clean sheet of parchment paper. Sprinkle with the crushed peppercorns, and chill or freeze before serving.

FRIENDLY FANGATING TIP: My favorite thing about this recipe (aside from the taste)? If you transport these to a tailgate and they come up to room temperature before you eat them, the raspberry goodness on the inside just oozes into your mouth after you bite into the chocolate coating. It's possibly one of the greatest sensations on earth. Just be sure these nuggets don't sit out in the heat for too long, or they'll turn into a chocolatey mess.

PEANUT BUTTER CRACKER JACK S'MORES

MAKES **12**

When it comes to dessert, there is little (perhaps other than chocolate) that I love better than freshly made whipped cream. And I cannot urge you enough to make it from scratch. It's so easy to do—and it saves you from the nuclear-proof stuff at the grocery store that will likely be fresh until the year 2057.

Making the rest of this sweet treat is such a cinch—it takes no time at all but it's packed with flavor, crunch, and creaminess. If you're serving these in the parking lot, my suggestion is to make them there. They don't travel super well and are best served immediately.

12 graham crackers, halved

$^1/_2$ cup smooth peanut butter

1 (1-ounce) box Cracker Jack, pulsed twice in a food processor

WHIPPED CREAM

1 cup heavy whipping cream (must be cold)

2 tablespoons confectioners' sugar

$^1/_2$ teaspoon pure vanilla extract

1. Make the whipped cream: Combine the cream, sugar, and vanilla in a large bowl. Using a whisk or handheld mixer, beat together until soft peaks form. (You may have leftover whipped cream. Feel free to cover and return to your fridge for later treats.)

2. Make the s'mores: Top half the graham crackers with a dollop of peanut butter, and spread it evenly. Top the peanut butter crackers with a dollop of whipped cream.

3. Sprinkle the Cracker Jack bits on top of the whipped cream, and then cover with the remaining crackers. Serve immediately.

FRIENDLY FANGATING TIP:

Instead of, or in addition to, the Cracker Jack bits, you can also lightly sprinkle your s'mores with my Hungry Fan™ Pumpkin Spice blend for a pumpkin-y spin on this dessert. It's really yummy!

BASKETBALL CAKE POPS

MAKES 6 DOZEN

I debuted this recipe on *Late Night with Seth Meyers.* It was such a treat to demo because my sous chef for this dessert was none other than the super-talented fashion designer Zac Posen. Granted, these cake pops were supposed to be designed to look like little basketballs, but who am I to tell Zac Posen how something should look? In the end, he decorated a few to look like basketballs, and then free-styled the rest. And they were all equally delicious.

1 box vanilla or chocolate cake mix (plus ingredients listed on the package)

8 ounces vanilla frosting

2 (16-ounce) packages vanilla CANDIQUIK® coating

¹/₂ ounce orange food coloring (oil- or powder-based only)

72 lollipop sticks

Styrofoam block, big enough to hold all sticks upright

Black decorating gel or 2 ounces dark chocolate, melted

1. Make the cake according to the directions on the cake mix box. Let cool completely.

2. Crumble the entire cake into a large bowl. Add the frosting, and mix thoroughly. Using your hands, roll the cake mixture into 1-inch balls, and place on a baking sheet. Chill for 1 hour in the refrigerator.

3. Melt the CANDIQUIK® coating in the Melt and Make Microwaveable Tray™ according to the package directions. Add the orange food coloring until you reach your desired color; remember, you want these to look like basketballs.

4. Dip ¹/₂ inch of a lollipop stick into the melted CANDIQUIK®, and then insert that candied end into a cake ball. Repeat with the remaining sticks and cake balls, inserting them into the Styrofoam block and returning them to the refrigerator. Taking only a few cake balls from the fridge at a time, dip the cake pops in the CANDIQUIK®, allowing excess coating to drip off. Stick the pops in the Styrofoam block, and let them set. Repeat with the remaining cake balls.

5. Once set, pipe on a basketball pattern with the black decorating gel, and serve.

FRIENDLY FANGATING TIP: To make these cake pops look like basketballs, I use orange food coloring and black decorating gel. Feel free to use white food coloring and red gel to make baseball pops; brown food coloring (or chocolate syrup) and white gel to make little football pops (just adjust the ball shape a bit); or even yellow food coloring and white gel to make tennis ball pops. You get the idea.

GUINNESS CUPCAKES WITH BAILEY'S FROSTING

MAKES **16**

I know, the sound of beer—especially such a hearty stout—in a dessert may seem strange. Beer in chili or in batter for frying, okay. But with chocolate in a cupcake? Yes! I kid you not, this tastes good. Really, really good. The Guinness actually adds crazy depth to the chocolate flavor (meaty, if you will) that's pretty hard to match. And don't even get me started on the Bailey's frosting. I have to summon every ounce of personal willpower not to just eat all the frosting up before icing these cupcakes. I first came up with this recipe for March Madness a few years ago, as it falls right around St. Paddy's Day. But I see no reason why you can't make these cupcakes year-round. They're one of my favorite desserts that I've ever come up with. I hope you enjoy them as much as I do!

8 tablespoons (1 stick) unsalted butter, at room temperature

1¼ cups dark brown sugar

2 large eggs

1½ cups all-purpose flour

½ cup unsweetened cocoa powder

1 teaspoon baking soda

¼ teaspoon baking powder

¼ teaspoon sea salt

¾ cup (plus an extra splash) Guinness Extra Stout

BAILEY'S IRISH CREAM FROSTING

8 tablespoons (1 stick) unsalted butter, at room temperature

2 cups confectioners' sugar

2 tablespoons Bailey's Irish Cream

1. Preheat the oven to 350°F. Line a 16-cup muffin tin with cupcake liners.

2. Cream the butter and brown sugar in a stand mixer until light and fluffy. Slowly mix in the eggs, one at a time, until well blended. Set aside.

3. Sift together the flour, cocoa, baking soda, baking powder, and salt in a medium bowl.

4. Beating on low speed, gradually add the flour mixture to the creamed butter and eggs, alternating with the beer until the batter is well blended.

5. Fill each cupcake liner about two-thirds full with batter. Bake for 15 to 18 minutes, until a toothpick inserted into the center of a cupcake comes out clean.

6. Meanwhile, make the icing: Cream the butter and sugar in the bowl of a stand mixer until light and fluffy. Add a little Bailey's at a time, mixing well, until you achieve the consistency you prefer. Set aside, being careful not to let the frosting get too warm. (You can stick it in the fridge if you'd like.)

7. Once the cupcakes are done baking, remove them from the oven, and let them cool. Spread the Bailey's frosting on the cupcakes, and serve.

BEER SNO-CONES
(AKA GRANITAS FOR GROWN-UPS)

SERVES **6**

You know how you can't freeze vodka? Well, I wondered what would happen if you tried to freeze beer. Not to mention that I thought grown-up sno-cones sounded pretty awesome, especially for a hot day. In Italy, frozen ice is called a granita. So if you want to get fancy with this dish—which really isn't fancy at all—you can call it a granita and your friends might think you're quite the chef. I suggest you make this with stout beer (and it works better if it's flat), but you can also make this with a malt beverage such as Smirnoff Ice. Or, you can get even fancier and combine Smirnoff Ice and Red Stripe and call it a Summer Shandy Granita.

2 (11.2-ounce) bottles stout beer, like Guinness

²/₃ cup packed dark brown sugar

1. This is quite possibly the easiest dessert to make. Simply stir the beer and brown sugar together in a high-sided bowl, and pour the mixture into an 8-inch square baking dish. Let freeze for 1 hour, until you see ice crystals forming at the edge of the baking dish.

2. Using a fork, mix the icy part of the granita into the rest of the beer mixture in the dish. Continue to do this every 45 minutes or so, until the beer is totally frozen into what will look like an Italian ice texture. This could take 3 to 4 hours.

3. To serve, simply scoop into a cup.

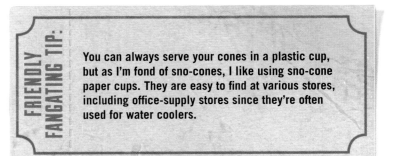

FRIENDLY FANGATING TIP: You can always serve your cones in a plastic cup, but as I'm fond of sno-cones, I like using sno-cone paper cups. They are easy to find at various stores, including office-supply stores since they're often used for water coolers.

TEAM USA FRUIT SALAD

SERVES **10 TO 12**

This is another super-simple dessert that's easy-peasy to make. And it's quite refreshing. As you can see, this fruit salad is composed of fruits that are red, white, and blue(ish) in hue, which is my spin on patriotic sportsfood. This is a great dish to serve during the Men's or Women's World Cup, the Olympics, the Ryder Cup, and so on.

½ seedless watermelon, cut into bite-sized pieces

1½ cups quartered strawberries

2 Honeycrisp apples, peeled, cored, and chopped

1 cup fresh blueberries

1 cup fresh blackberries

⅓ cup Lillet Blanc

2 tablespoons fresh lemon juice

2 tablespoons honey

2 tablespoons chopped fresh mint

Toss the fruits together in a large bowl. Whisk together the Lillet, lemon juice, honey, and mint in a small bowl. Pour the dressing over the fruit, and toss well. Let stand for 30 minutes, stirring occasionally, to allow the fruit to soak up the flavors.

This is me in my official Team USA mittens, issued to Team USA for the 2014 Winter Olympic Games in Sochi, Russia.

POPP'N PEACH COBBLER

CONTRIBUTORS: **JAUNÉ AND ANTWAAN RANDLE EL** | SERVES **6 TO 8**

I adore Jauné and Antwaan Randle El. They, like many of the athletes and athletes' spouses featured in this book, are friends of mine from grad school. Both are incredibly kind and thoughtful and are such loving parents to their kids. But one of my favorite things about the pair is that they both bring a little something different to the table. Antwaan's loud, booming voice and unmistakable laugh are impossible not to recognize anywhere. And he makes everyone smile pretty much all the time. Jauné is seemingly the quiet one—until she decides to speak—and what comes out of her mouth is consistently profound and wise. I love that about her. And I love this recipe that they shared with me—as I'm sure you will, too.

2 (14-ounce) packages roll-out piecrusts, thawed if frozen

3 (15.25-ounce) cans sliced peaches in syrup

4 tablespoons salted butter

1 teaspoon fresh lemon juice

1 teaspoon lemon zest

1 teaspoon pure vanilla extract

1/4 teaspoon ground nutmeg

Dash of ground cinnamon

1 tablespoon all-purpose flour

Ice cream, for serving

1. Preheat the oven to 350°F.

2. Roll out both piecrusts so that they fit perfectly into a 9-inch pie dish. Place one piecrust into the pie dish and bake for 15 minutes.

3. Meanwhile, drain the peaches, reserving the syrup. Combine the peaches, butter, lemon juice and zest, vanilla, nutmeg, and cinnamon in a medium saucepan.

4. Whisk 1/4 cup of the reserved syrup and the flour in a small bowl until smooth. Add to the pan with the peach mixture, and cook over medium heat for 5 minutes, or until the mixture boils and thickens.

5. Pour the peach filling into the prebaked piecrust. Place the remaining rolled piecrust on top, pressing the edges together to seal. Cut slits in several places in the top crust. Bake for 55 minutes, or until the top crust is golden brown.

6. Cool the cobbler for 15 minutes, and then serve warm with ice cream.

TASTY TIDBITS

There's a scene in the movie *Silver Linings Playbook* during which Robert De Niro's character, who is a huge Eagles fan, is watching the game against the Washington Redskins and he calls out Antwaan by name. That was a "whoa" moment for me. It's not every day your friend gets a shout-out from Robert De Niro himself in a movie! And that shout-out was well deserved: Antwaan had a stellar nine-year NFL career during which he was first-team All-Pro in 2005, a two-time AFC champion (in 2005 and 2010), and Super Bowl champion (XL) in 2005, when his Pittsburgh Steelers beat the Seattle Seahawks. Incidentally, he also made history during that game with his famous touchdown pass. To this day, that is the only time a wide receiver has thrown a touchdown pass in a Super Bowl.

DRINKS

If I had to generalize, I'd say most sports fans consume beer when watching sports. And that's easy—just go buy some! (Or if you're super adventurous, you might try brewing your own, but that is admittedly outside my expertise for now.)

For those of you who want to mix it up a little bit, here are some adult beverages for you to try. Bust out your martini shaker and muddler and start practicing cutting that lemon rind into a swizzly shape!

Just as a heads-up for you fans who like gear, you may have noticed several recipes in this book that call for the Hungry Fangating™ Bag for slow cooking. Believe it or not, it can also function as a cooler, keeping your beverages cold for hours! Just throw 'em in the bag, seal it up, and off you go! Whenever I do my TV cooking segments, I bring two Fangating™ Bags—one for hot and one for cold food or drink items. I hate to sound like a product pusher, but I'm all about making the most of the fangate experience, and my Fangating™ Bag can be a big help. Just sayin'…

Watermelon Cooler (page 234), The Manhattan (page 233), Mango Caipirinha (page 235), Sazerac Cocktail (page 237), and The Detroit Red Wing (page 236)

BLOODY MARY

MAKES **2**

There is so much in this Bloody Mary, it's nearly a meal. But I happen to enjoy extensive garnishes. This recipe makes enough to fill two individual tumbler glasses, so if you want to mix up a large batch or even a pitcher, just increase all the ingredients equally and accordingly.

$^1/_2$ cup Pomì tomato sauce, or to taste

1 teaspoon pepperoncini juice

1 tablespoon green olive juice

$^1/_4$ teaspoon Sriracha sauce

$^1/_4$ heaping teaspoon prepared white horseradish

$^1/_2$ heaping teaspoon whole-grain mustard

2 sprinkles freshly ground black pepper

$^1/_8$ teaspoon garlic powder

1 sprinkle ground cumin

1 sprinkle ground ginger

1 teaspoon Worcestershire sauce

1 teaspoon beef or vegetable broth

$^1/_8$ teaspoon celery salt or sea salt

2 teaspoons fresh lemon juice

2 shots vodka, or to taste

Generous sprinkle of Cajun seasoning, optional

$^1/_4$ teaspoon anchovy paste, optional

Ice cubes

4 to 6 green olives, for garnish

2 pepperoncinis, for garnish

Celery slices or 2 stalks celery, for garnish

2 slices thick-cut bacon, cooked until crispy, for garnish, optional

1. Combine all the non-garnish ingredients in a pitcher. Whisk or mix well. Pour into two tumbler glasses, and add the ice cubes.

2. Place the olives on a toothpick with a pepperoncini on one end. Add the toothpicks to the drinks with a celery slice or two and, if you'd like, throw in a slice of crispy bacon as well.

FRIENDLY FANGATING TIP:

My Hungry Fan™ Barbecue Spice Blend makes for a great twist—you can just mix it right into this recipe in lieu of the Cajun seasoning for a BBQ Bloody Mary. I'd start with ½ teaspoon per glass and add more as desired.

BEERMOSA

MAKES **1**

You've heard of mimosas—made by combining Champagne and orange juice. They're delicious and great for a swanky brunch, but they're hardly a fangating go-to. Too frilly. That said, I dig the bubbles in the orange juice. So instead, I offer beer as a substitute for Champagne. It's got bubbles, right? For this recipe, I like to use a Hefeweizen, as it already has a citrusy flavor profile and goes nicely with orange juice. You can also try a pilsner (or any other beer you like, for that matter, save for porters or stouts, which I think are too "meaty" for a drink like this).

1 (12-ounce) bottle beer
(preferably Hefeweizen)

¹/₂ cup orange juice
(I like freshly squeezed)

1 orange slice, for garnish

Combine the beer and orange juice in a tall glass. Garnish with the orange slice, and serve cold!

THE MANHATTAN (PICTURED ON PAGE 230)

MAKES **1**

My ode to New York, New York—where I have lived since 2011. I used to be a huge Knicks fan as a kid. And now I can't help but cheer for the Rangers—they have great fans and it's fun to join in the revelry with my neighbors. This recipe is an easy one, and it's aptly named since it's classy, stylish, and delicious. I've been getting into Manhattans more and more as of late, and so I share this recipe—from the Big Apple to you.

Ice cubes

1 ounce sweet vermouth

2 ounces rye

3 dashes Angostura bitters

Dash of maraschino cherry juice

2 maraschino cherries

Place the ice in a cocktail shaker. Add the vermouth, rye, bitters, and cherry juice. Shake well, and then strain into a martini glass. Add the cherries, and serve.

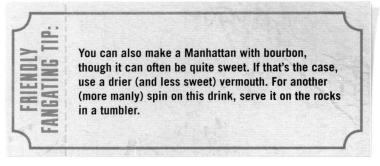

FRIENDLY FANGATING TIP:

You can also make a Manhattan with bourbon, though it can often be quite sweet. If that's the case, use a drier (and less sweet) vermouth. For another (more manly) spin on this drink, serve it on the rocks in a tumbler.

WATERMELON COOLER

(PICTURED ON PAGE 230)

MAKES **2**

Watermelon is one of my favorite fruits. It's so refreshing and just screams summer. I eat it plain, I often put it in my salads, and I also find that it's delicious to drink! I came up with this recipe a few years ago after visiting an organic farm in Riverside, California. The farmers sent me home with fresh watermelon, freshly picked lemon basil, and some lemons off their lemon trees. I was like a pig in you know what (to keep with the farm theme). I whipped out my blender and some vodka I had in the freezer and came up with this refreshing drink (for grown folks). Hold the booze and you've got a great drink for everyone.

¹⁄₄ large watermelon, seeded and roughly chopped

¹⁄₄ cup water

Juice of 1 lime

Several sprigs fresh mint, to taste

4 shots citrus vodka

1 tablespoon Mint Simple Syrup (recipe below)

Combine all the ingredients in a blender. Blend on the smoothie setting until not too pulpy. Pour into a martini shaker with several pieces of ice; shake, strain, and serve in two (ideally, chilled) martini glasses.

MINT SIMPLE SYRUP (MAKES ABOUT 1¹⁄₂ CUPS)

1 cup sugar

1 cup water

Stems from 1 bunch mint

Combine the sugar, water, and mint stems in a small saucepan. Cook over medium, stirring occasionally, until the sugar has dissolved. Remove from the heat, and let cool. Strain to remove the mint. Refrigerate in an airtight container for up to 2 weeks.

MANGO CAIPIRINHA

(PICTURED ON PAGE 231)

MAKES **1**

I originally published this recipe on Celebrations.com as their resident sportsfood expert in anticipation of the 2014 World Cup in Brazil. The Caipirinha is a famously delicious cocktail from Brazil. It's made with cachaça, Brazil's most popular distilled spirit, that's made from sugarcane juice. With the 2016 Summer Olympic Games also taking place in Brazil, this is a good recipe to master so you can thematically fangate as you cheer on your favorite Olympians.

½ lime, quartered into wedges

2 teaspoons brown sugar

¼ to ½ cup puréed fresh mango, to taste

Ice cubes

¼ cup cachaça

1. Reserve one lime wedge for garnish. Combine the rest of the lime and the sugar in a serving glass. Using a wooden spoon or muddling utensil if you've got one, mash the lime and sugar together.

2. Stir in the mango purée. Add some ice cubes and the cachaça. Stir well, garnish with the reserved lime wedge, and serve.

PUMPKIN SPICE BEER (MAKES ABOUT 1½ CUPS)

SERVES **1**

I am a sucker for pumpkin-spiced anything. I love pumpkin pancakes, waffles, chai teas, and lattes—and I looove pumpkin spice beer. Because this particular beer flavor is only available in the fall—and sometimes during only a small segment of the fall season—I have attempted to hoard it. But try as I might, it just doesn't last. In fact, it gets downright skunky, and I'm back to the drawing board, waiting for fall to roll around again. Epic fail. So I put my little thinking cap on, turned my apartment into a *Breaking Bad*–style spice lab (it was a mess!), and came up with an organic pumpkin-spice blend that you can mix into your pancake or waffle batter, your coffee, tea, and even—yes, even—your beer! Any kind of beer. Go crazy, and have fun with it. And drink up any time of year!

1 teaspoon Hungry Fan™ Pumpkin Spice Blend, or more to taste

1 (12-ounce) bottle of your favorite beer

1. The spice blend is best dissolved if you put it in your glass first and then pour in the beer. You don't need to stir—simply swirl lightly.

2. If you decide to pour the beer first, add the spice blend into the beer a little at a time and swirl, allowing it to dissolve. Or use a spoon to gently stir. Serve and enjoy.

THE DETROIT RED WING

(PICTURED ON PAGE 231)

MAKES **1**

In my final nod to hockey fans, I had to include the Red Wings. I remember 1998's Stanley Cup Final quite well. It was the first time in the history of the Washington Capitals franchise that they made it to the Stanley Cup. And they had to take on the Detroit Red Wings, who had won the Stanley Cup the year before. (Eek!) It didn't bode super well for Washington, sadly. I was in attendance for Game 4 in Washington and witnessed the clean sweep by the Detroit Red Wings. That win represented Detroit's ninth Stanley Cup and the last sweep in a Stanley Cup Final to date. In an ode to such a historic win, I give you The Detroit Red Wing cocktail.

Ice cubes

6 tablespoons cinnamon Schnapps

¾ cup natural ginger ale

1 teaspoon minced fresh mint, optional

Fill a tall cocktail glass with ice. Add in all the other ingredients. Cheers!

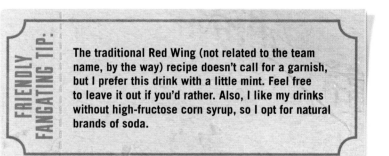

FRIENDLY FANGATING TIP: The traditional Red Wing (not related to the team name, by the way) recipe doesn't call for a garnish, but I prefer this drink with a little mint. Feel free to leave it out if you'd rather. Also, I like my drinks without high-fructose corn syrup, so I opt for natural brands of soda.

SAZERAC COCKTAIL

(PICTURED ON PAGE 231)

MAKES **1**

I had the good fortune to attend Super Bowl XLVII in New Orleans. (It was a big party in the Big Easy, which happened to immediately precede another big party—aka Mardi Gras.) While down there, I visited some of New Orleans' most famous bars (there are many) and had my fair share of Sazeracs, a cocktail that originated in New Orleans in the mid 1800s. One of its defining characteristics is that it must be made with whiskey or cognac, as it's named for the Sazerac de Forge et Fils brand of cognac brandy. Here's a heads-up: This cocktail is a kick in the pants. Enjoy carefully (wink wink)!

¹/₄ teaspoon absinthe

1 teaspoon Simple Syrup (recipe below)

¹/₄ teaspoon bitters

¹/₄ cup rye whiskey or cognac

Lemon rind twist

Ice cubes, optional

1. Chill a 3¹/₂-ounce cocktail glass.

2. Pour the absinthe in the glass, and swirl so it coats the insides of the glass. Pour out the remaining absinthe (or leave it in; just know it will create a strong licorice-flavored drink).

3. Add the Simple Syrup, bitters, and whiskey.

4. Run the lemon rind around the rim of the glass and throw it in, or use it as a garnish on the rim. Serve with or without ice cubes.

SIMPLE SYRUP (MAKES ABOUT 1¹/₂ CUPS)

1 cup sugar

1 cup water

1. Combine the sugar and water in a small saucepan over medium-high, stirring frequently, until all the sugar has dissolved.

2. Remove from the heat, and let cool.

FRIENDLY FANGATING TIP:

Be sure when purchasing the absinthe that it contains wormwood. Real absinthe is made from the flowers and leaves of that plant, along with green anise and sweet fennel. If you can't find absinthe, you can substitute anise liqueur. You'll be left with a bunch of Simple Syrup. Just keep it in an airtight container in the fridge for up to 6 months—it can be used in many other cocktails...

RYE WHISKEY BLUE VALENTINE

MAKES **A STRONG PITCHER (BEWARE)**

I confess I haven't catered to hockey fans as best as I possibly could have throughout this book. And I am a hockey fan! (I actually briefly worked for the Washington Capitals when I was younger.) This drink is an ode to the fans of the Toronto Maple Leafs who are great through thick and thin—and it's been a bit of a roller coaster over the years. Thus, I thought I'd offer something a little on the strong side. Like bourbon, American rye is made in new charred oak barrels, imparting an oaky, caramel, and vanilla flavor that I thought would lend well to this drink. (Feel free to use Canadian rye whiskey as well.)

Ice cubes

⅓ handle Blue Curaçao

⅓ handle rye whiskey

¼ handle peach Schnapps

½ cup natural lemon-lime soda

¾ cup fresh lime juice

Fill a large pitcher about halfway full with ice. Add all the other ingredients, and stir well.

TASTY TIDBITS

I find the whole whisky versus whiskey thing a bit confusing. So I did some research to find out if there's a difference. Here's what I found: Apparently there is a difference and that one little "e" is actually pretty significant. Whisky (no "e") denotes Scotch whisky and Scotch-inspired liquors. Whiskey (with an "e") refers to Irish and American liquors. So, if you forget to drop the "e" in Scotland, you might find yourself in a pretty big pickle.

THE ROCKET

MAKES **1**

To continue my ode to hockey fans of the north, I thought I'd include a recipe for the fans of the Montreal Canadiens, a team with a rich history of Stanley Cup wins. This is more of a tribute recipe, as the athlete for whom this drink is named is no longer with us. All you Canadiens fans, I know you're nodding your heads right now. How can you forget Joseph Henri Maurice "the Rocket" Richard? The Canadiens retired his number 9 in 1960, and 38 years later, the Maurice "The Rocket" Richard Trophy became the NHL's annual award for the league's leading goal scorer of the regular season.

1 cup crushed ice

³/₄ cup Smirnoff Ice

2 tablespoons grenadine

3 tablespoons Blue Curaçao

1. Fill a tall cocktail glass with the ice. Then pour the Smirnoff Ice over it.

2. Tilt the glass on a bit of an angle, and then pour in the grenadine carefully, focusing on pouring down the side of the glass and not splashing off the ice.

3. Then carefully pour the Blue Curaçao as you just did the grenadine. Bottoms up!

TASTY TIDBITS

The Rocket played 18 seasons for the Canadiens. He was the first player in NHL history to score 50 goals in a single season (which he did in 50 games between 1944 and 1945), and he was the first NHLer to reach 500 career goals. The Rocket was part of eight Stanley Cup championship teams, which included a winning streak of five straight years between 1956 and 1960.

BASICS

I am a big fan of making my own condiments. Nothing against the store-bought brands, but so many of them are jam-packed with preservatives and other chemicals that I'd rather not eat them. Condiments are actually pretty easy to make and will last you a little while if you put them in an airtight container and store them in the fridge. Here's a bunch of condiment basics that should keep your fridge pretty well stocked for a while.

Ketchup (page 245), Dijon Mustard
(page 246), Healthy Homemade Mayonnaise
(page 250), and Pumpkin Butter (page 249)

HUMMUS (MAKES ABOUT 1½ CUPS)

You'll often find za'atar spice used in Middle Eastern cuisine. It's a combination of flavors including lemon peel, sesame seeds, salt, and sumac. I think it gives this hummus an extra-awesome flavor. That said, this recipe is great on its own. I leave it up to you!

1 (15-ounce) can chickpeas, drained, rinsed, and de-skinned

4 to 5 ice cubes

Juice of 1 lemon

2 cloves garlic, crushed

2 tablespoons extra virgin olive oil

Pinch of sea salt

2 teaspoons za'atar spice, or to taste, optional

1. Blend the chickpeas in a food processor, adding 1 ice cube at a time as you go. (This helps promote a creamier, smooth texture.) Once blended, transfer to a bowl, and add in the lemon juice, garlic, olive oil, and salt. Mix well.

2. If you desire a runnier texture, feel free to stir in a little water.

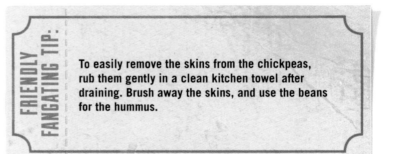

FRIENDLY FANGATING TIP: To easily remove the skins from the chickpeas, rub them gently in a clean kitchen towel after draining. Brush away the skins, and use the beans for the hummus.

TZATZIKI (MAKES ABOUT 1½ CUPS)

Tzatziki is one of my favorite condiments. It may not seem like the obvious go-to condiment for game day, but it's great on potato skins in lieu of cheese or sour cream. It also goes great on my Mediterranean Nachos, page 40. I love dipping sliced cucumbers and even tortilla chips in it—I can eat an entire bowl of it in one go, no problem!

1 cup reduced-fat (2%) plain Greek yogurt

2 cloves garlic, crushed

Juice of 1 lemon

1 sprig dill, finely chopped

½ small cucumber, finely diced

2 tablespoons extra virgin olive oil

Sea salt and freshly ground black pepper

Combine all the ingredients in a bowl, season with salt and pepper, and stir well.

KETCHUP (MAKES ABOUT ³/₄ CUP)

With so many ketchups on the market—both organic and nonorganic—you might question the need to make your own. That's fair. But this recipe is so easy to make, and what I like most is that it's a cinch to add new flavors to make it your own signature condiment. For instance, you could add some chipotle hot sauce to make chipotle ketchup, extra garlic, or even truffle oil. Have fun with it, and happy dipping!

2 tablespoons plus 2 teaspoons cane sugar

¹/₄ cup water

1 cup Pomì finely chopped tomatoes

2 tablespoons Pomì tomato sauce

2 tablespoons tomato paste

1 tablespoon distilled white vinegar

¹/₂ teaspoon onion powder

¹/₂ teaspoon garlic powder

¹/₄ teaspoon celery salt

¹/₂ teaspoon sea salt

¹/₄ teaspoon freshly ground black pepper

1 whole clove

1. Dissolve the sugar in the water in a medium saucepan over low. Add in all the other ingredients and stir well. Cover and bring to a boil for 2 minutes. Then reduce the heat to a simmer, and cook, uncovered, for 20 minutes, stirring frequently.

2. Remove from the heat, discard the clove, and blend the mixture with an immersion blender. Strain through a fine-mesh strainer, using a spatula to press out as much of the ketchup as possible. Discard the solids.

3. Serve at room temperature or chilled.

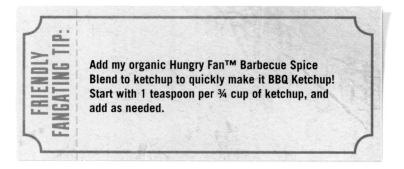

FRIENDLY FANGATING TIP:

Add my organic Hungry Fan™ Barbecue Spice Blend to ketchup to quickly make it BBQ Ketchup! Start with 1 teaspoon per ¾ cup of ketchup, and add as needed.

DIJON MUSTARD (MAKES ABOUT 1½ CUPS)

I'm a mustard girl through and through. I have been known to eat a good Dijon mustard right out of the bottle with a spoon (don't judge, we all have our things). While Dijon is my favorite, with some recipes, including my Cornflake Chicken Tenders (page 170), a nice honey mustard hits the spot. If you're aiming for a honey Dijon, omit the sugar entirely in this recipe and use 3 tablespoons of honey.

1½ cups dry white wine

½ cup white wine vinegar

3 cloves garlic, finely chopped

1 large yellow onion, chopped

⅔ cup mustard powder

2 tablespoons raw honey

1 tablespoon extra virgin olive oil

2 teaspoons fine sea salt

1 tablespoon minced
fresh tarragon, optional

1. Combine the wine, vinegar, garlic, and onions in a medium saucepan, and bring to a boil over high. Reduce the heat to medium, and simmer, uncovered, for 5 minutes, stirring frequently, until reduced slightly.

2. Allow the contents of the saucepan to fully cool in order for the flavors to incorporate and mellow, and then strain through a fine-mesh strainer. Discard the onions and garlic chunks, and return the liquid to the saucepan.

3. Add the mustard powder, and whisk well until smooth. Add the honey, olive oil, and salt, and heat over medium, stirring constantly, until the mixture thickens, about 10 minutes. Remove from the heat.

4. Stir in the tarragon, if desired. Then spoon the mustard into a clean glass jar, and let it cool completely, uncovered, on your countertop, ideally overnight.

5. Seal the jar tightly, and, for optimal flavor, let it sit for 2 weeks before serving. (You have to let the goodness marinate in itself for a bit.) This keeps in your fridge for up to a year.

COCKTAIL SAUCE (MAKES ABOUT 1 CUP)

Ah yes... another condiment I have been known to stealthily eat straight out of the bottle. (My trick is to add a little extra onto an empty oyster or clam shell... shhh.) I'm all about spicy cocktail sauce, so I like to add more horseradish to this cocktail sauce once it's prepared, especially if I'm serving it with chilled shrimp cocktail. Just a heads-up, if you're using freshly ground horseradish, you will need less horseradish.

1 tablespoon sugar

$^1/_3$ cup water

2 tablespoons tomato paste

$^1/_2$ cup Pomì finely chopped tomatoes

2 tablespoons distilled vinegar

1 heaping tablespoon prepared white horseradish

1 teaspoon sea salt

1 tablespoon Worcestershire sauce

$^1/_2$ teaspoon onion powder

$^1/_2$ teaspoon garlic powder

1 teaspoon anchovy paste

$^1/_2$ teaspoon red pepper flakes, or less to taste

1. Dissolve the sugar in the water in a saucepan over low. Add all the other ingredients, and stir well. Cover and bring to a boil for 1 minute. Then reduce the heat, and simmer for 10 minutes, until thickened.

2. Let cool to room temperature, or refrigerate before serving.

BASIC GUACAMOLE (MAKES ABOUT 2$^1/_2$ CUPS)

There are about a bagillion ways to make guacamole (including my Bacon Guac recipe on page 52). But it's always good to have one super-solid, go-to recipe nailed down that you can bust out when needed. This is that recipe!

2 ripe avocados, pitted, peeled, and mashed

$^1/_2$ teaspoon sea salt

$^1/_2$ teaspoon freshly ground black pepper

3 teaspoons fresh lime juice

$^1/_3$ cup diced red onion

2 tablespoons finely chopped fresh cilantro, plus more for garnish

Combine all the ingredients in a serving bowl, and mix well. Garnish with additional chopped cilantro, and serve.

SALSA ROJA (MAKES ABOUT 3 CUPS)

This recipe is a simple and delicious tomato-based, roasted chile pepper salsa. It's great for game day, but it can also last for a few weeks in the fridge should you decide to make it in bulk.

$^1/_2$ habanero chile

1 jalapeño chile

1 Fresno or mirasol chile

6 baby carrots

Extra virgin olive oil

$^1/_2$ red bell pepper, seeded and roughly chopped

$^1/_2$ yellow bell pepper, seeded and roughly chopped

$2^1/_2$ tomatoes off the vine

3 cloves garlic, peeled

1 small sweet onion, diced

$^1/_4$ cup thinly sliced green onions

3 tablespoons tomato paste

$^1/_2$ teaspoon sugar

$1^1/_2$ teaspoons sea salt

2 teaspoons distilled vinegar

1 tablespoon fresh lime juice

1. Preheat the oven to 400°F. Line a baking sheet with aluminum foil.

2. Rub all the chile peppers and carrots with olive oil in a large bowl. Transfer to the prepared baking sheet, and roast for 7 minutes. Using tongs, flip the vegetables over, and return them to the oven for about 8 minutes. You will know the chiles are done when their skins have blistered. (The carrots are done then, too.) Let cool.

3. Alternatively, roast the chiles and carrots directly over a flame if you have a gas stovetop. Using tongs, hold the chiles over a medium to medium-high flame until the skin blisters (and if it's the carrots, until the carrots brown).

4. When cool enough to handle, carefully remove the blistered skins of the chiles. Then use a knife to carefully remove the veins and seeds from the chiles (take care not to touch your face and eyes especially). Mince the roasted chiles, and dice the carrots. Set aside.

5. Gently pulse the red and yellow peppers, tomatoes, and garlic in a food processor. You don't want to make soup, you just want the processor to chop 'em for you. If you prefer a soupier consistency, go ahead and pulse some more. (I just like my salsa chunky.)

6. Transfer the tomato base to a serving bowl, and add the roasted chiles and carrots, the sweet and green onions, the tomato paste, sugar, salt, vinegar, and lime juice. Mix well, and serve.

PUMPKIN BUTTER (MAKES ABOUT 3 CUPS)

This is basically autumn in a jar. I love it. I can't help it. It's really good all by itself, eaten straight with a spoon. Or you can slather it all over toast for breakfast, or use it on my Sweet-and-Savory Prosciutto Grilled Cheese (page 103).

1 sugar pumpkin (about 1 foot in diameter) or 2 (16-ounce) boxes pumpkin puree

Extra virgin olive oil

$^1/_2$ cup apple cider

3 tablespoons dark brown sugar

3 tablespoons organic maple syrup, or more for extra sweetness

$^1/_2$ teaspoon sea salt

1 teaspoon bourbon vanilla extract

1$^1/_2$ teaspoons fresh lemon juice

$^3/_4$ teaspoon ground nutmeg

1 heaping tablespoon ground cinnamon

1. Preheat the oven to 350°F. Line a deep baking dish with aluminum foil.

2. Cut the top off the pumpkin just below the stem. Cut the pumpkin in half vertically. Scoop out all the stringy stuff and seeds. (I roast my pumpkin seeds, blotted dry, with a little salt and red pepper flakes alongside my pumpkin.) Toss the stringy stuff and the seeds if you don't want to use them.

3. Pour 1 to 2 tablespoons olive oil into each pumpkin half, and use a brush to spread the oil all over the inside of the pumpkin, so both inside halves are coated but not greasy. Place them on the prepared baking dish, and roast for 50 minutes.

4. Let the pumpkins cool for 5 to 10 minutes. Then remove the skin by wedging a spoon between the skin and flesh and scooping out the flesh.

5. Place the pumpkin flesh in a food processor, and add all the other ingredients. Pulse until fully puréed. Refrigerate until ready to use.

6. Alternatively, if using pumpkin puree, just place the puree in the prepared baking dish, and roast for 50 minutes. Transfer to a medium saucepan over medium, stir in the rest of the ingredients, and bring to a boil. Reduce the heat to low, and simmer until thickened, about 1 hour 15 minutes. Let cool to room temperature, and then refrigerate until ready to use.

HEALTHY HOMEMADE MAYONNAISE (MAKES ABOUT 1 CUP)

This recipe makes a good amount of mayo, so I recommend that you store it in a jam jar, or something similar, in the refrigerator and use it for sandwiches, as a base for aïoli, or in dips. Mayonnaise recipes usually call for ¾ cup of oil for every egg yolk. To me, that's a ton of oil. And it's usually canola oil, which isn't the healthiest oil out there. So I fixed all that and came up with a delicious, zesty mayonnaise made with a *much* healthier avocado oil and more yolks!

3 large egg yolks

2 teaspoons white wine vinegar or Champagne vinegar

1 tablespoon fresh lemon juice

1 teaspoon sea salt

³/₄ cup avocado oil

1. Whisk together all the ingredients except the avocado oil in a medium bowl until well blended, about 1 minute. I use a handheld or stand mixer.

2. Continue to whisk as you slowly (slowly!) pour in the oil, a little at a time (you won't get the creamy mayo texture if you pour in too much oil at once). Continue to pour in the oil little by little as you whisk away. You will notice the color of the mayo change and the consistency get fluffier. Once it has reached a consistency you like, you're done!

BBQ SAUCE (MAKES ABOUT 1²/₃ CUPS)

Not to toot my own horn, but this is my pretty-darn-tasty-go-to BBQ sauce recipe. I've been known to put a little extra sauce on my plate just to wipe it off with my finger, a little extra bread, or a tortilla. Check out the Slow-Cooked BBQ Pulled Pork Quesadilla recipe on page 148; it's just one of the many delicious things you can make with this sauce.

1 large shallot, minced

2 tablespoons salted butter

1 cup Pomì tomato sauce

1 cup apple cider vinegar

2 tablespoons tomato paste

1¹/₂ tablespoons yellow mustard

1 tablespoon Worcestershire sauce

1 teaspoon molasses

¹/₃ cup dark brown sugar

2 teaspoons sea salt

2 teaspoons freshly ground black pepper

1 teaspoon cayenne pepper, or more to taste

1 teaspoon Smoulder smoky seasoning blend or hickory spice mix

Sauté your shallots in the butter in a skillet over medium until they begin to caramelize, about 10 minutes. Lower the heat, and add the tomato sauce, vinegar, tomato paste, mustard, Worcestershire sauce, molasses, brown sugar, salt, pepper, cayenne, and Smoulder seasoning. Stir to combine and simmer for 15 minutes, stirring occasionally.

METRIC EQUIVALENTS

The information in the following charts is provided to help cooks outside the United States successfully use the recipes in this book. All equivalents are approximate.

COOKING/OVEN TEMPERATURES

	Fahrenheit	Celsius	Gas Mark
Freeze Water	32° F	0° C	
Room Temp.	68° F	20° C	
Boil Water	212° F	100° C	
Bake	325° F	160° C	3
	350° F	180° C	4
	375° F	190° C	5
	400° F	200° C	6
	425° F	220° C	7
	450° F	230° C	8
Broil			Grill

LIQUID INGREDIENTS BY VOLUME

$1/4$ tsp	=					1 ml		
$1/2$ tsp	=					2 ml		
1 tsp	=					5 ml		
3 tsp	=	1 Tbsp	=	$1/2$ fl oz	=	15 ml		
2 Tbsp	=	$1/8$ cup	=	1 fl oz	=	30 ml		
4 Tbsp	=	$1/4$ cup	=	2 fl oz	=	60 ml		
$5 1/3$ Tbsp	=	$1/3$ cup	=	3 fl oz	=	80 ml		
8 Tbsp	=	$1/2$ cup	=	4 fl oz	=	120 ml		
$10 2/3$ Tbsp	=	$2/3$ cup	=	5 fl oz	=	160 ml		
12 Tbsp	=	$3/4$ cup	=	6 fl oz	=	180 ml		
16 Tbsp	=	1 cup	=	8 fl oz	=	240 ml		
1 pt	=	2 cups	=	16 fl oz	=	480 ml		
1 qt	=	4 cups	=	32 fl oz	=	960 ml		
				33 fl oz	=	1000 ml	=	1 l

DRY INGREDIENTS BY WEIGHT

(To convert ounces to grams, multiply the number of ounces by 30.)

1 oz	=	$1/16$ lb	=	30 g
4 oz	=	$1/4$ lb	=	120 g
8 oz	=	$1/2$ lb	=	240 g
12 oz	=	$3/4$ lb	=	360 g
16 oz	=	1 lb	=	480 g

LENGTH

(To convert inches to centimeters, multiply the number of inches by 2.5.)

1 in	=					2.5 cm		
6 in	=	$1/2$ ft			=	15 cm		
12 in	=	1 ft			=	30 cm		
36 in	=	3 ft	=	1 yd	=	90 cm		
40 in	=					100 cm	=	1 m

EQUIVALENTS FOR DIFFERENT TYPES OF INGREDIENTS

Standard Cup	Fine Powder (ex. flour)	Grain (ex. rice)	Granular (ex. sugar)	Liquid Solids (ex. butter)	Liquid (ex. milk)
1	140 g	150 g	190 g	200 g	240 ml
$3/4$	105 g	113 g	143 g	150 g	180 ml
$2/3$	93 g	100 g	125 g	133 g	160 ml
$1/2$	70 g	75 g	95 g	100 g	120 ml
$1/3$	47 g	50 g	63 g	67 g	80 ml
$1/4$	35 g	38 g	48 g	50 g	60 ml
$1/8$	18 g	19 g	24 g	25 g	30 ml

INDEX

ACKNOWLEDGMENTS

To start your own brand from nothing takes a lot—lot—of work. It also takes a ton of support from friends and loved ones.

When I started my blog in 2011, I didn't know where it would take me. Since its inception, I have had wonderful people in my life who have helped me in so many ways to get to where I am today.

A huge, heartfelt thanks to my parents for their love and support. If anyone knows about trailblazing, it's my dad. He's always been such an amazing role model and has a heart of gold. And if anyone knows how to calm me down when I get fussy and stress (which I do often), it's my mom. She's strong and soothing at the same time. Together, they are my rock, and none of this would be possible without them.

To KK, thank you for helping me develop my palate from such a young age. Your cooking is incredible. Thank you for being my first teacher and my second mother.

My sister, Jocelyn, is the most fun person to eat out with (and one of the funniest). Thank you for always splitting every dish with me. There's truly no better way to taste everything on the menu! (Especially Buffalo wings—which we have tried the world over.)

To Garrett, my favorite coffee table dining companion. Thank you for such amazing, loving support—and for being my guinea pig. I love you.

To Margot, you are the catalyst that made this all possible—and a wonderful sushi-eating buddy. Thank you so, so much.

To Anja, you seriously rock. I so enjoyed getting to know you throughout this process, and I couldn't have done it without your amazingly positive attitude and thoughtful hand-holding. And if you ever need a BBQ-eating buddy in Birmingham, I'm your girl.

To the whole Time Inc. team in Birmingham, thank you. I had such a blast shooting the photos for this book. You are all so talented and quite possibly the nicest people I have ever met. We must tailgate again sometime.

To Ben, Mark, and Kyle, you guys were such an incredible help. Thank you for believing in the value of this project and allowing me to benefit from your sportstastic expertise.

I met Lamin, my Whole Foods guru, serendipitously, and he is not only an expert in food retail, but a dear friend who shares a love of sports and lunch. Thank you for all your support, your help finding ingredients, and enough coconut water to sustain me through the entire book-writing and spice-making process. (Go Arsenal!)

Ellie, thank you for your chemistry know-how. I'm so grateful for the dinner invites and the use of your lab!

I owe a huge thank you to all the athletes who participated in this cookbook. Thank you all for sharing with me and the rest of your fans a little insight into some of your favorite things to eat.

And to Michael Mina, thank you for the incredible recipes. You're such a talented chef, and I'm so excited to include your contributions in this book!

And lastly, I could not publish a game day cookbook without acknowledging the two people who introduced me to sportsfood and Super Bowl parties: Charlie and Elaine Castle. I deeply miss Mr. Castle, his grilling mastery, and most-delicious food (most of which he'd bring freshly caught from the Eastern Shore). And Mrs. Castle's salads were what first got me into tinkering in the kitchen. My salads are pretty good nowadays, but Mrs. Castle's will always be the best.

A portion of the proceeds of this book will be donated to the many foundations and charities founded by the incredible athletes who participated in this book.